THE GROUNDS OF GAMING

DIGITAL GAME STUDIES

Robert Alan Brookey and David J. Gunkel, editors

THE GROUNDS OF GAMING

NICHOLAS TAYLOR

INDIANA UNIVERSITY PRESS

This book is a publication of

Indiana University Press
Office of Scholarly Publishing
Herman B Wells Library 350
1320 East 10th Street
Bloomington, Indiana 47405 USA

iupress.org

First Printing 2024

Cataloging information is available from the Library of Congress.
978-0-253-07122-4 (hdbk)
978-0-253-07123-1 (pbk)
978-0-253-07124-8 (web PDF)

CONTENTS

Acknowledgments   *vii*

Introduction: Men, Place, and Games   *1*

1. Frames: Extractive Logics in Play   *33*

2. Circles: It All Starts at Home   *64*

3. Grids: LAN Parties and the Infrastructural
   Grounds of Gaming   *103*

4. Platforms: Making Space for Collegiate Esports   *135*

5. Pockets: Practicing Safe Storage at Games
   Industry Conventions   *169*

Conclusion: Boundaries, (Re)taking the Field   *202*

Bibliography   *213*

Index   *241*

ACKNOWLEDGMENTS

PERHAPS IT IS FITTING FOR a book about location and play to have been written across many different places, the process subject to multiple dislocations and relocations. About half of these essays were written over the pandemic, during those brief but welcome times when I was able to squirrel myself away for writing retreats in cabins in the North Carolina woods or summer homes on its beaches. The other half was written in cafés, libraries, and on trains in Finland, particularly in the small town of Vaasa, where my family and I stayed during the 2022–23 academic year. In fact, as I write this, it is almost midnight on a warm July evening in Vaasa, and our apartment is illuminated (and overheated) by what feels like early afternoon sunshine. Place matters as much to how we write and think as to how we play and game. But for a book that has been in the making for twelve years and counting (seriously?!), the list of places where the actual writing came together tells just one small part of the story.

First, I am incredibly grateful to Allison Blair Chaplin and Sophia Herbert at Indiana University Press, who guided me through this process so patiently and expertly, and to Robert Brookey and David Gunkel, the series editors for Digital Game Studies. They had to wait most of the pandemic between approving the proposal and receiving the full draft. More importantly, though, they expressed confidence and support in the project at key inflection points over the long process—the first, when I contacted them after a years-long pause to see whether they were still on board, and the second, when I realized the degree to which the project needed to center *ground* and its manifold meanings and complexities rather than the initial proposal's more unidimensional focus on gender.

Though I departed North Carolina State University (NCSU) in 2022, this book was made possible by the encouragement and material support of colleagues and friends I met during my decade in Raleigh. Steve Wiley served as a mentor, department coconspirator, and fellow writing retreat-er, and his feedback on key parts of this book (particularly the introduction) was invaluable. The warmth and generosity of his and Myriam's friendship are a large part of what made NCSU, and Raleigh, such a welcoming home for so long. They represent the best of what we left when we moved.

I was lucky to have two department heads during my time at NCSU, Kenneth Zagacki and Jessica Jameson, who made space within the Department of Communication (both materially and discursively) for postdisciplinary research and teaching on games. Grant Bollmer not only provided a sounding board for my more obtuse ideas (some of which made it into the book) but also offered sage guidance on various aspects of the writing and publishing process. The same goes for Andrew Johnston; I am thankful to Andrew for the grace, humor, and levelheadedness he showed in accepting the news of my departure, which required him to take on an administrative position a year early and under challenging conditions. Though they both left North Carolina shortly after we arrived, Jeremy Packer and Sarah Sharma made indelible impressions on this book and on my intellectual and professional journey over the long, long course of its writing. In particular, Sarah provided an early staging ground for what would become chapter 2 when she invited me to speak at the McLuhan Center in Toronto in 2018 and later, when the work appeared in *Re-understanding Media*, the edited volume she and Rianka Singh put together. Jeremy, for his part, put the idea for a book in my head—casually, over a lunch of North Carolina barbeque (eastern style, obviously)—long before I think I was ready to undertake writing one.

I am very fortunate to have been deeply involved with the Communication, Rhetoric, and Digital Media (CRDM) PhD program during my time at NCSU. For a book project that centers on infrastructure, CRDM was itself infrastructural: my work was enriched by the energy, creativity, and intellectual generosity that circulates through that community of students, faculty, and alumni. This included, especially, the direct support and input provided by current and former CRDM students on specific chapters in this book.

Katreena Alder and I worked together closely on the study of domestic gaming setups discussed in chapter 2. Max Renner lent his labor and time to much of the ethnographic work that forms the basis of chapter 4, on collegiate esports. My collaborator and advisee Bryce Stout has been indispensable to my ongoing work with collegiate esports, both in this book and elsewhere. Bryce will continue to be instrumental to NCSU's efforts at building a sustainable and equitable esports program. Aaron Dial contributed to the study of games industry conventions reported on in chapter 5; his curiosity and keen intellect gave that study much more depth and dimension than it would have had otherwise. I am also grateful for the relationships I have had with many other CRDM alumni and for the casual conversations and formal collaborations we shared, which in some way or another informed the shape and direction of this book: Sarah Evans, Kristina Bell, Jessica Elam, Megan Fletcher, Brandon Rogers, Eddie Lohmeyer, Alex Monea, Joel Schneier, Brent Simoneaux, Madison Schmalzer, Robyn Hope, Malcolm Ogden, Gayas Eapen, Alex Sutter, Matt Howard, and Chris Kampe.

Going back even further, I should acknowledge the opportunities provided by John Murray and the team he led at SRI and by Jennifer Jenson and Suzanne de Castell. Their collaboration provided the administrative framework and funding for the local area network (LAN) event fieldwork I draw on specifically in chapters 1 and 3. I am also grateful to Kelly Bergstrom, Glenn Gray, and Kyle Leveque, my travel and fieldwork companions on many of these ethnographic encounters.

Of course, I need to acknowledge the dozens of research participants I spoke to, hung out with, and learned from: esports administrators, players, and spectators; LAN organizers, attendees, and staff; and games industry workers. I hope that if you have a chance to read this book, it does justice to the experiences and perspectives you shared with me.

If my time in Raleigh provided the material and impetus for the book, our stay in Finland during the 2022–23 academic year cleared space for me to complete it. Fritjof Sahlstrom and Matilda Ståhl made possible the extraordinary opportunity to serve as research fellow in the Faculty of Education and Social Welfare at Åbo Akademi University in the first place. Matilda did so by judging me worthy of serving as the opponent for her excellent dissertation. Fritjof did so by deftly posing the question "Well, what if you came here for a year?" (while just as deftly gutting fish outside in the bitter cold) during my initial visit to Vaasa. The support of Katarina Heikius and the board of Högskolestiftelsen i Österbotten provided the means for Danielle, Ben, and I to make a home for the year in the little town on the west coast of Finland.

Matilda Ståhl and Yvonne Backholm-Nyberg were instrumental to my efforts at finishing the book and allowed me to share some of its core ideas via the Supporting Play Symposium they organized at Åbo Akademi University in December 2022. More than this, they were incredibly generous with their time and hospitality. Fredrik Rusk's camaraderie and collaboration over my year in Finland grounded me in more ways than one. Through our runs and lunchtime chats, I was able to gain a grasp of the terrain, both physical and ideological, of my host country; the projects he and Matilda invited me into, which I worked on while wrapping up this writing, helped return me to my roots in qualitative social science, with all its messy entanglements and ethical obligations. I am grateful for an intellectual kinship with Matilda and Fredrik that crosses institutions, borders, and languages. *Tack så mycket.*

Thanks to the vibrant games research community in Finland and in Scandinavia, I was given multiple opportunities to pilot material from these chapters in the form of invited talks and keynotes. I am so very grateful to Olli Sotamaa, Jaakko Stenros, Frans Mäyrä, and Heikki Tyni for welcoming me in Tampere for the Oasis Lunchtime Series in October 2022 and again for the Party! Seminar in May 2023; to Maria Ruotsalainen, Raine Koskiima, and Marko Siitonen for inviting me to talk to the Games Research Group in Jyväskylä in March 2023; to Lina Eklund, Jon Back, and Björn Sjöblom for arranging my keynote at the Nordic DiGRA symposium in April 2023; and to Usva Friman and Mikko Meriläinen for letting me present at the Finnish Games Research Symposium in May 2023. At each of these venues, I was given space to talk to folks about contexts and events taking place an ocean away in Canada and the United States, and together, we did the work of puzzling out what travels from one gaming context to the next and how, through gaming's manifold global infrastructures. *Kiitos paljon.*

My colleagues in the Department of Communication and Media Studies at York University provided the space and support for me to wrap up this book. As strange as it was to carry out the first year of my time (back) at York so far away in Finland, Ganaele Langlois, Rianka Singh, Kelly Bergstrom, Robert Gehl, and others made me feel like I was a welcome part of their community of thoughtful and conscientious media scholars. The editor and publisher would like to thank the Faculty of Liberal Arts & Professional

Studies, York University, Toronto, Canada, for the financial support it provided to this work.

I am grateful to the networks of games researchers whose insights have been so generative to this project: Aaron Trammell, Florence Chee, Seth Giddings, Mia Consalvo, Kishonna Gray, Will Partin, Rainforest Scully-Blaker, Felan Parker, Bart Simon, Gerald Voorhees, Shira Chess, Alison Harvey, Chris Paul, Sam Tobin, Tom Apperley, Ergin Bulut, Stefanie Boluk, Patrick LeMieux, Jennifer Whitson, Emil Hammar, Adrienne Shaw, Souvik Mukherjee, and Soraya Murray, to name but a few. While I hesitate to place this book wholly "in" game studies—despite appearing as part of Indiana University Press's Digital Game Studies series—the work of critical, feminist, queer, antiracist, and postcolonial game studies scholarship remains utterly foundational to my work.

I feel it is appropriate to acknowledge T. L. Taylor and Emma Witkowski together in the same paragraph. So much of this book began as conversations we three had, whether in person, over messaging apps, or in my head, about what competitive gaming is and ought to be; what truly matters in the doing of ethnography and maneuvering through academia with its manifold injustices; and how to be a good academic citizen and community member. Plus, there was that incredible fieldwork trip to Jönköping for DreamHack in the summer of 2016.

Though they are separated by distance and have not yet met in person, I also want to acknowledge in the same breath the contributions made by Chris Ingraham and Stephanie Fisher. Both have been staunch supporters of this project, confident in its direction and the worth of its contributions, even (and especially) when I was not. We three share more than a love of *Zelda*, LEGO, and *Pokémon GO*: Chris and Stephanie are also, in their own distinct ways, my role models for how they put their considerable intellectual acumen and envious amounts of energy to making their world(s) better. My own world is certainly better for their friendship.

So much of this book is about those less-visible relations of support, care, and regeneration that make our mundane moments of play possible. Of course, the same is true of academic work. Seth and Leilani, Kellee and Geoff, and Juan and Marguerite made our little pocket in Raleigh utterly magical for many years. I want to thank Sarah, Mike (West), Nolan, Isla, Evie, Margaret, Hermas, Lesley, Shane, Nicole, Emmett, and Edie for always being *there*, even when we have been so far away. I have learned so many invaluable lessons from my father, Mike Taylor (a.k.a. Grumpy), through his quiet but steadfast support and his deep curiosity. Not the least of these lessons is how to build true and lasting friendships with women, including, especially, partners. And I am grateful to Mary Elizabeth Taylor, who, through her own brilliant example of a life lived well, taught me how to cultivate care and nurture creativity wherever I am and in whatever I do.

Finally, I am most grateful to Danielle and Ben. You two felt the pressures and strains of this process as acutely as I did, if not more. Ben, your thoughtfulness, humor, and curiosity are a constant source of wonder and inspiration. Danielle, you allowed me to lock myself way in the woods or the office when I needed to and helped me work through countless thorny problems this book posed, both conceptual and logistic. Together, we have never backed down from a challenge or said no to adventure, and that has sustained me in ways I find hard to fully express.

Artist Statement about the Cover

SOFT CHAOS COOPERATIVE

For this cover, we wanted to create a space that seemed slightly surreal and out of place: a gaming setup in the middle of a forest. On closer examination, however, you can see that there are wires everywhere, and despite its apparent positioning "off the grid" (quite literally floating above one), it is still connected.

We built a world in engine and combined it with common art store assets and digital painting techniques. We wanted to contrast the idea of a digital readymade, using some of the first results in the asset store, with bespoke customization. In this way, we are engaging with contrasts between concepts of home and the domestic, as explored in the book, and the sort of flat-pack, mass-produced furniture and tech consoles found in the homes of many people who play games.

And of course, as game designers, we wanted to make the cover playful by turning it into its own little game. Moments and stories from the book are hidden throughout the cover art—see how many you can find!

THE GROUNDS OF GAMING

INTRODUCTION

Men, Place, and Games

Staging the Mancounter

Every couple of months from 2015 to when we left Raleigh in summer of 2022, I would invite a friend—and, for a time, neighbor—over to play video games. These sessions were far from the spontaneous "Hey, want to come over and play Nintendo after school (or class, or work)?" that constituted so much of my social life as a child and young adult, the only barriers to which were getting the requisite parental approval and perhaps making sure most of the next day's schoolwork was done. These gaming nights had to be planned well in advance. They were coordinated through consultation with our partners, opportunistic alignment of fluctuating work and social schedules, and availability and desirability of particular games: mostly first- or third-person shooters, sometimes sports games, sometimes party games. We would play games that I do not often play by myself and in which my friend, who was an avid *GoldenEye* and *Halo* player back in his college days (but now games only rarely), had some residual competency.

To prepare for these sessions, I would gather my Sony PlayStation 4 (PS4) and one of my computer monitors from the third floor of our tall but tiny house in Raleigh, grab a portable speaker from the second floor, and arrange them on the kitchen island countertop on the first floor. Wires and cords would get strewn across the counter, dangling off the edge. I always strived to set this ad hoc gaming apparatus up before my friend's arrival but rarely managed to do so without some hitch: a game needed updating because I

1

had not played it in a while, the temperamental portable speaker would not connect properly, or the batteries on one or both of the PS4 controllers were dead. This was a consistent enough occurrence that fiddling with the setup became part of our pregaming ritual as much as catching up on each other's lives—a settling in of technologies, bodies, and affects.

We timed sessions to take place on weeknights, often when our partners had other plans, in the hours in between when our children went to bed and when we ought to have gone to bed. The two of us would sit on barstools about a half meter apart, drinking overpriced craft beer, eating corn chips, and playing games. We began these sessions when my friend lived right across the street and we had both become new parents; his eldest was born five weeks before our child. We used the time to chat about parenthood, work, family, politics, our mutual friends. We disclosed things—it was fairly early on during one of these sessions, for instance, that he informed me he and his spouse had bought a new house and were moving out of our neighborhood.

Both of us consider ourselves and each other to be committed and involved parents and partners, concerned with a fair division of labor with our respective spouses when it comes to domestic work. We took care to ensure that sessions neither inconvenienced our partners nor intruded into our social or professional obligations. They occurred in the interstitial periods of our lives as spouses, fathers, friends, and workers. They were ethereal and ephemeral; they left no trace, save for one or two social media posts or inside jokes about one game or another. They took place and, temporarily, took up space on the kitchen counter as an unstable, "janky" apparatus.[1] At the same time, these sessions were built on the sedimented cultural foundations of mine and my friend's individual experiences playing other games with other people, mostly white men, in other places and times. What made these sessions work, socially if not always technologically, was the solidity of that sedimentation: the ability for a gaming arrangement similar enough to the kinds we enjoyed as children, teenagers, and young adults to constitute a kind of social foundation, one more stable and functional than the technical apparatus itself.

We dubbed these sessions "mancounters" as a bad joke, and, like a lot of bad jokes, the name stuck. The term makes sense for a couple of reasons, one spatial and one temporal. First, it is a somewhat deprecatory riff on "man caves," domestic spaces dedicated wholly to forms of male homosociality and centered around rituals of competition and dramatized violence such as video games or, more commonly, sports spectatorship.[2] Unlike the cave, the counter is ad hoc, temporary, and opportunistic. It occupies an intensely social and shared space (like many modern houses, the open kitchen was the focal point of our home) repurposed for a slightly more exclusive sociality. I could set it up in ten minutes, however imperfectly, and take it down in five after my friend left, redistributing its components to their proper place in our house. As a gaming space, the mancounter was as unobtrusive and undemanding as the man cave is territorial and fixed. It is certainly a stretch to characterize as feminist any space in which two straight, white, economically advantaged, cis male settlers play games, but as a gaming arrangement, it was at least careful of the space it temporarily occupied. The mancounter tried not to manspread.[3]

"Mancounter" is also a portmanteau of "man" and "encounter," where more temporal connotations come into play. It evokes forms and practices of white masculine contact that are illicit, or at least invisible and inaccessible to outsiders: the public washroom, the pool hall, the bathhouse. Like these other transient encounters, the mancounter was a momentary reprieve from the normative rules governing public interactions between those involved (most often, but not always, white men).[4] This is not to say there were no rules to the mancounter. Rather, it was a reprieve from the responsibilities that characterize the everyday, a way of invoking, briefly, past periods of our lives when gaming with friends was much more mundane and accessible, or when—given his family's move to a new neighborhood and, later, the pandemic—spending time with each other did not require so much effort. Like other ostensibly casual forms of homosocial rendezvous, mancounters were made possible by meticulous coordination and staging.

Video games played a crucial role in these occasions. For starters, I would go to some lengths planning which games we played; mancounters were not simply staged but curated as well. In the weeks leading up, I would check in with my friend about possible options, texting him links to trailers for games he might find enjoyable. I would search review sites, watch Twitch.tv (Twitch) streams, and consult co-optimus.com, the long-standing website that rates and reviews games featuring cooperative, colocated play, to get a feel for games. The games needed to be approachable enough in terms of narrative and given our middling competencies to avoid causing too much frustration—in other words, they needed to offer relatively casual experiences, at least for players with some preexisting knowledge of genre conventions, mechanics, and interfaces. They could be neither attentionally nor temporally demanding. Sometimes we took turns—life or level—as with *Titanfall 2* or *The Division 2*. Sometimes we played split-screen co-op, as with *Borderlands 3*. Sometimes we played the game over multiple sessions, as with *Battlefield 1*, completing the campaign over multiple mancounters. As a general rule, the games we played in these sessions were *only* played in these sessions, again marking the mancounter as a space and time apart from our normative, day-to-day realities.

The games that interested us the most were big-budget first-person shooters (FPS), games normally associated with hypermasculine characters and themes, narratives of militarized conquest, and play experiences centered around violent movement through gamespace.[5] Neither of us found an explicit ideological purchase in these games—quite the opposite. The hackneyed plot and cel-shaded postapocalyptic wasteland of *Borderlands 3* were not the main draws for us, and while we may have applauded the inclusion of more racial and gender diversity in *Battlefield*'s cast of playable characters, we were by no means invested in their appearances and backstories. Rather, these games drew us in because my friend and I shared a similar level of competency with the genre's mechanics and conventions; we did not have to put much effort into learning controls, competencies with which had been inscribed into our bodies through more intensive play sessions, decades earlier, of *Goldeneye*, *Halo*, and the like. The mechanics of the games we leaned toward, like the arrangement of the mancounter itself, called back to times when playing alongside masculine friends was woven into the fabric of our respective lives.

Men at Play

As a site of hypothetical scholarly interest, the mancounter can be approached in any number of ways, consistent with the multidisciplinary tangle of game studies scholarship. We might inquire into the motivations of participants for playing certain games or try to measure the effects of playing these games on our self-efficacy, empathy, aggression levels, or ability to navigate three-dimensional environments. We might wonder about the design and arrangement of interface elements and how these aid in our enjoyment (and continued use) of the game or system. We might consider the formal rules and mechanics of the games themselves to understand how these systems work together (or do not) to create a play experience. We might ask what forms of perception and attention the games demand of players and what sorts of affects they induce. We might inquire into the forms of monetization and surveillance implanted in the games and how, through our play, we create value for game publishers. And we might certainly consider their representational politics, asking how the militarized themes, characters, and environments of the games we gravitated toward further extend the conjoined projects of patriarchy, capitalism, and white supremacy. This latter set of approaches has been among the most well used and oft cited in scholarly understandings of how games and associated communicative practices aid in the construction and circulation of masculinities, particularly those trafficking in reactionary and hyperexclusionary logics.[6]

These approaches—and in particular, critical studies of gaming using player-centered, representationalist techniques—have pulled together a remarkably comprehensive sketch of the figure who has long stood at the center of gaming. This figure is predominantly white (or, not uncommonly, Asian), cisgender, heterosexual, and male.[7] From early childhood, he has enjoyed near-unfettered access to games, gaming technologies, and sites of play.[8] He is well accustomed to having his gaming experiences, preferences, and embodied competencies taken very seriously by the games industry, so much so that he regards attempts to cater to other demographics as an affront, if not threat, to his way of life and source of identity.[9] His mastery of games is expressed in statistical terms—refresh rate, rate of fire, lag time, damage over time, damage per second, frames per second, critical hit percentage, subscription counts, gear score, player ranking—and he has a deep familiarity with the numerical substrata of games that allows him to hone the efficiency and effectiveness of his in-game exploits.[10] He acquires these competencies through online forums, YouTube videos, and other platforms and has even dabbled in producing his own content. These platforms are some of his primary tools for cultural and rhetorical gatekeeping, for insisting on the sorts of competencies, dispositions, and literacies that mark one as "in" games culture.[11] He is acutely aware of the increasing mainstream visibility of gaming culture, which he views with some irony while enjoying the increased range of lifestyle products (drinks, furniture, pharmaceuticals) that cater to authentic players like him.[12] In theory, he does not mind the presence of women, trans, nonbinary, queer, BIPOC, or differently abled gamers—he may even boast of his affiliation with them—so long as they can hold their own and take a joke.[13] He insists that gaming is a true meritocracy and dismisses any evidence to the contrary as smug wokeness or SJW (social justice warrior) bullshit.[14] He frequently finds common cause with other elements of the perpetually aggrieved manosphere, such as incels, the alt-right, ethnonationalists, and antifeminists, but he would not describe himself as particularly political.[15] He is just here to game.

As indicated by the detail and breadth of this composite sketch, this subject has been extensively documented. We know "that guy" very well, and we know what forms of cultural expression he relies on and traffics in for his sense of belonging.[16] The particular gendered subjectivity he embodies has been given several names: "technicity," "technomasculinity," or just plain "gamer."[17] Ergin Bulut describes this set of dispositions succinctly—it "becomes visible through good command of computer knowledge, machinic manipulation, passion for games, antiauthoritarian work attitude, or ordinary use of language that bears the imprints of gendered imaginations and assumptions."[18] But as comprehensive as this picture is, it tells us little about the material conditions that allow for the emergence and continued presence of the subject. Instead, these approaches tend to take as a priori the fact of the player's engagement with the game. In the varied and otherwise distinct approaches to making sense of the mancounter listed above, what seems to matter most is what happens between screen (and, occasionally, input device) and player. Spatiotemporal arrangements like the mancounter, not to mention more stable domestic gaming setups, local area network (LAN) parties, esports houses, games industry conventions, and so on, tend to fade from view in scholarly accounts of gaming, masculinity, and whiteness—at most, they are the inert backdrops, the "meatspace," for the more spectacular and perhaps more immediately problematic performances of masculinity staged by the game itself. And yet, the places where games are played, discussed, bought, sold, watched, and made are intensely generative and agential sites of political and cultural production: they enable certain subjects to cultivate the competencies, cultural practices, social futures, and embodied identities related to games, while disallowing others. In order to grasp their cultural significance and possibly intervene into the long-standing inequities associated with them, I believe we need to decenter interactions between player and game—at least temporarily—and foreground the spatial dimensions and place-based practices through which gaming's connections to white masculinity are reproduced. As a first step toward this project, I want to outline how I understand masculinities themselves, particularly in relation to (i) other axes of privilege and oppression (most notably, race) and (ii) technological artifacts and practices—including, but by no means limited to, games and gaming devices.

Hegemonic Masculinity and Whiteness

Like many masculinities scholars, I find Raewyn Connell's work on masculinities and her theorization of "hegemonic masculinity" in particular (both in her own work and in collaboration with James Messerschmidt) to be an indispensable touchstone in conceptualizing what masculinities are and how they operate. Connell and Messerschmidt define masculinities as "configurations of practice that are accomplished in social action and, therefore, can differ according to the gender relations in a particular social setting."[19] Masculinities are multiple, historically and geographically situated, and shaped by intersecting systems of race, sexuality, class, age, language, and so on. Regardless of iteration, all masculinities are based on and work to reproduce connections between masculinized bodies and power— political, economic, technological, cultural, physical. Masculinities are modes of embodying, in practice, the unequal distribution of rights, privileges, resources, and responsibilities within gender hierarchies meant "to guarantee the dominant position of men and the subordination of women."[20] Any particular iteration of masculinity, even one rooted in parody or subversion, will embody some aspect of this hierarchically organized distribution. What makes a given formation of masculinity "hegemonic" is not whether it is enacted by a majority of men; few men are capable of fully embodying hegemonic masculinity. Rather, a formation of masculinity becomes hegemonic in the extent to which it supports hegemony—the process of securing consent for the dominant social, political, and economic order. Hegemonic masculinity therefore undergoes constant transformation and renewal as the conditions of hegemony change. As one brief example, we might look to the value placed on "hustle" and "grind" in contemporary masculinities. These terms have become increasingly detached from their initial connotations among African American communities and now underscore men's capacity to find success and fulfillment in a late capitalist society in which work is increasingly platformized and precarious through an entrepreneurial ethos and sheer grit. As an emergent paragon of masculinity, the hustling, risk-taking (and frequently, white) self-starter—whether ride-share driver, video game livestreamer, or app developer (maybe all three)—helps shore up and legitimize the ascendancy of "platform capitalism" and the attendant prioritization of corporate profit above all else.[21]

As indicated through these examples, the interplay between hegemonic masculinity and race, colonialism, and class is central to contemporary understandings of masculinities. The "playful subject" courted by the games industry (and constitutive of much of its workforce), and the figure who populates the (mostly) US- and Canada-based gaming contexts I consider in this book, accrues his privilege from intersections of hegemonic masculinity with whiteness and settler coloniality.[22] In his examination of the origins of tabletop gaming culture in model railroading clubs and wargaming communities, Aaron Trammell foregrounds whiteness as a foundational condition for what he calls the "networks of privilege" formed via these early "geek" hobbies. Through careful historical analysis, Trammell shows how the activities of model train communities and wargaming hobbyists unfolded in the "white male enclaves" of the suburban, postwar United States: a racialized geography formed through the white flight of the 1950s and 1960s as middle-class white families moved from cities to suburbs, motivated in part by consumer comforts and in part by fears of Black civil unrest.[23] According to Trammell, present-day geek hobbyists are inheritors of a historically subordinate masculinity utterly reliant on and imbricated in the privileges that come with whiteness—what Ergin Bulut calls "the sociocultural infrastructure behind discourses of fun, success, or escapism."[24] By situating the emergence of tabletop hobbyism within the racial dynamics of post–World War II America, Trammell offers a mode of intersectional analysis regarding whiteness and masculinity that is well needed in studies of leisure media, a vital touchstone for the project I take up in this book.

Where Trammell's work excavates the racial dynamics of tabletop gaming, Ergin Bulut's *A Precarious Game: The Illusion of Dream Jobs in the Video Game Industry* undertakes a similarly intersectional consideration of labor relations in contemporary game development. Bulut's analysis unfolds from a simple but provocative question: who works so that we can play?[25] If the term "networks of privilege" guides our attention to the racialized economic, political, and geographic conditions that allow for the hegemonic status of white masculinity within gaming cultures, "ludopolitics," the term Bulut offers for power relations animating the games industry, situates this concern within a global political economy. Bulut emphasizes that the costs of white masculinity's propensity for play—whether over beers at the mancounter or at work in a game development dream job—are rarely exacted on these playful subjects themselves. Rather, their playfulness is paid for by their partners in the form of domestic labor and the work of social reproduction; by the poor (often Black and Indigenous) urban communities that are displaced when video game companies push for the "revitalizing" gentrification of Canadian and American city centers; and by workers in the Global South, whose dangerous and dehumanizing labor provides for the circuits of extraction, processing, and disposal of materials the games industry requires.[26] Under late-stage capitalism, in which exploitation and precarity are features, not bugs, "one's creative pleasure and escapism are enabled by somebody else's pain"—pain distributed according to logics of patriarchy, white supremacy, and colonialism.[27]

Taken together, these concepts—networks of privilege and ludopolitics—highlight the ways in which whiteness and hegemonic masculinity intersect in both historical and present-day gaming contexts. Moreover, Trammell and Bulut employ an understanding of whiteness as a structural construct that, like hegemonic masculinity (and operating in tandem with it), is continually reconstituted through legal frameworks, civic and political apparatuses, racial ideologies, economic systems, and technologies; as succinctly stated by Trammell, "white people enjoy cheaper mortgage rates, more just treatment by police, better jobs, and the freedom to speak their mind without fear of retaliation."[28] We can add to this list the ability to enjoy digital games without race-based harassment, marginalization, stereotyping, and violence.[29] This systemic understanding of whiteness operates against a strain in "critical whiteness studies" to understand racism as something that can somehow be solved by "converting white people" to antiracist beliefs.[30] White supremacy will not be dismantled simply by folks like me learning to unpack their privilege knapsack, but rather by challenging the infrastructural operations of whiteness as it circulates through our institutions as well as through our everyday interactions with each other.[31]

Technogenders, Cultural Techniques, and Apparatuses

Of vital importance to this understanding of masculinities is the insistence that they are not just sets of norms, mediated prescriptions for and representations of manliness. They are also constituted through nondiscursive practices, including "wage labor, violence, sexuality, domestic labor, and child care as well as through unreflective routinized actions."[32] We might extend this argument further and insist that masculinities (like all gendered subjectivities) are constituted through technological processes that define and fix our bodies as "male" or "female" in order to assign them to their proper place within a gender hierarchy, one historically based on Victorian ideals of sexual dimorphism. Such is Paul B. Preciado's central thesis articulating the notion of "technogender": that "male and female are terms without empirical content beyond the technologies that produce them."[33] Preciado's understanding of technology is akin to Bernhard Siegert's concept of "cultural techniques," defined as the concretization of "signs, instruments, and human practices . . . into durable symbolic systems."[34] Technologies, understood through the lens of cultural techniques, are always both material and discursive and are fundamentally engaged in the production of difference.[35] As an example, we might look to the gender reveal party as a cultural technique for the production of a gendered subject before birth: a binding together of scientific instruments (the ultrasound), artifacts (cupcakes, confetti, explosives, balloons), signs (binary codes expressed through color, language, and iconography used to designate gender), spaces and place-making practices (the backyard, the nursery), and organic beings (parents, friends and family members, fetus). The result is the ascription of the unborn child to dimorphic gender regimes, accomplishing one of the most powerful and agential forms of belonging in white patriarchal capitalism—and only occasionally at the cost of human injury or environmental devastation.[36]

In Preciado's work, technogenders are cultural techniques that, like gender reveal parties, hair grooming devices, hormone treatments, clothing, skincare products, contraceptives, sex toys, piercings, weddings, bathrooms, mancounters, and so on, work on and through our bodies to produce gender difference. It is worth quoting Preciado in full to appreciate their understanding of gender as biotechnological artifice (and the artifice with which they express this insight).

> The certainty of being a man or a woman is a somato-political biofiction
> produced by a collection of body technologies, pharmacologic and audiovi-
> sual techniques that determine and define the scope of our somatic
> potentialities and function like prostheses of subjectification. Gender is
> an operational program capable of triggering a proliferation of sensory

perceptions under the form of affects, desires, actions, beliefs, and identities. One of the characteristic results of such a technology of gender is the production of inner knowledge about oneself, with a sense of a sexual self that appears to be an emotional reality that is evident to consciousness. "I am a man," "I am a woman," "I am heterosexual," "I am homosexual," "I am transsexual": these are units of specific knowledge about oneself, hard biopolitical nuclei around which it's possible to assemble an entire collection of discourses and performative practices.[37]

Technogenders thus constitute the means through which we understand and (re)make ourselves, and are understood and (re)made by others, as gendered subjects; they are key building blocks in the production of masculinities, among other gender formations.

In keeping with Preciado's own concern with understanding how gendered subjects are brought into being, I lean on the Foucauldian notion of the *apparatus* to understand how cultural techniques of gender (as well as cultural techniques for the production of other intersecting forms of difference such as race and class) are assembled to construct a particular masculine subject central to, and centered in, digital play. Michel Foucault defines an apparatus (*dispositif* in French, which might also be translated as "device" or "operation") as a network of "discourses, institutions, architectural forms, regulatory decisions, laws, administrative measures, scientific statements, philosophical, moral, and philanthropic propositions . . . the apparatus itself is the system of relations that can be established between these elements."[38] The concept—generative, if initially nebulous—has been adapted further by Jeremy Packer, who rearticulates it as a system of relations that has as its goal the production of a particular subject.[39] Within this system, or "machine of subjectivization," Packer sees media playing a vital role: media are the instruments that bind and hold elements of the apparatus together.[40] If, for instance, we consider the apparatus of home cooking and its relatively recent alignment with the formation of a white, upper middle-class masculine subject, we might consider how media texts (cookbooks by and for men, social media, television shows, movies featuring hypermasculine chefs) and media instruments (kitchen gadgets such as immersion circulators, black rubber gloves, instant-read thermometers, digital scales, and other devices that amplify power and precision) work to bind the man-who-cooks-at-home to a set of embodied practices and discourses that make cooking a visible, highly technologized, and legitimate investment of time, energy, and capital. To take an example from my own work on white masculinity and esports, we could see how the hypermediated domain of contemporary esports spectatorship functions as an apparatus of "kinaesthetic masculinity": "the potential, through the aestheticization of masculine bodies in violent motion, and the capture, storage, and distribution of their athletic performance, to provide other masculine subjects in other places and times with a feeling of belonging to the activity—of virtually being there."[41] Here, the crack *Counter-Strike* or *Valorant* player is encouraged to imagine that he can make it as a streamer or professional esports athlete provided he hustles and grinds hard enough to ascend through the "toxic meritocracy" of competitive gaming.[42] Through livestreaming platforms and infrastructures for networked play, he need not simply follow his favorite streamers' exploits; he may in fact participate in and *best* those exploits.

Applied to understandings of masculinity and gaming, these related concepts of *technogender, cultural techniques,* and *apparatus* provide means of considering how gaming masculinities are made possible through the arrangement of various systems, practices, and technical artifacts, many of which are well documented by scholars of gender and gaming: crunch time; workplace harassment; racist and misogynistic language in game chat and on forums, Twitch streams, and YouTube videos; game advertising; esports scholarships; gaming chairs; avatar customization systems; energy drinks; and so on. These become components in machines of subjectivization that produce predominantly white masculine identities rooted in and expressed through an intensive investment in gaming practices—the dominating esports athlete, the charismatic Twitch streamer, the entrepreneurial game developer, the hardcore PC rig builder and case modder, the responsible dad who games. All of these masculine subjectivities have in common (and indeed, are made possible by) a privileged relationship to the technologies, infrastructures, and places associated with intensive gaming.

Inverting the Game Studies Gestalt

While we know a great deal—perhaps too much—about these playful subjects and their interactions with gaming and its related communicative practices, we know much less about the spatial and temporal arrangements that make these interactions possible. And yet, such arrangements reveal much about the contemporary cultural politics of digital gaming and the relations of power and conditions of privilege and oppression that video gaming engages. For instance, returning to the mancounter, consider how gender, race, class, and mobility all come into play in the following:

- My friend could travel from his gentrified neighborhood in downtown Raleigh to mine and back, at night, without fear of harassment or violence, particularly at the hands of the police. His mobility and bodily autonomy are relatively unfettered.

- We both have spouses who were able to attend to our young children should they require nighttime attention and care, and we had no other dependents living with us whose comfort and safety we needed to consider (e.g., elderly parents).

- The house my spouse and I owned in Raleigh had an open concept kitchen as well as other areas for leisure and socialization, such that I did inconvenience her too much by hosting an occasional mancounter in the kitchen.

- The mancounter built on our respective earlier experiences with co-located gaming in dorm rooms, parents' basements, friends' houses, and so on; these histories were made possible in part because my friend and I belong to a demographic that has consistently been *the* target audience for video games and game systems.

- My friend and I both had steady, white-collar jobs that allowed us to not only own homes but also set aside time in the evening for occasional gaming sessions; we enjoyed (and still do) a degree of temporal autonomy, of command over our own time.

- Our access to media equipment and infrastructures such as high-end gaming gear and reliable internet connectivity was, for us, an unremarkable condition of our lives as middle-class, white, settler, cis men dwelling in an urban, technology-rich area.

These are just some of the more obvious forms of mobility and agency the mancounter leveraged as a spatiotemporal arrangement that allowed my friend and I to reproduce bonds through colocative gameplay. Even as a relatively benign and unobtrusive playground for white masculinity, the mancounter relied on and, crucially, reproduced boundaries: between male and female, play and work, white and Black, insider and outsider, belonging and isolation. Foregrounding the mancounter's operations *of* and *in* place not only gives us a richer understanding of the patterns of privilege and oppression that shape contemporary digital play but also increases the breadth of resources, both theoretical and practical, that we can turn to in order to intervene into gaming's persistent involvement in the production of inequality. In doing so, we necessarily shift our attention away from the playful white masculine subject and his ludic preferences. This figure remains present throughout this book, but he is, for the most part, silhouetted. He recedes from view in the following essays so that we may instead focus on the arrangement of physical gaming sites, the other humans and nonhumans who populate them, the infrastructures that connect them, and the relations of power that determine who is allowed to enter, and stay, and in what capacity.

To use a distinction introduced by Gestalt psychology and popularized in media studies by Marshall McLuhan, players and the games they interact with constitute the *figures*—the attention-grabbing, semiotically hypercharged, and endlessly problematized beacons of scholarly and public interest—while the spatiotemporal arrangements I dwell on here form the *grounds*.[43] This book is centrally concerned with effecting an epistemic inversion between the grounds of gaming and its figures, particularly relating to our understanding of games, whiteness, and masculinity.

Space, Place, and Games

At the root of this investigation are two interrelated questions. The first is how we *make space* for games, and the second is how games take part in *making place*. As the shape of these questions suggest, I am indebted to the distinctions cultural geographers made between space and place; specifically to the work of feminist cultural geographer Doreen Massey in theorizing the dynamic relationships between space, place, gender, ethnicity, and class. Throughout her prolific work, Massey articulates definitions of space and place as produced by, and productive of, social relations—and therefore, of power. "The spatial," for Massey, is "constructed out of the multiplicity of social relations across all spatial scales, from the global reach of finance and telecommunications, through the geography of the tentacles of national political power, to the social relations within the town, the settlement, the household and the workplace."[44] To state that society is spatially organized, therefore, is to recognize the role of space in producing and shaping social relations.

Massey's conception of space and place broadly parallels, and occasionally intertwines with, the Marxist geography of Henri Lefebvre. Each are concerned, in Massey's words, with understanding space as "both an arena of action and potentially enabling/productive of further effect."[45] That is, space is not simply the inert backdrop on which the social unfolds—an empty container awaiting human agency—but product and productive of social relations. Like Massey, Lefebvre's writings on space are too wide ranging and evolving to pin down to a single, pithy formulation, but his conception of a "spatial triad" comes close. As articulated by David Harvey, Lefebvre's spatial triad models a dialectical relationship between embodied and material experience of space; perceived dimensions of space as represented through everyday media and academic disciplines dealing with space; and imagined space, communicative practices that "seek to generate new meanings or possibilities" for how we interact with space (we might include video games among such "spaces of representation").[46] Lefebvre's conception of space, and this triad in particular, have been put to use by other critical scholars who, like me, are interested in better understanding the ways that the contexts of digital play shape (and are, in turn, shaped by) gaming cultures' long-standing inequities along lines of gender, race, and class.[47]

Despite this precedent for favoring Lefebvre in scholarly considerations of gaming's spatial practices and politics, my own approach throughout this book leans more heavily on Massey's work. This choice is due, in large part, to my commitment to an explicitly feminist project of articulating the spatial dimensions of gaming's gender-based marginalizations and oppressions. Massey's conception of spatial practices seems to be grounded in a profoundly relational understanding between space and time, gender and other categories of difference, local and global scales: a capacity and an insistence on seeing these as mutually constituted and in continual transformation rather than as fixed abstractions. Ultimately, to echo Gillian Hart in her account of becoming a geographer, my primary reliance on Massey (instead of other cultural or critical geographers) has less to do with a sense that one set of theories is better than others and more to do with pragmatic deliberation and a sense of intellectual and ethical kinship. I am, like Hart, in complete agreement with Massey regarding the importance of critical theorizations of space and place—that they "are not just part of academic debates, but

constitute key analytical and political resources in the increasingly dangerous conditions in which we find ourselves."[48]

Bringing this sensitivity toward space into conversation with media
studies necessitates what Lisa Parks and Nicole Starosielski term an "infrastructural disposition" toward media—how people and resources are geographically and culturally distributed, how they are connected by multiple,
overlapping communication networks, and how such networks of distribution and circulation allow and inhibit certain forms of mobility and agency.[49]
Understanding the mancounter in infrastructural terms, for instance, requires attending to (or at the very least, acknowledging) processes of gentrification and racialized patterns of wealth concentration that shape the
neighborhoods in Raleigh where we lived; colonial histories through which
we come to dwell, work, and play on land that was stewarded for millennia
by the Tuscarora and Catawba peoples before their violent dispossession;
infrastructures that provide our home with electrical power and internet
connectivity, to say nothing of running water and easy access to food and
alcohol; and global systems of game production that extract, process, and
circulate raw materials, labor, data, and so on, allowing me enjoy the latest
game without leaving my house. These considerations are incommensurate
with any notion of space as "flat, immobilized surface" or as the container
in which things happen.[50] We cannot grasp the cultural significance of the
mancounter, as mundane and unexciting as it might be, solely through what
happened "in" our kitchen (or for that matter, "in" the game), separable from
the social and material relations outlined above. The same goes for any gaming arrangement.

Place can be defined in similarly relational and temporal terms. If the
spatial is "formed out of social interrelations at all scales," writes Massey,
then place "is a particular articulation of those relations, a particular moment in those networks of social relations and understandings."[51] A place
arises out of the unfolding, in time, of spatial relations: the mancounter
becomes a place of homosocial bonding between two friends through the
arrangement of spatial conditions (gentrified neighborhood; single-family
home; central, open-plan kitchen) and temporal relations (after children's
bedtime; spouses otherwise occupied; alignment of two white-collar workers' social and professional schedules). Crucially, for Massey, places serve
as sites for the construction of subjectivities, and in turn, certain subjects
become associated with certain places—a "double articulation" in which

place and subjectivity are coconstructed.[52] A central premise of this book is that the intertwined megastructures of patriarchy, colonialism, capitalism, and white supremacy work, in part, by facilitating fixed boundaries around the spaces of play, boundaries that *make place* in part by delineating which subjects can and cannot participate.

While not explicitly invoking Massey's double articulation, a similar understanding of the coconstitutive relationship between place and subject formation is offered by Paul B. Preciado in their account of how white, middle-class masculinity was reimagined throughout the 1950s and 1960s by *Playboy* magazine. Preciado recounts Hugh Hefner's efforts to construct a novel masculine subjectivity, both in *Playboy's* editorials on the swingin' bachelor pad and all the things it ought to house and through Hefner's own well-publicized and extensively documented architectural projects. Decades before feminist cultural theorists and cultural geographers articulated the coconstitutive relationship between place and subjectivity, suggests Preciado, Hugh Hefner had keyed on the insight that to build a new masculine subjectivity, one had to first construct his dwelling.[53] Hefner's place-making activities served as incubator, a "biopolitical, surrogated womb," for the "indoor man": the subject who transforms domestic space from a feminizing domain of housekeeping and social reproduction into a masculine world of media mastery, playful hedonism, aesthetic refinement, and heterosexual conquest.[54]

This book is indebted to Massey and Preciado's separate but thematically connected projects of conceptualizing the inequitable distribution of cultural, economic, technological, and legal resources and privileges in terms of spatial and temporal dimensions—their insight that we become subjects, in part, through what kinds of *places* become possible for us and give us a sense of belonging. It is my contention in this book that a full reckoning of digital play as an agential site of cultural production and subjectivity formation cannot be achieved without an understanding of how games *make place*. With this brief overview of space and place, I turn to the book's key questions.

Key Questions

The book first poses the question, How do we adapt our physical surroundings to house, support, and power digital gameplay—not just in our homes but in convention centers, stores, university campuses, game development

offices, and so on? This line of inquiry owes much to studies of media domestication, in particular to Lynn Spigel's landmark work exploring the
ways US-based media industries, in the decades following World War II,
encouraged families (mothers in particular) to "make room" for the TV, placing the TV at the spatial and affective center of the suburban, white home:
the nucleus of the nuclear family.[55] As I explore more fully in chapter 2,
on domestic gaming setups, my book builds on and extends a robust body
of ethnographic and critical work that explores how the organization of
gaming technologies in homes reflects and organizes gendered differences
in leisure time and practices.[56] Later chapters move beyond the home to
include nondomestic spatial arrangements: LAN parties (chap. 3), college
campuses (chap. 4), and games industry conventions (chap. 5). These chapters are indebted to scholarly explorations of how our built environments are
transformed for the production and play of video games. Such a broad geographic sensitivity is demonstrated in Ergin Bulut and Aphra Kerr's separate
accounts of how tax subsidies and zoning regulations make certain regions
and municipalities more attractive for game companies, spurring further
forms of gentrification, and Nicholas Dyer-Witheford and Greg de Peuter's
consideration of the zones of extraction and disposal required to make and
discard of gaming hardware and of the necropolitical, neocolonial regimes
that arrange these place-making practices.[57] Aided by such orientations, the
chapters collectively constitute an *infrastructural* understanding of gaming
and its inequities: a blueprint, or the makings of a blueprint, of how arrangements of gaming bodies, technologies, and ideologies circulating across different spaces and times tend to prioritize certain forms of participation and
belonging while making others improbable or unsafe.

The second set of questions concern *place*. How do particular configurations of gaming technologies, in homes, convention centers, classrooms, and
so on, serve to bind certain social relations in place? What sorts of boundaries—material, discursive, infrastructural, economic, legal—are constructed
around physical sites of gaming? Inversely, how does the presence of games
and gaming technologies in certain places constitute such boundaries? For
whom does the presence of a monitor connected to an Xbox console running
Madden, for instance, signal that a location is potentially inhospitable or
even unsafe? In the terms offered by Massey and Preciado, the sites of intensive gaming I consider in this book build on historical forms of place making
that privilege the intersections of masculinity, whiteness, and computational

mastery in order to quite literally keep certain people out. To return to the mancounter, it is not *just* a place; it is more accurately a *place-making practice* in which my friend and I rehearsed our privileged subject positions as parents, partners, and workers who had (so we told ourselves) earned a momentary reprieve from our cares via colocative gaming experiences that called back to our histories as members of gaming's core demographic. The mancounter may be a relatively benign instance of masculine place making, but it is one made possible by other spatiotemporal practices, historical and current. These include not only the forms of racial, gendered, classed, and colonial exclusions mentioned above but also the technogendered practices of my childhood, in which my parents allowed the Nintendo Entertainment System to stay in my bedroom, ensuring I had unfettered access and my sister only a contested and negotiated access to the family gaming console. In a similar vein, each of the sites of intensive gaming and games-related work I examine in this book are continuations and refinements, under emerging technical and economic transformations, of the long-standing project in which we become subjects according to the place-making practices that are made (in)accessible to us, which is to say that games are a powerful tool in the disciplinary project of keeping people in their proper place.[58]

Relocating Play

Paying attention to physical sites of gaming and the conditions that make them possible is in keeping with the (now lengthy) "materialist turn" in media studies more broadly and game studies more specifically.[59] Despite this turn, the prevailing mode in which game studies scholars conceptualize the spatial is via consideration of the *virtual* spaces we navigate through play. There are notable exceptions, of course, but the overarching concern of game studies scholars with regard to questions of space is nonetheless to understand players' experiences of inhabiting and moving through digital gameworlds. As outcomes of machinic processes (altered by player input) made possible by global infrastructures of power and connectivity, gamespaces remain wholly a part of the material world and are not some alternative, autonomous domain. Yet games allow for the simulation of movement, *as if* they offer an objective reality. While scholarship on games and space often acknowledges that gameworlds are created through the intentions of game designers working through the technical and aesthetic capabilities of code, platform, and game engine, it frequently takes as its analytical starting point players' movements in digital gamespace. This is perhaps best articulated by Espen Aarseth's foundational work on games as "allegories" of space. Aarseth notes that games are centrally concerned with "spatial presentation and negotiation" accomplished through the computational production of visual representations of space and thus "already dependent on our bodily experience in, and of, real space."[60]

Scholarship on gamespace that builds on and extends from Aarseth's work largely sets aside the balance he strikes between acknowledging gamespace's machine-generated, simulated nature on one hand and the perception of movement it enables on the other in favor of exploring the perceptual phenomenon of ludic movement. The result is a sort of phenomenological privileging of the player's (and by that, we can mean, researcher's) experience of gamespace: it is experienced *as* space, so it must *be* space—or at least, can be treated as space for the sake of analysis and discussion. One consequence of this premise is a kind of slipperiness and uncertainty regarding the ontological status of gamespace, particularly in relation (and frequently, in comparison) to actual space. Actual space enters the discussion as a rich site for appropriating certain techniques of analyzing and engineering spatial experiences, as in Michael Nitsche's look at how games borrow from architecture and theater or Nokkvi Bjarnason's consideration of how we might position gameplay as a form of travel.[61] At other times, real space is posited, briefly, as that which we escape by entering gamespace, which furnishes a sense of lived space unavailable to those whose economic precarity means they may never experience home "as a fixed or congruent physical or familiar site."[62] What was initially treated in Aarseth's foundational text as a hallucination or allegory of actual space constituted through material and symbolic processes instead becomes an ontologically parallel, and perhaps more welcoming, domain.[63] Thus, we have earnest and robustly theorized accounts of gameplay that talk of players "teleporting" into games, "crawl[ing] through the frame," being "transported" into a new world.[64] Through such rhetorical and analytical techniques, the notion that games constitute a separate spatial domain has become firmly established; it has become a matter of fact rather than a matter of concern, enabling scholars to apply theories initially intended for

the analysis of physical space, like Massey's or Lefebvre's, to our phenomenological experiences of games without much modification.[65]

The result is an apparent divide that becomes the work of games (and
game designers) to cross through particular techniques. A first-person
camera, an intuitive interface, atmospheric audio cues, and a fine-tuned
choreography between players' skill levels and a game's challenges are all
particularly lauded for their ability to transport players from the real world
into gamespace. Such bridges are described in terms of perceptual states—
"flow," "immersion," "presence"—that are notoriously difficult to measure
but nonetheless discussed frequently in objective, quantifiable terms (i.e.,
high vs. low presence).[66] While the specific nuances and conceptual affordances of these different terms are a matter of some debate, they are generally
understood as states of perception that arise from the player's engagement
with properties of the virtual environment and are accomplished primarily
through an alchemical combination of the aforementioned design elements.
Little to no mention is made of the material conditions that must be met
in order for flow, immersion, or presence to become possible: no children
tugging at your arm or cat walking across your keyboard, no disruptions
to electrical power and internet connection, no discomfort or strain felt in
the wrists, eyes, ears, bottom, no pressing obligations or lingering anxieties
about your safety. The inhabitant of gamespace, immersed in the virtual
environment, is thus frequently assumed to be a subject for whom spatial,
temporal, embodied, and material conditions pose no constraints. Our capacity to experience and theorize games in these terms, as parallel, discrete
spaces, presumes that our bodies and material surroundings have become
infrastructural: preconditions for the experience largely disappearing from
view.

In the materialist approach I espouse here, phenomenological experiences of transportation are by no means discounted or discarded as irrelevant; rather, they are *grounded*, informed by a sensitivity to the conditions
that make them possible and the attendant relations of power that allow
such uninterrupted stability. Another starting point for this book, then, is
the acknowledgment that this stability—this capacity for the surrounding
material and technical apparatus facilitating gameplay to fade from attention, whether on the part of players or scholars—is an *accomplishment born
of privilege* and ought to be understood as such. It is produced through the

inequitable distribution of and access to resources, spaces, and times of digital play accrued over generations and frequently distributed along lines of gender, race, class, geography, ability, age, language, and so on. Here, again, I lean on Trammell's articulation of "networks of privilege" and the connections it builds between the practices of white male hobbyists and the racialized and gendered geographies of suburban America. I also return to Bulut's concept of ludopolitics, the insight that white masculinity's propensity for certain kinds of technology-intensive, resource-hungry fun, whether at play or at work, is almost always the product of exploitive labor relations operating along lines of race, gender, class, and coloniality. Not only do these concepts offer intersectional understandings of masculinity and whiteness, but they are also attuned to the multiple temporal and social scales at which systems operate—a perspective that is both intersectional and *infrastructural*. Beginning from this acknowledgment allows us to understand how certain forms of masculinity, afforded by white privilege and rooted in ludic mastery, constitute an infrastructure for so many gaming cultures.[67] I mean this in a very literal sense: using the tools of empirical and archival research I employ in the following chapters, we can track the movement of communicative practices, texts, clothing styles, bodily comportments, and technological artifacts that, taken together, constitute a distribution system for gaming masculinities. This infrastructure allows for the unfiltered circulation of gendered codes and protocols that make certain kinds of racialized, classed, technocentric masculinity endlessly available while throttling other forms of gender expression—not necessarily making them impossible but making them laborious and unsafe.

Chapter Overview

The chapters in this book draw from nearly fifteen years of qualitative, and mostly ethnographic, activities across dozens of primarily English-speaking sites in the Global North: from esports club meetings and training sessions on university campuses to internet cafés in Canada to large-scale LAN parties in England and Sweden to esports tournaments and games industry conventions in the United States. That said, the chapters are bound thematically rather than methodologically. They are constructed through a variety of qualitative and humanistic knowledge-building traditions, including visual discourse analysis of online forum posts (chap. 2), qualitative fieldwork at gaming tournaments (chaps. 1 and 3), a longitudinal connective ethnography of campus-based competitive gaming communities (chap. 4), and a novel twist on the interview technique known as photovoice (chap. 5). I delve further into my use of and indebtedness to specific methodological approaches in individual chapters. Tying them all together is an underlying set of ideas, which I have covered in this introduction, around how to look for and make sense of the connections between various place-making practices: hegemonic masculinity and whiteness; networks of privilege and ludo-politics; technogenders, cultural techniques, and apparatuses; figure and ground; space and place. In the following chapters, I employ these ideas as tools for connecting separate case stories into an infrastructural mapping of masculinity and digital play in which the circulation of specific formations of white masculinity is foundational to the place-making practices of gaming in specific contexts.

Each chapter is offered as a distinct essay (truly embracing the French root of that word, from "attempt") to map connections between digital games, race and colonialism, masculinities, and place-making practices. Furthermore, each chapter has a separate motif: a geometric shape that I provide as a sort of iconographic shorthand for the diagram of power I see operating through relations between bodies, technologies, and space within a given context.[68] Over the course of each chapter, these motifs are developed into more than metaphors; they are revealed as cultural techniques, again invoking Siegert's generative term for the concretization of semiotic and material practices into more or less stable arrangements that mean and do certain things. Cultural techniques embody logics—ways of interpreting and arranging the world—and, as such, they are fundamentally engaged in the production of boundaries, categories, and differences.[69]

The first chapter takes up the motif of *frames*, offering an account of my own agency in studying gaming communities and producing accounts of their manifold inequities and exclusions. As a cultural technique of representation, a frame centers attention on a given phenomenon while necessarily bracketing off things outside the frame (including, conventionally, the framer's own agency). Providing an epistemic and ethical foundation for subsequent chapters, this chapter integrates media theorists' problematizations of contemporary datafication apparatuses with anticolonial critique and critical environmental communication, moving past a one-dimensional understanding of my positionality and considering the sets of relations between land, study participants, and myself that I have relied on and helped reproduce through my ethnographic fieldwork. The chapter proceeds through reframing a fieldwork story from a large-scale LAN party in 2011, during which I inadvertently participated in an act objectifying a promotional worker. Rather than offering simple self-flagellation or performative positionality statements, my reflections on this story explore the complexities of conducting research on and in locations frequently characterized by gender violence and made possible through legacies of colonialist violence. By centering the grounds, discursive and material, of this interaction at a LAN party, this chapter highlights the extractive logics at work in both contemporary gaming and in a lot of contemporary games research. Furthermore, it foregrounds the relationships of digital play and digital games research to land, the material foundation for communicative action, thereby creating a frame for later chapters and their explorations of the space-making and place-taking operations of digital play.

The geometric motif for chapter 2 is the *circle*. In the work of Johann Huizinga, a cultural historian writing in the early to mid-twentieth century, the "magic circle" is meant to describe the enclosing of a ritual space designated for games within which normal social relations and hierarchies are temporarily suspended.[70] I recast this much-maligned concept in order to understand domestic gaming setups as material arrangements of temporal and spatial privilege within which the masculine player can escape—not real life, but the labor of social reproduction and the restitutions of feminism. Drawing from research on the domestication of media, this chapter examines photographs of domestic gaming setups posted on gaming forums and asks what they tell us about how participants in this masculinized play culture make space for gaming in the home. This work is based on visual qualitative analysis of data gathered from the 2007 and 2015 editions of the online community NeoGAF's annual "Show Us Your Setup" threads, in which members upload and comment on pictures of their domestic gaming arrangements. Based on an empirical consideration of how arrangements of screens, cords, controllers, chairs, and so on are presented in these photographs, the chapter offers a schema for classifying different kinds of domestic gaming setups: *hearth, bunker,* and *cabinet.*

After defining these types of gaming setup, the chapter considers the histories and cultural politics of each and reverse engineers their archetypal users. The hearth lies at the heart of a family's domestic media use, much like the TV was imagined as the center of postwar family life. It is the setup of the dad, the husband, the family man, looking to unwind. The bunker is the bare-bones, technology-centered setup of the solitary gamer, a defensive fortification from which he can exert agency and survive in a world he finds increasingly hostile or inhospitable. The cabinet, like its Renaissance-era historical namesake, is a space meant to showcase its inhabitant's cultural status and wealth, primarily through the curation of rare, exotic, and expensive artifacts: curios from the Orient in the case of the Renaissance bourgeois, limited edition bobbleheads and obscure anime posters in the case of the contemporary cabineteer. As this overview illustrates, different kinds of gaming setups, like the culturally adjacent man cave, have complex historical trajectories and legacies; each of these mundane arrangements is associated with different aesthetics, cultural practices, and, in Preciado's terms, "technohabits of the male body."[71] If, as this chapter suggests, domestic arrangements of space and media technology are incubators for different sorts of masculine subjects, it behooves us to understand what sorts of masculinities are in play in each and how these arrangements engage in boundary-making practices by which "magic circles" become real—if not entirely actual.

Chapter 3 uses the geometric motif of the *grid* in order to produce a cultural-infrastructural diagram of the LAN party, returning to the ethnographic fieldwork at the series of LAN events that fill the frame in chapter 1. LAN parties vary widely in scope and can involve anywhere from a few dozen to tens of thousands of gaming enthusiasts who travel often substantial distances, with their PCs in tow, to play, watch, and talk games over the course of several days. But these events are all grids: ordered arrangements of bodies and machines configured according to the demands and capacities of local and global infrastructures. As a cultural technique for segmenting space and its contents, converting position into quantifiable location, the grid is *the* logic of the LAN party. Seating arrangements and IP addresses alike are affixed to players and their machines; seen from above, LAN parties look like big grids of bodies tethered to computers, and as I show in the chapter, much of the culture of these events can be at least partially attributed to this arrangement.

Drawing from observations and interviews at many such events, primarily a series of LAN parties in England but also a large-scale games and digital culture festival held regularly in Sweden and numerous, smaller events in

Canada and the United States between 2008 and 2018, this chapter considers LAN parties in terms of the material and infrastructural contexts in which they take place. Where previous accounts of LAN parties focus on the social activities of participants, seeing these as more or less contained by the virtual spaces of games and the physical spaces of the event floor, this chapter asks how intersecting layers of infrastructure—networks of electrical power, sanitation, connectivity, transportation—and their attendant mobilities quite literally come to matter in shaping the gendered and racial conditions of access that characterize these public play contexts. Centrally, it illustrates the ways in which considerations around electric power and connectivity, including how and where to come by them cheaply, can become transduced into instances of gendered and racial power and social (dis)connectivity as events are situated in locations and at times that make them accessible primarily to those with privileged social and spatial mobility. These and other instances, what Paul Dourish calls the "relationship between infrastructure and experience," are explored through a series of vignettes that interweave performances of white, cisgender gaming masculinity at LAN events with insights into the infrastructural and geographic conditions that make such performances possible.[72] I show how the visibility and inescapable agency of grids as a technique for managing LAN parties work to ensure that a particular sort of gaming arrangement and corresponding set of masculine technogenders—namely, the bunker from chapter 2—come to dominate these gaming LANscapes.

Engaging the turbulent domain of American and Canadian collegiate esports, chapter 4 considers possibilities and limitations for equity and inclusion in university-based competitive gaming cultures. In this chapter, I turn to the motif of the *platform*, a key concern of critical media theorists and political economists. Platforms are cultural techniques of connection, elevation, and capture. I draw from the rich terrain of platform studies to understand the relationship between the contemporary neoliberal university and collegiate esports. In Canada and the United States, university campuses represent a site of intensive investment for an esports industry eager for continued expansion. Postsecondary institutions have responded, formalizing the long-standing and vibrant culture of competitive gaming on campuses into official esports clubs and, in a growing number of instances, varsity esports programs. Such initiatives often involve corporate partnerships and sponsorships, providing top collegiate esports talent with everything from practice space to scholarship funding to team nutritionists and psychiatrists. Making use of long-term connective ethnographic research with the esports community at a large American university, work that also included esports administration and advocacy, this chapter explores the material and infrastructural conditions for inclusivity in collegiate esports as both networked gaming and academic institutions become increasingly "platformized."[73]

Within a broader system of neoliberal governance, and under threat from shrinking budgets and growing public distrust in the traditional goals of postsecondary education, universities are turning to esports as a way to stand out in an increasingly crowded market, equating esports with success in the economically performative fields of science, technology, engineering, and math (STEM). Under these constrained conditions, esports programs are following the lead of professional esports organizations: paying lip service to gender inclusivity but doing little in the way of challenging a status quo in which masculine players are best positioned to succeed. In a logic that stretches back to the establishment of many public American schools, made possible through the government's donation of lands bought through Indigenous dispossession and genocide (circling back to the anticolonial perspectives engaged in chap. 1), universities find ways to allocate scarce resources—including, and especially, space—to support esports programs yet deem inclusivity too costly. Though the chapter is skeptical regarding the capacity of the platformized university to "do" esports in a way that is sustainable, equitable, and inclusive, it concludes by articulating practical solutions that collegiate organizers and administrators might consider to transform their local esports communities into engines of equity rather than exclusion and exploitation.

Chapter 5 employs the motif of *pockets*. In it, I (virtually) trail behind games industry workers as they navigate the hallways and event spaces of games industry conventions such as the Game Developers Conference (GDC) and the Montréal International Game Summit (MIGS). These multiday events, held at large convention centers, operate as platforms by which the games industry connects its multiple publics (workers, entrepreneurs, advertisers, journalists, academics, students, fans) for purposes of networking, marketing, recruiting, and, not infrequently, partying. The context for this chapter is the persistent state of public relations crisis the games industry finds itself in regarding its support of gendered violence: the steady stream of sexual harassment allegations and reports of hostile work environments

against studios both large and small and the vociferous reactions by antifeminist gaming communities against any and all efforts to address the
exclusions that characterize cultures of intensive gameplay and production.
Despite their importance to the economic and cultural reproduction of the
games industry, conventions such as GDC and MIGS have received scant
academic attention. This chapter specifically centers the experiences and
perspectives of women and nonbinary games workers (most of whom are
white) attending these and other industry conventions, relating stories of
the work they carry out in order to keep themselves and their colleagues safe
at such events—safe from burnout, exploitation, germs, and perhaps most
acutely, gender-based harassment and violence.

The motif of the pocket becomes a way to theorize this labor of care for
self and others. Pockets become not just clothing features but also place-
making practices that carve moments of rest and invisibility out of the fabric of events that otherwise valorize, and frequently demand, always-on
networking and potentially dangerous forms of visibility. In doing so, the
chapter follows the work of feminist media theorists who recenter *storage*
into accounts of media as not just a technical problem but a very human
one. Games industry conventions pose acute problems of storage for women
and nonbinary attendees, such that what they put in their pockets—and
what pockets are made available to them—become questions of safety and
survival.

The book's conclusion takes the *boundary* as its motif, foregrounding a
cultural technique that runs through each of the previous chapters' considerations of gaming and its manifold exclusions. Eschewing the usual
boundary-setting work of academic book conclusions, this short piece considers *origins*: specifically, it relates one story (among many) of how the
field of game studies came into being and how its canon was established.
The story invites us to consider what would happen if game studies scholars
took *Beyond a Boundary*, an autobiographical look at cricket under conditions of colonial rule by the Marxist historian and Pan-African activist
C. L. R. James, as canon instead of the translocal, transhistorical theorizations of games and play constructed through the colonialist armchair eth-
nologies of Johann Huizinga and Roger Caillois. In imagining an alternate
historical and epistemic ground for game studies, I posit that efforts to *re-
place* gaming's normative spatial practices, to rearrange the usual configurations of space, subjectivity, and play, is already well underway by feminist,

queer, and BIPOC games organizers, researchers, and activists in games and that we ought to follow their lead.

As this chapter overview makes apparent, the project uniting these various essays is an attempt to put games, literally, in their place. I insist that the connective threads between the place-making practices approached in each chapter are not only conceptual but also material and infrastructural as well. Whether it is young men packing up their bunkers and cabinets (chap. 2) to take to a LAN party (chaps. 1 and 3), or collegiate esports boosters (chap. 4) handing out business cards at a games industry convention (chap. 5), these sites—and others beyond the purview of this book, like esports houses, game production studios, domestic live streaming setups—are connected in ways that have often gone neglected in critical scholarship on gaming. If we can follow these connections through the infrastructural approach espoused in this book, we might begin to understand how certain formations of masculinity are, themselves, infrastructural to the production of digital games; how logics of exclusion circulate as readily as power, technologies, bodies, and connectivity; and how the task of challenging gaming's long-standing patterns of marginalization might involve thinking and acting as if the mundane and material grounds of gaming matter at least as much as gaming's hypervisible and well-documented figures.

NOTES

1. I am grateful to Madison Schmalzer for her definition of "jank," which she describes as "a player's perception that a video game does not behave in the ways that it should." For Schmalzer, jankiness interrupts the smooth operations of a game and allows us to glimpse the underlying mechanics—and sociotechnical relations. This is a productive way to approach the jank of a video game setup: to ask what sorts of material conditions are best suited for it and what in turn enables those conditions. Schmalzer, "Janky Controls and Embodied Play."

2. Rodino-Colocino, DeCarvalho, and Heresco, "Neo-orthodox Masculinities on Man Caves"; Smith, "This Guy Studies Man Caves for a Living; Here's What He's Learned."

3. Jane, "'Dude ... Stop the Spread,'" 459. My analysis of the mancounter appears in a more concise form in ToDiGRA, where it is used as an example of a "postdisciplinary" approach to gaming. Taylor, ", "Postscript: On Postdisciplinarity."

4. Ward, *Not Gay*.

5. The FPS genre is the subject of numerous academic works, but *Guns, Grenades, and Grunts: First-Person Shooter Games* remains a comprehensive and critical foun-

dation, particularly for its attention to militarism and gender. Voorhees, Call, and Whitlock, *Guns, Grenades, and Grunts*.

6. Salter and Blodgett, *Toxic Geek Masculinity in Media*; Cote, *Gaming Sexism*; Paul, *Toxic Meritocracy of Video Games*; Phillips, *Gamer Trouble*.

7. Fickle, *Race Card*; Patterson, *Open World Empire*; Trammell, *Privilege of Play*.

8. Johnson, "Technomasculinity and Its Influence in Video Game Production"; Kocurek, *Coin-Operated Americans*; Bulut, *A Precarious Game*.

9. Voorhees and Orlando, "Performing Neoliberal Masculinity"; Srauy and Palmer-Mehta, "Tools of the Game"; Parisi, "A Counterrevolution in the Hands"; Chess and Shaw, "A Conspiracy of Fishes, or, How We Learned to Stop Worrying about #Gamergate and Embrace Hegemonic Masculinity."

10. Donaldson, "Mechanics and Metagame"; Boluk and LeMieux, *Metagaming*; Taylor and Elam, "'People Are Robots, Too.'"

11. Cote, *Gaming Sexism*; Phillips, *Gamer Trouble*; Salter and Blodgett, *Toxic Geek Masculinity in Media*; Rusk and Ståhl, "Esports."

12. Trammell, "Deodorizing the Geek Gamer."

13. Gray, "Intersecting Oppressions and Online Communities"; Taylor, Jenson, and de Castell, "Cheerleaders/Booth Babes/*Halo* Hoes."

14. Chess and Shaw, "A Conspiracy of Fishes, or, How We Learned to Stop Worrying about #Gamergate and Embrace Hegemonic Masculinity"; Paul, *Toxic Meritocracy of Video Games*.

15. Cross, "'We Will Force Gaming to Be Free'"; Boluk and LeMieux, *Metagaming*; Ging, "Alphas, Betas, and Incels."

16. Bergstrom, Fisher, and Jenson, "Disavowing 'That Guy,'" 234.

17. Of course, there are important nuances separating these terms, and they come out of distinct theoretical and methodological trajectories. This being a composite sketch, these distinctions are glossed over somewhat. For "technicity," see Bulut, *A Precarious Game*; Dovey and Kennedy, *Game Cultures*. For "technomasculinity," see Johnson, "Technomasculinity and Its Influence in Video Game Production"; Kocurek, *Coin-Operated Americans*. For critical takes on the "gamer" as cultural identity, see Shaw, "Do You Identify as a Gamer?"; Williams, "Death to the Gamer."

18. Bulut, *A Precarious Game*, 63.

19. Connell and Messerschmidt, "Hegemonic Masculinity," 836.

20. Schippers, "Recovering the Feminine Other," 94.

21. Rosario, "When the 'Hustle' Isn't Enough"; Hill, "Hustle Ethic and the Spirit of Platform Capitalism"; Srnicek, *Platform Capitalism*.

22. Bulut, *A Precarious Game*, 10. I develop my understanding of settler colonialism more fully in chapter 1.

23. Trammell, *Privilege of Play*, 13.

24. Bulut, *A Precarious Game*, 37.

25. Here, "we" can refer to anyone who is able to participate intensively in any ludic hobby. But more specifically, for both me and Bulut, "we" refers to the white masculine subject centered by the games industry and mainstream gaming cultures: the "we" of the contemporary Canadian or American game development studio and the "we" of the mancounter.

26. Bulut, *A Precarious Game*, 10–11.

27. Bulut, *A Precarious Game*, 27. This stark relation is also at the core of Aaron Trammell's critical retheorization of play from the perspective of Black phenomenology (Trammell, *Repairing Play*).

28. Trammell, *Privilege of Play*, 8.

29. Fickle, *Race Card*; Fletcher, "Esports and the Color Line"; Gray, "Intersecting Oppressions and Online Communities"; Patterson, *Open World Empire*.

30. Blaisdell and Taylor Bullock, "White Imagination, Black Reality," 5.

31. Alexander, *New Jim Crow*; Benjamin, *Race after Technology*.

32. Connell and Messerschmidt, "Hegemonic Masculinity," 14.

33. Preciado, *Testo Junkie*, 101.

34. Geoghegan, "After Kittler," 67.

35. Winthrop-Young, "Material World."

36. Morales and Waller, "A Gender-Reveal Celebration Is Blamed for a Wildfire."

37. Preciado, *Testo Junkie*, 117.

38. Foucault, *Power/Knowledge*, 194.

39. Packer, "Conditions of Media's Possibility," 20.

40. Packer, "Conditions of Media's Possibility," 27.

41. Taylor, "Kinaesthetic Masculinity and the Prehistory of Esports."

42. Paul, *Toxic Meritocracy of Video Games*.

43. Molinaro, McLuhan, and Toye, *Letters of Marshall McLuhan*, 478.

44. Massey, *Space, Place and Gender*, 4.

45. Massey, "Masculinity, Dualisms and High Technology," 495.

46. Harvey, "Flexible Accumulation through Urbanization Reflections on 'Postmodernism' in the American City," 254–57.

47. Chief among these are Ergin Bulut, whose ethnographic documentation of game development I discuss in more detail above, and Önder Can and Max Foxman, who offer a nuanced consideration of three esports venues in Ankara, Turkey. Bulut, *A Precarious Game*; Can and Foxman, "Out of the Café and into the Arena."

48. Hart, "Becoming a Geographer," 85.

49. Parks and Starosielski, "Introduction," 5.

50. Massey, *For Space*, 4.

51. Massey, *For Space*, 5.

52. Massey, *For Space*, 7.

53. Preciado, *Pornotopia*, 33.

54. Preciado, *Pornotopia*, 33.

55. Spigel, *Make Room for TV*, 38.

56. Harvey, *Gender, Age, and Digital Games in the Domestic Context*; Tobin, *Portable Play in Everyday Life*; Simon, "Beyond Cyberspatial Flaneurie"; Flynn, "Geography of the Digital Hearth"; Chambers, "'Wii Play as a Family.'"

57. Kerr, *Global Games*, 150–59; Bulut, *A Precarious Game*, 73–88; Dyer-Witheford and Peuter, *Games of Empire*, 222–24.

58. The capacity of games to hold us in place took on a very literal meaning during the pandemic, when the WHO recommended video gaming as a key technique for occupying oneself during lockdowns. Gaming became the killer app for stay-at-home orders.

59. Packer and Wiley, *Communication Matters*; Sharma, *In the Meantime*; Jayemanne, "Game Studies' Material Turn."

60. Aarseth, "Allegories of Space," 162.

61. Nitsche, *Video Game Spaces*; Bjarnason, "Playing as Travelling."

62. Taylor, "Toward a Spatial Practice in Video Games."

63. Aarseth himself leans into the long history in science fiction of imagining cyberspace as a domain ontologically distinct from the real world.

64. Nitsche, *Video Game Spaces*, 63; Muse, "Event of Space," 191; Lombard and Ditton, "At the Heart of It All."

65. The distinction between "matters of concern," in which the status and relations of a given set of phenomena are not at all certain, and "matters of fact," in which they have become settled, is from science and technology studies (STS), specifically the work of Bruno Latour. See Latour, "Why Has Critique Run out of Steam?," 225.

66. Lombard and Ditton, "At the Heart of It All."

67. I am indebted to Laine Nooney for offering the idea that gender itself can be thought of in infrastructural terms. Nooney, "A Pedestal, a Table, a Love Letter."

68. Foucault, *Discipline and Punish*, 171.

69. Siegert, *Cultural Techniques*, 13.

70. Huizinga, *Homo Ludens*, 11.

71. Preciado, *Pornotopia*, 19.

72. Dourish, "Protocols, Packets, and Proximity," 185.

73. Nieborg and Poell, "Platformization of Cultural Production," 4276.

1

FRAMES

Extractive Logics in Play

Leaning Out

Let us start with a fieldwork story. It is from Insomnia 42, a local area network (LAN) event held in the spring of 2011 at a horse racing venue just outside of Newbury, a town in England halfway between London and Bristol. Insomnia 42 was the last LAN that Multiplay, the hosting organization, held at this idiosyncratic site—the event was later moved to a more proper convention hall. I discuss this LAN series in more detail in chapter 3. It was my second time attending an Insomnia event; my research activities were part of a larger study aimed at producing a multifaceted picture of how massively multiplayer online games (MMOGs) stage and mediate player interaction. Expressed in the ominous language of the government program funding our team (and four others, most of which were made up of university-based researchers and US-based nonprofit research organizations), the aim was to "infer real life characteristics from in-game behaviors."[1] The government program impelled researchers to adopt an objective stance toward the processes of game-based observation and data gathering—a gaze on game-based activities "from nowhere," as Donna Haraway describes.[2] Two of the teams relied heavily on player data recorded automatically by game servers without players' explicit consent, handed over to researchers by MMOG publishers. Our own team sought a balance between a positivist, big data–driven approach (which the program managers saw as necessary to create statistically sound criteria for figuring out participants' identity markers from their in-game activities) and the kind of feminist, constructivist research in which I was trained during my graduate education. In other words, we sought to tack between the epistemologically and ethically distant poles of "god tricks" and "situated knowledges."[3] Thankfully, our colleagues on the project, data scientists and analysts accustomed to working with interdisciplinary teams and trained in creative, rigorous analyses of large datasets, supported us in this effort. They saw our insistence on face-to-face interaction with participants as providing a kind of "ground truth" for the connections their quantitative inquiries could establish between participants' demographics and what they did and said in game.

My and my colleagues' visits to LAN events occurred among other research activities, including observing people playing in university-based computer labs; together, these activities constituted the basis for a material bridge connecting players' in-game actions to their embodied identities. This work was often logistically complex and emotionally draining. During my forays at large-scale LAN events, the multiplicity of data collection methods at our disposal coupled with the twinned imperatives of recruiting as many participants as possible and ensuring that all facets of each participant's data (survey, interview, observations, and server logs of instrumented gameplay) were properly labeled and sorted meant that I often understood myself less as a researcher and more as a mobile social science laboratory. Conventional ethnographic concerns around rapport building were balanced with a desire to *process* participants through the media instruments designed for the study: sign here, check this box and that box, navigate your browser tab to this URL, enter your unique user ID here, speak into this device, type into that one, and so on. I found myself primed toward a highly instrumental view of attendees, whom I saw as potential sources of data, singled out for recruitment based on what I perceived to be their openness (were they chatting with their neighbors, or did they have headphones on, intently focused on their screens?) as well as their potential added value to our study (were they playing games for which we had not yet gathered data?). Once I had them signed up for the study, my aim was to get them through as efficiently as possible.

The interaction I describe below occurred during my first full day of fieldwork at Insomnia 42; it was midafternoon, and I was still acclimating to the time zone and the venue, preparing for the frequently disorienting task of carrying out ethnographic work in a strange place. The horse racing track's viewing areas were split into multiple large rooms across several floors, and the LAN organizers used the disjointed arrangement of spaces to section- alize attendees. Small groups (under twenty participants) could rent one of the booths in the upper floor, which offered better views of the world outside and, more importantly, privacy. These were most used by esports organiza- tions for intensive training purposes, though some were booked by MMOG "clans," affiliations of players who migrate together from one game to the next and whose members pool their resources for the weekend. The middle floor was reserved for competitive first-person shooter (FPS) play, the walls and windows covered in black curtains to blot out any distracting natural light; the lower floor, adjacent to the modest event stage and close to the largest of the venue's bars, was for more casual MMOG play.[4]

I had arrived in the early afternoon and was walking the lower floor, scouting for MMOG players. I spotted a group of attendees I had met on my trip to Insomnia 40, months earlier at the same venue. They were part of a gaming clan made up mostly of white men (and some women) in their late twenties and early thirties. The popular MMOG *World of Warcraft* (WoW) was their primary fixation at the time. As I had learned from my interviews with them at the previous LAN, they treated Insomnia events as a chance to hang out for four days playing in close proximity. They seemed like they had spent a great deal of time together, in networked play as well as in person; their bodies and gear extended into each other's stations, snack wrappers and beverage cans (primarily beer and energy drinks) intermingling with cables and extraneous clothing and bedding into a continuous mass of stuff piled under and behind their row of computers.

During a lull in their WoW play, I walked over to where seven of them, all white men, sat closely together. I was greeted with some warmth; a few smiled or nodded from their seats, and some stood up to slap me on the shoulder or shake my hand. Two exclaimed, "Hey, it's the Canadian!" in reference to what was apparently the most notable thing about me from our last encounter. I explained that I had returned to continue the same research project as the first time we had met, now with a networked, instrumented game they could play together that would automatically collect behavioral data. They all agreed to try it out. Consent forms were distributed and signed, and I helped them log into the browser-based game. Built specifically for the research project, it invoked the look and feel of isometric, fantasy-themed role-playing games (RPGs) from the mid-90s and early 2000s like *Diablo* or

Baldur's Gate, albeit without the polish. It was loaded with a built-in surveillance apparatus accessible only to the developers and our research team. Once the participants were logged in to the game, I wandered off to give them time alone to play. When I checked back with them fifteen minutes later, I saw that most of them had progressed in the game; they had finished a number of quests and advanced their characters past the point where the game allowed them to select more powerful character classes. Their initial concentration had given way to trash-talking each other and the game. A few had alt-tabbed away from the game to go on Internet Relay Chat (IRC), Steam, and various music and video platforms, exhibiting the kind of fluid, multilayered communicative media practices characteristic of participants at large-scale LANs.[5]

Two had their heads together and were giggling over what was transpiring in an IRC channel, and I walked over to ask them about it. They responded that the LAN had just been visited by a group of promotional models representing one of Insomnia's corporate sponsors.[6] The models were circulating the LAN, handing out swag. As I looked on, these two participants communicated via IRC with attendees in other sections of the horse racing track in an attempt to have their confederates locate a model and "send her over" to their area. They were sheepish yet determined in their aim, and after five minutes, a young woman arrived in uniform (pink nylon hot pants and a matching halter top, with a more modest fleece vest over top), bearing candies emblazoned with the company's logo. She came with a small amount of fanfare from the group, including high fives between the two participants who had successfully lured her over via IRC collusion. After some back-and-forth with a couple group members, she agreed to pose for a photograph. The two IRC operators held items that had some significance to the group as inside jokes; one held a pineapple with writing on it in front of his chest (I never learned what it said) while another hoisted a plush pig between himself and the model. I could guess based on the impish grins and surreptitious glances at the model that their meanings were sexualized. They insisted I be in the shot as well, despite my reluctance. In the photograph they later emailed me, I am at the edge of the image, looking incredibly uncomfortable. I am not in physical contact with any of the clan members, who crowd around the promotional model in the middle of the shot; rather, I am leaning away from them in an unsuccessful effort to stand outside the frame.

The above account has been reproduced, with some minor modifications, from a 2018 article in the Danish media studies journal *MedieKultur* for a special issue on games and research methods edited by Emma Witkowski and Torill Mortensen. In the piece, I reflect on the interaction and what it communicates (via the photograph, printed in the article) about the tensions involved in critically studying masculinity and gaming while embodying a cisgender masculine identity. My analysis leans heavily on cyberfeminist theory and feminist ethnography to interrogate my ambivalent presence in the photograph: someone who is at once reluctantly in the frame, part of the interaction, and in a position to critically reflect on and make professional use of the interaction and my agency in it.[7] My initial plan for this chapter was to lightly revise the journal article, an idea to which the journal's editors generously agreed. For reasons I explore in this chapter, however, this plan became unfeasible to me as I reread the article and, with the benefit of hindsight and an emerging commitment to other knowledge traditions, reflected on what *else* the above interaction communicates about my activities and orientation as a researcher. Here, I mean the relations I have leveraged and helped shape through my work as a scholar and ethnographer trained in feminist modes of data collection and analysis yet steeped in legacies of colonialism and the privileges that come with my embodied identity. In the initial article, I use the interaction to theorize how my own agency and social location allow me to pass as a legitimate participant in masculinized gaming contexts even as I seek to document the exclusions that characterize gaming cultures. But as the opening chapter of this book about the infrastructural role of white masculinity in gaming's place-making practices, this story is put to different use: it is about the importance of place, of material as well as social location, and of the extractive relationships to land and people on which intensive gaming activities (including, crucially, games research itself) rely so heavily.

Rather than *reproducing* the account of my awkward interaction at a LAN and the attendant analysis, then, this chapter attempts to *reframe* it. Reframing, as I practice here, is a matter of rearranging the central elements in the interaction (the clan members, the model, myself) into a new composition that reveals different connections. If the original frame invited a feminist critique of the figures—foregrounding yet another instance in which women are harassed, marginalized, and objectified in gaming cultures while illuminating my own ambivalent involvement—the reframing I offer in this chapter problematizes the *grounds*, both intellectual and material, that made this interaction possible in the first place. I am referring to the extractive logics that shape and rationalize much of the research done on gaming communities, reproducing the long legacies of scientific research enacted in service of "settler capitalism." This term describes an economic system that relies on access to and exploitation of lands on which Indigenous people were (and continue to be) violently displaced through imperial settlement for the purpose of accumulating material wealth—wealth that is then hoarded by the capitalist class and redistributed in ways that tend to deepen racial, gendered, classed, and colonial systems of oppression.[8] Applied to the study and play of games, settler capitalist logics frame the communicative activities involved in digital play as raw material to be extracted without consequence, as if the data produced through our engagement with games are separable from the embodied and localized contexts of play, not to mention the infrastructures that make those circuits possible. Thus, as starkly articulated by the program directive that brought me to Insomnia events—figure out markers of players' identities by recording what they do in games—one of the pernicious effects of settler capitalism and its technoscience is to sever the connections between gaming technologies, humans, and land.

Reframing the interaction between the model, players, and me using the tools of anticolonial critique marks a provisional step toward reckoning with the troubling legacies within which the interaction unfolded. I do so with the awareness that this exercise ought not be considered a "decolonization" of my research practices, and I do not name it as such. As a white settler born and raised on unceded Anishinabe Algonquin territory (Ottawa, Ontario, Canada), I have been able to live and carry out my academic work in Toronto, Canada; Raleigh, North Carolina; and Vaasa, Finland, in universities built on and enriched through multiple distinct histories of colonial settlement and Indigenous dispossession. I have done so while profiting both intellectually and materially from the ongoing relations of exploitation and harm enacted through settler capitalism. I am grateful for the insights made by anticolonial scholars that, at least within the Canadian context I call home, decolonization must entail a material reconciliation with Indigenous genocide, an enactment of Indigenous sovereignty, and a repatriation of Indigenous land.[9] I draw on anticolonial critique carefully and gratefully, not as a performative gesture that somehow decolonizes my research but because it invites me to consider how the practices of knowledge production at work in the interaction described above remain tethered to fundamentally extractive and exploitative technoscientific legacies—and how studies of digital play and its manifold inequities and injustices might be done otherwise.

There are, of course, other traditions I might draw from to reframe this interaction, to reorder its composition so it makes sense in other ways. A primarily Marxist rendering, for instance, might ground contemporary gaming and games research first and foremost within the unfolding legacies of capitalism and consider what this episode at a LAN reveals about relations between workers (and players) on one hand and those who own the means of production and exchange on the other: game publishers, academic publishers, and the institutions that support their exploitative regimes. This is an urgent set of concerns, particularly given the multiple crises associated with our current political economic order, and there is certainly no shortage of scholarly work that speaks to these concerns.[10] But I step into conversation with anticolonialist research here because it invites me to figure out how I might more respectfully begin to stand with individuals and communities carrying out feminist and anticolonial projects, having spent a great deal of my career cataloging gender-based damage.[11] The modest aim of this chapter, then, is to figure out where and how I *have* stood. This is why I begin by relating and reframing an interaction in which I stood awkwardly, trying desperately to lean out of the frame while still very much in (and of) the composition.

Framing Framed[12]

I have opted against reprinting the actual photograph of the promotional model, clan mates, and myself here, though curious readers can look up the article if they really want to see it. Its exclusion underscores a point that became clear to me on rereading the original article in *MedieKultur*. If the photograph captures a moment in which the group of attendees has successfully manipulated events so that the promotional model poses with them—if indeed the photograph serves as both the record of this manipulation and the technical apparatus of the model's objectification—then publishing it in this book would arguably reproduce the exploitative logics the photograph documents and enacts. The photograph positions her as a prop for the participants' horny pranks. In a pattern that echoes the gendered and racialized dynamics in so many forms of play, she works so that they can have a bit of fun; if they are the playful subjects, she becomes, at least momentarily, the object.[13] But it also positions her as a data point in the repeated rediscovery of what we already know about how gender operates in so many masculinized cultures and contexts of intensive play such as this one.[14] Furthermore, we do not need to actually see the photograph to consider the conceptual fecundity of *framing* to understand the dynamics at play. Consider the following:

- The photograph visually frames the interaction. It provides the limits of representation such that what is *in* the frame, and the composition of those contents (the smiling attendees surrounding the promotional model; me, at the edge, trying to lean out), is captured and stored, and everything else is excluded.

- The promotional model has been framed (set up, manipulated into a compromising situation) by the clan mates and their confederates.

- Through the analytical frame of white, Western feminist critique, the photograph becomes visual evidence of the ongoing objectification of women in gaming cultures.

- Through this analysis, the promotional model is *reframed*: she is at once the focal point of a bounded visual representation, the mark in a manipulative scheme, and mute proof that women are frequently rendered either invisible or hypervisible in gaming cultures.[15]

The frame is the central motif of this chapter; as a start, it provides a generative means for exploring reflexivity, agency, and the reproduction of social worlds in and through qualitative research. But framing is also an intervention into the world, a means of arranging objects, people, and ideas into a particular composition for a particular set of purposes. It is a cultural technique for defining the borders of what is visible and knowable. Furthermore, for the entwined projects of capitalism and colonialism in particular, framing is a key technique in the instrumentalist relation to the world that converts land and its inhabitants into resources for capitalist production and the ecocidal, genocidal goal of endless accumulation. Theorizing frames and their work enables a better understanding of the conjoined logics of representation and extraction that define contemporary settler capitalist technoscience. It is therefore worth considering some of the key ways frames have been understood within and across the intellectual traditions I draw on most in this chapter: media history, sociology, critical media studies, environmental communication, and anticolonialism. In particular, I seek to reconnect two broad notions of framing—one immaterial and epistemic and the other resolutely physical—to theorize framing as a material-discursive configuration of our social and physical worlds. From there, I undertake the central work of this chapter: a *reframing* of the narrative involving the MMOG clan members, the promotional model, and myself. The aim is to arrive at a better understanding regarding the ways we theorize and enact relationality in games research—how and where we stand in relation to gaming's figures and the epistemic and material grounds of colonial encounters.

Frames as Cultural Techniques

Visual media provide perhaps the most obvious and ubiquitous instances of frames. A frame fixes the limits of a given image. Susan Sontag famously writes that "photographs are experience captured"; if so, the frame is the boundary between what is captured and what is not.[16] Anything inside its boundary is fixed, made ready for consideration and analysis. In representational terms, it becomes visual content. Anything outside is either deemed irrelevant or deliberately left to the imagination. For visual media like photography, the frame functions as an ocular-epistemic enclosure—in Karen Barad's terms, a "boundary making practice" delineating what is visible and knowable from what is not.[17] Friedrich Kittler in *Optical Media* provides what can be read as a history of framing and its technical and epistemological operations, though he does not frame his account in these terms. In his story of how film and photography came into being, Kittler delves into the role Renaissance artists, architects, and military strategists played in devising ways of visually capturing reality. At one point, he attempts to deconstruct the process that inventor and artist Filippo Brunelleschi may have used to create his small, hyperaccurate painting of the Baptistry in Florence—the painting that (according to Kittler) introduced linear perspective into European art and established the foundation for geometrically accurate and, to employ a deliberate anachronism, photorealistic visual media. Extending the detective work of art historian Shigeru Tsuji, Kittler describes the setup Brunelleschi plausibly used: he employed a camera obscura to project the flipped image of the Baptistry on a surface and then placed on top of it a rectangular frame made out of paper with a grid overlay subdividing the projected image into smaller units.[18] Accordingly, the combination of camera obscura, grid, and frame "allowed geometrical constructions to be performed . . . to such a high degree of accuracy that the resulting drawing obeyed all the laws of linear perspective."[19] As this account suggests, frames mediate the technical operations of capture and processing.

The frame is also the fundamental unit for animated media—the single image that, when projected in sequence with other images, creates the illusion of motion. Indeed, animation has been defined as "the art of manipulating the invisible interstices that lie between frames."[20] As media theorist Andrew Johnston points out, the technical and aesthetic accomplishment shared by animation, cinema, and video games, in which we perceive fluid motion through the rapid succession of frames, is fundamentally bound up with transformations in our perception and understanding of temporality.[21] Those involved in intensive (and most often networked) gameplay are intimately aware of the technical operations required to generate fluid motion through computational manipulation of frames, with the dreaded lag most often registering as a drop in frames per second (FPS) that can render games unplayable.[22] For esports athletes, speedrunners, and others involved in highly attuned modes of gaming, frame rates are discussed, fussed over, exploited, and felt in the body. They can spell defeat, open a window of opportunity, and form the technical basis for a gaming community's aesthetic identity.[23]

In relation to visual media, then, frames are cultural techniques for both containing and preparing representations—readying representations for the machinic operations of animation to create the perception of motion and vitality and for the aesthetic operations of display, such as hanging on a gallery wall or resting on an office desk.[24] If we are to understand framing as a technical and aesthetic process mediating capture and circulation, then arguably every act of representation involves—requires—framing.

Given their mediating function, it is not surprising that frames show up repeatedly as epistemic and hermeneutic devices in studies of communicative action and more broadly in scientific knowledge production, which, after all, is fundamentally engaged with both representing and capturing the world. Note the ubiquity of the word "framework" to refer to a given set of epistemic commitments and the ways these commitments make certain aspects of our world (un)knowable and (un)representable. A key inflection point for grasping the significance of frames in studies of communication and media (including studies of digital games) is Erving Goffman's text *Frame Analysis: An Essay on the Organization of Experience*. Goffman's earlier work *The Presentation of Self in Everyday Life* is credited with advancing a dramaturgical orientation to sociology, conceiving social orders as structures reproduced through microsocial interactions that are themselves staged and performed.[25] But the motif he employs in *Frame Analysis* is rooted more squarely in visual media than in drama. Borrowing from Gregory Bateson, Goffman describes frames as the "basic elements" out of which we craft interpretations of events, shaped by broader (and often opaque) systems of governance. Frames provide an organizational "structure of experience" through which our interactions with each other become comprehensible.[26] While this schema is certainly complementary to the dramaturgical emphasis of *The Performance of Self in Everyday Life*, it is important to note the shifts between the two works. In a sense, the frame replaces the stage as the apparatus through which the social unfolds; interpretation, rather than performance, becomes our foundational capacity for participation in social worlds. It is as if we are observers first and participants second to the spectacle of human interaction.[27]

In the hands of mass communication theorists and others interested in political communication, Goffman's notion of framing becomes a way to understand the role of communications media in shaping how we interpret the world. Framing has long been part of the media effects researcher's tool kit, alongside "agenda-setting theory" and "priming."[28] Eschewing the material histories of visual media and their technical operations that Kittler (among others) illuminates, the media effects tradition largely views frames as immaterial and psychological, operating primarily, if not exclusively, through language. It is still rooted in an ocular-centric epistemology, however; framing is a matter of arranging "slices of observed, experienced, and/or recorded 'reality' . . . such that a new angle of vision, vantage point, and/or interpretation is provided."[29] Where mass communication theorists primarily conceive of framing as a linguistic process aimed at manipulation and control, game studies scholars deploy the concept mostly to consider the ways players negotiate social and psychological boundaries between games and real life.[30] Jonas Linderoth, for instance, builds from Gary Fine's Goffmanian analyses of tabletop gaming to ask how WoW players in a roleplay-focused guild switch in and out of various interactional frames to stay in character, primarily through linguistic utterances.[31] Linderoth's careful analysis of players' in-game textual communication shows how, for these players, "immersion" in the diegetic world of the game must be continuously and often arduously maintained through collective investment in a "sociodramatic" frame.[32] Holin Lin and Chuen-tsai Sun take a slightly different tack in their look at the relationship between *Dance Dance Revolution* players and spectators in a public arcade while still working with Goffman's core interpretive schema. In their account, frames are constituted not through what players say to each other in game but rather how arcade attendees of different skill levels arrange themselves in relation to each other and to the gaming apparatus: clear social and physical boundaries demarcating highly skilled from unskilled players, for instance, versus more open circulation between playing and watching among evenly matched players.[33] The underlying epistemic orientation in Goffman's *Frame Analysis*—that we are all both observers of and participants in social worlds—is brought to the fore in this productive consideration of playing and watching digital games, as Lin and Sun schematize relationships between skill, modes of engagement, and physical space.

In much of this work by games scholars and media scholars, the use of frames as a way to understand communicative action seems removed from the history of frames as mediators between capturing and codifying representations of the world and readying them for storage and circulation. This abstraction is somewhat ironic, given the foundational technical work frames carry out in and for games themselves (alluded to above), in which frames act as the technical unit of representation out of which is constructed the perception of smooth and unbroken movement through gamespace. Given these separate trajectories, we are left holding a bifurcated frame—in one hand, its seemingly immaterial epistemic and interpretive functions and, in the other, its material and technical dimensions. To put these pieces back together so as to provide a reconsideration (a reframing) of the interaction I described at the outset of this chapter, I turn to one more consideration of framing, offered by anticolonial and environmental scholars.

Enframing the World

In *Pollution Is Colonialism*, Métis scientist Max Liboiron articulates the ways in which colonial technoscience—including, crucially, environmental science—relies on and exploits land once stewarded by Indigenous peoples.

Liboiron engages the notion of "enframing" (*Gestell*, in German), first articulated by Martin Heidegger, to help explain the logic undergirding contemporary capitalism's rapacious relationship to land. Enframing is a process of revealing nature in a way that makes it ready for extraction; this process is the defining characteristic of modern technology.[34] In Liboiron's words, "this process makes the various relations of Land into a unidirectional relation called Resource for anticipated settler use."[35] They describe enframing as a central characteristic of both capitalism and colonialism, which are united in their "analogous relational logics." In Liboiron's words, "the model of capitalism and imperialism is one of incessant increase and expansion for settler futures, both of which require access to Land."[36] Enframing is a precursor technique to the extractive projects carried out by agents of settler capitalism: a "fundamentally communicative act accomplished through language and mathematical representation" aimed at articulating the steps through which resources might be extracted, risks might be mitigated (or outsourced), and wealth might be accrued from working the land.[37] Such work involves, among other things, the sciences of geography and geology, land surveys (a key instrument of early colonialism in which land, once violently dispossessed, was rendered an "object of calculation"), economic analyses, risk assessments, and corporate and state propaganda.[38] For instance, in his examination of the Hanford reservation (America's primary plutonium facility during World War II and later the site of one of the largest environmental cleanups in the world), William Kinsella describes how developing a particular section of the Columbia River in Washington for plutonium refinement extended and intensified "the ongoing colonization" of the area. It also enveloped people—settler and Indigenous residents of the area as well as site workers—in the same extractive logics, as either (human) resources or logistic hindrances to the task of transforming land and water into components for a machinery of nuclear production. In bringing a Heideggerian philosophy of technics in dialogue with environmental communication, Kinsella's work shows how enframing is a mediated and mediating process, a matter of measuring and quantifying land in order to ready it for extraction.[39]

These two instantiations of framing as cultural technique—one, a visual instrument for freezing a representation in place and, the other, a way of viewing land, its inhabitants, and relations in instrumental terms—are bound by a central logic of capture. Capture can be relatively banal (capturing a moment on camera) or monumental (capturing the flow of a river in order to cool massive nuclear reactors). In what follows, I show how both of these instantiations of framing were in play in the research project that brought me to the horse-racing-venue-turned-LAN to study MMOG players. After all, the same fundamental concern with capture that animates framing as a cultural technique brought me to the Insomnia LAN event, in which my task as a qualitative researcher on a large-scale study of MMOG play was to extract data from attendees. Thus, even though the research itself did not engage Indigenous populations or their lands directly, the research program was thoroughly conditioned by relations both to study participants and to land that might best be described as colonial.[40] The program has this in common with much contemporary social scientific research on digital (and, particularly, networked) games. In what follows, I discuss two sets of relations that framed my fieldwork: relations between players, social scientific knowledge production, and instruments used to frame players as sources of data; and relations between digital games and land. Clarifying the first set of relations allows me to better articulate where I stand in relation to the individuals and communities I have studied and within legacies of colonialist technoscience. Clarifying the second set of relations helps to situate land "at the forefront of critique and theory" and lays the groundwork for subsequent chapters in which I more fully engage the infrastructural character of white, settler masculinities in the space-making and place-taking capacities of digital play.[41]

Extractive Logics in Games Research

The research project that brought me to the horse racing track outside Newbury lasted from 2009 to 2012. Roughly corresponding with this period, a technological and economic imperative toward automated data gathering and analysis began transforming the games industry, along with many other areas of life. Players became positioned as both sources of data extraction and populations on which new strategies of behavioral prediction and control are operationalized. These joint projects have proved to be a source of lucrative partnership between academia and industry; for many social scientific games researchers, the rush to instrument games for data collection and to make sense of the resultant troves of data has offered opportunities to prove their value to games companies.[42] Prior to 2009, when the MMOG project

I was part of began, quantitative social scientists had already demonstrated that large-scale analyses of players' in-game activities could be useful to both games industries and state agencies, often working with data obtained directly from game publishers. But while both automated data gathering and social scientific analysis of large datasets on players had become established by the late 2000s, the period of time between 2009 and 2012 seems, in retrospect, to have been formative. During the height of MMOG research in the late 2000s and early 2010s, the same period as our research at LAN events, scholars such as Nick Yee, Dmitri Williams, and their associates produced prolific and highly cited scholarship based on massive amounts of data gathered automatically on players' in-game behaviors.[43] In addition to pathologizing certain player practices ("gender-swapping" with avatars, for instance), this work proceeds on the basis that players' informed consent to participate in research based on their in-game activities is rendered irrelevant by their coerced agreement to the games' End User License Agreement, the same flimsy cover that serves as the legal framework for the surveillant regimes of contemporary platforms.[44]

Around this same time, big data–driven work on MMOGs also paved the way for the wholescale instrumentation of esports and mobile games, such that it is unthinkable for many in the game development and esports industries to *not* engage in systematic data capture.[45] In 2011, Riot Games, the publisher of *League of Legends* (LoL), implemented a giant data apparatus. This machinery of collection, analysis, and data-driven design would later lead to one pundit calling the game the "largest virtual psychology lab in the world."[46] The year after, Valve, the publisher of numerous networked FPS games (including esports staple *CS:Go*) and of the game distribution platform Steam, hired economist Yanis Varoufakis to help run the virtual economy of the team-based FPS *Team Fortress 2*. Varoufakis, who later became the finance minister of Greece (and who tried, unsuccessfully, to shift the country out of its cycle of bankruptcy and austerity), wrote that Valve offered an economist's "paradise": the ability to run social scientific experiments on the totality of a given population without the need for sampling, to observe the results in real time, and to tweak accordingly.[47] Developers themselves, at least those with deep pockets, now not only instrument their games but also hire their own data analytics teams.[48] This trend certainly enriches the datafication industry, but—according to Jen Whitson—it may be driving further gender-based exclusion in games development and stifling innovation, at least among small-scale publishers.[49] Studies of player practices under these emergent "surveillant assemblages," like the research undertaken by Aphra Kerr and her colleagues, strike a similarly skeptical tone with regard to the increased use of data analytics in games, at least when analytics drive the use of opaque automated tools to curtail forms of player behavior that game companies consider undesirable.[50]

The discourse surrounding and supporting this technological imperative toward data gathering and analysis abounds with metaphors of capturing and processing natural resources: "raw" data on players can be "mined" through automated techniques such as machine learning to process insights about player activity, which can then be operationalized as strategies for attracting and retaining players, curbing unwanted behavior, and offering in-game purchases. And the booming mobile gaming market, having tuned data analytics toward the kinds of predatory techniques used by the gambling industry, employs terminology for high-rolling casino spenders ("whales") to describe players willing to spend large sums on in-game purchases. Such metaphors are more than rhetorical flourish: they are framing devices for the extension of settler capitalist logics and techniques of governance.

Numerous critical media theorists and anticolonial scholars have located the datafication of communicative action (including but certainly not limited to gaming) in broader histories in the intertwined development of colonialism and capitalism. Marc Andrejevic, following the lead of legal and colonial historians, likens the "separation of users from their data"—the central condition of participation on social media platforms—to the land enclosure movement in England in the seventeenth and eighteenth centuries, in which "common" land intended for shared, public use was appropriated by the state, parceled out, and sold off, becoming private commodity.[51] Perhaps the most explicit invocation of the connections between contemporary regimes of datafication and histories of forceful dispossession and extraction is Nick Couldry and Ulises Mejias's articulation of "data colonialism" offered in their book *The Costs of Connection: How Data Is Colonizing Human Life and Appropriating It for Capitalism*. For Couldry and Mejias, the rise over the last two decades of the "social quantification sector" (the multifaceted set of industries carrying out the digitization of social and communicative action in video games and elsewhere) heralds a refinement of the extractive regimes that fueled the dispossession of Indigenous societies from their lands and the conversion of those lands into raw material for the growth of European imperialism and its emerging modes of capitalist production.[52] The authors seize on rhetoric, pushed by big data proponents, that frames data as "the new oil": a naturally occurring resource that lies dormant under the surface, ready to be pulled out, processed, and converted into fuel for powerful forms of economic production.[53] The epistemology undergirding this agential and well-circulated (albeit sloppy) metaphor sees communicative action, and the social production of subjectivity, as the largely immaterial grounds for this new form of colonialism. In Couldry and Meijas's words:

> The colony is not a geographic location but an 'enhanced reality' in which we conduct our social interactions under conditions of continuous data extraction. The resources that are being colonized are the associations, norms, codes, knowledge, and meanings that help us maintain social connections, the human and material processes that constitute economic activity, and the space of the subject from which we face the social world.[54]

At times, Couldry and Meijas's analysis proceeds through a series of further parallels between historical colonialism, which they see as concluded, and this new regime, in which it is not land but the grounds of social belonging that are framed as exploitable resource. For instance, they compare contemporary End User License Agreements to the Spanish conquistadors' *Requerimiento* of 1513: the first are written in obtuse jargon that coerces us into legally dubious and exploitative terms in order to participate in networked services, while the second was a document read aloud (in Spanish) informing the Indigenous audience of what would later be termed the Americas that their lands now belonged to the papacy and that resistance was punishable by genocide.[55] At the same time, Couldry and Meijas emphasize throughout their book that they are not interested in mere parallelism, as if there is simple "one to one correspondence" between "using an app to share pictures of cute cats and participating in a process that decimated the natural resources and Indigenous populations of vast areas of our planet."[56] Rather, echoing Marx, they view historical colonialism as providing for the "primitive accumulation" of natural resources that enabled the construction of industrial-era communication and transportation infrastructures, legal frameworks, hierarchies of racial, ethnic, and gendered difference, and knowledge-building practices in which information is gathered from the colonies and sent to the imperial metropole in order to generate new techniques for imperial control. These systems, in turn, constitute the foundations for the emergent order of data colonialism.[57] In its most trenchant moments, Couldry and Meijas's book carefully explores how the "social quantification sector" is an extension and refinement of colonial logics of dispossession and extraction operating through the capture of data. It is not only that the logics of extraction further colonial arrangements; "the human and environmental relations of production remain characteristically colonial."[58]

While *Costs of Connection* is primarily focused on close examination of the various processes through which our personal data is extracted, processed, and used against us, it is worth interrogating Couldry and Meijas's somewhat ambivalent stance regarding the historicity of colonialism. Contrary to what they say, colonialism is not behind us because it is not an "event"—rather, it constitutes the material and discursive "milieu" in which we continue to work, play, and communicate, including the ways we construct and circulate knowledge.[59] For instance, the data collection and analysis instruments I used in my fieldwork for recording players' demographic information have their origins, as tools of statistical governance, in the empire-building projects of early social science.[60] The survey, the census, and other means of systematically gathering information about people's identities and proclivities were used to subject colonial populations to imperial rule, the raw data traveling from peripheries to metropoles along the same transportation and communication infrastructures that circulated more material instruments of colonization.[61] These tools did to Indigenous peoples (and, eventually, everyone else) what the geographical survey did to the land they stewarded: demarcated boundaries, extracted information, and processed the framed objects for remote governance. If the effect of the geological survey was to produce abstract notions of space amenable to Western legal notions of ownership and (dis)possession, the effect of the survey and the census was to produce categorizations of people amenable to ontological notions of human difference that rationalized the brutalization and enslavement of "lesser" peoples—producing, in both instances, a "rule by numbers."[62] The production, categorization, and operationalization of demographic difference, based on hierarchically organized constructions of race, gender, and ethnicity, remains as foundational to contemporary practices of governance—for instance, figuring out a person's background based on their in-game actions—as it was during more overt colonial rule.

In pointing to the connections between this colonialist legacy and some of the ubiquitous forms of data gathering I was tasked with carrying out in my fieldwork, I am by no means claiming that the LAN attendees I studied represent a particularly oppressed or colonized group. In fact, there is a small irony in traveling to the heart of what was once the British Empire, the imperial power responsible for developing so many techniques of statistical governance and remote administration, to extract data from players on behalf of agents of the current hegemonic metropole (recalling that our study was funded by the US government). Rather, I am pointing to what are some well-rehearsed arguments in anticolonial and postcolonial critique: that techniques of control initially developed for the rule of colonized subjects—the categorization of humans along hierarchies of difference and the (de)allocation of rights, resources, and privileges based on these categorizations—are foundational to contemporary governance and that digitization has been instrumental to the refinement, ubiquity, and power of these techniques. There is, however, a clear line to be drawn between pointing out that we are all subjected to and subjectivated by techniques of social control that have origins in European imperialism and claiming (as Couldry and Meijas seem to) that "we are all colonized." This much is made clear by the ways surveillant regimes continue to operate along and intensify the oppression, marginalization, and brutalization of individuals and communities that are constructed as inferior according to the intersecting hierarchies of colonialism, patriarchy, and capitalism.[63]

Extractive Logics in Games Industries

There is a tendency in much of the critical media scholarship on datafication and data colonialism to see the operations of the social quantification sector as primarily immaterial, proceeding through the capture and extraction of information in ways that are only tangentially, if not metaphorically, related to earlier regimes of colonial dispossession. Here and elsewhere, the work of anticolonial and Indigenous scholars provides a powerful reminder that the colonial project of converting stolen land into "natural" resources, made possible through Indigenous dispossession and genocide, is still very much with us, not a historical backdrop against which we can compare and draw metaphors for contemporary digital enclosure. Max Liboiron, for instance, notes that the enclosure movement was not simply a historical phase; it offered a blueprint adapted and applied to numerous colonial contexts, including "in the scrip system via the Dominion Lands Act of 1879, the largest Land fraud scam in Canadian history."[64] Digitization and datafication do not just share a common set of logics with colonialism—they are refinements of colonialism operating through *and frequently reproducing* its discursive and material foundations, particularly the framing of Indigenous land as exploitable resource. In what follows, I further rely on the insights of Liboiron and other Indigenous scholars, coupled with the work of scholars who consider the environmental degradation wrought by the social quantification sector, to think through relationships between data (including data on and from players), the manifold techniques through which data are produced and stored, and the unfolding legacies of Indigenous dispossession.

Games, like technology industries more generally, are not just involved in the extraction of data; they rely on arrangements of technology and capital historically rooted in and produced for colonial projects to carry out resource extraction, industrial production, and waste disposal, all for the production of surplus value from players and games industry workers. In *Games of Empire*, Nicholas Dyer-Witheford and Greg de Peuter illuminate many of these arrangements. They explore how rare minerals for game consoles are mined in former colonies in Africa; consoles are manufactured under exploitative conditions in China and Southeast Asia; and massive amounts of refuse generated by the games industry and its cycles of obsolescence are sent to landfills in South America and India.[65] Since *Games of Empire* was first published, our understanding of the environmental degradations caused by games (among other digital media) has kept pace with the rapid development of data centers and other energy-hungry components of the global infrastructure required for platform capitalism and its voracious appetite for raw data. Commenting on how the cloud has become an "ecological force," Steven Monseratte notes the tremendous amount of air conditioning required to prevent data servers in the state of Virginia's "data center alley" (responsible for "70 percent of the world's internet traffic in 2019") from overheating. As Monseratte notes, "the Cloud now has a greater carbon footprint than the airline industry."[66] At the same time, new media industries are a main driver of sustainable energy initiatives around the world; environmental media scholar Mél Hogan notes how companies such as Google and Amazon are investing considerably in sustainable energy and rolling out plans for carbon-neutral data centers. And yet, these initiatives are offset by the increasing energy demands of the tech industry's own operations. They are premised on the belief that capitalist accumulation can continue unfettered if provided the right technologies, "upholding the idea that perpetual growth is possible and economically desirable within these conditions."[67] Under this neoliberal (and, as Hogan points out, colonial) project, "Big Tech sees itself as 'partnering' with nature in order to maintain and grow its operations at a time of severe social and political unrest and environmental instability," as if the capitalist goal of endless accumulation could ever be commensurate with(in) a world of finite and diminishing resources.[68] The games industry is a key player here. According to one study published in 2016, the energy expenditures of the 134 million dedicated gaming devices in the United States alone—accounting for the upstream costs of data storage and distribution—are equivalent to 5 million cars, or 85 million refrigerators.[69] With the industry's push toward digital distribution, prompted by the data-extractive allure of platformization, gaming will likely drive the demand for large-scale data storage (and its associated carbon footprint) even further.[70]

Putting Land Back in Play

In pointing to the ways the games industry partakes in and abets this instrumentalist framing of our natural world, whether through its colonial circuits of production and waste or its push toward incredibly resource-intensive streaming distribution, my aim is to reassert the centrality of land in how we understand the manifold connections between colonialism and digital play. I see this perspective as adding valence to the already rich scholarship on how colonialism operates *through* digital games, scholarship that primarily engages in postcolonial critique of games' representations, mechanics, and surrounding discursive practices.[71] If we follow this generative line of critique offered by Soraya Murray, Souvik Mukherjee, Emil Hammar, and others and apply it to the popular mobile game *Temple Run*, developed by an "indie" game company in my former home of Raleigh, North Carolina, we might focus on the game's hypercolonialist narrative and imagery in offering players a range of white/European playable characters (including an actual Spanish conquistador) with which to raid an ancient Aztec temple while being chased by murderous monkeys.[72] The relationship to land that such a critical framing of *Temple Run* might illuminate, if it were more fully developed, is representational and ideological: the white, Western framing of Indigenous lands as savage and inhospitable yet endlessly open to (violent) extraction.[73]

In contrast, the kind of analysis I invite here considers the connections to *physical* land that this game makes possible within the milieu of contemporary settler capitalism. Just up the road from our old house in Raleigh (the site of the mancounters discussed in the introduction) sits Heights House, a boutique bed-and-breakfast that opened its doors in 2021. Offering views of the increasingly vertical Raleigh skyline, on land once stewarded by the Tuscarora and Siouan tribes, Heights House is a "pre–Civil War" (slavery era) Italianate building perched atop the crest of the hill that gives the Boylan Heights neighborhood its name.[74] Like other affluent neighborhoods in Raleigh, Boylan Heights was established as a white enclave under Jim Crow, governed by "explicit deed covenants" that prohibited Black inhabitants such that (as in many other regions in the American South) "Black exclusion from housing was codified by law, as well as by custom."[75] The building's recent and expensive revitalization was undertaken by a husband and wife team; the husband worked at Imangi, creator of *Temple Run*, and his brother is Imangi's founder. One of the top destinations in Raleigh for wealthy travelers and "staycationers" was made possible by video game money—specifically, by a game that capitalizes on the technical and economic conditions that make casual play on mobile devices so irresistible not only to players but also to developers, platform owners, and advertisers.

The relations to land that make possible this mobile game studio, and the boutique bed-and-breakfast it paid for, are less immediate and explicit than the game's Orientalist motifs, requiring different kinds of inquiry. We could certainly take into account the neocolonial arrangements of infrastructure that provide for the distribution of *Temple Run* and the circulation of data it extracts from players. We might also consider the colonialist framing of the land on which both Imangi's studio and Heights House sit: the ways video game companies exert outsize influence over city zoning regulations and processes of gentrification, for instance, such that moving their studios into certain neighborhoods presages the extraction of poor and/or marginalized residents.[76] Looking at the histories that shape these more recent transformations, we might further consider how this land was violently dispossessed from its original stewards by European colonizers; the ways the land's subsequent "owners" were enriched, however indirectly, through the slave economy of the antebellum South; the sordid politics of Jim Crow and, more recently, the carceral state that directs the colonial gaze inward, simultaneously marking Black bodies as unwanted (or at least highly suspicious) in places like Boylan Heights and as exploitable resources for ongoing enrichment.[77] Such are (some) of the colonial relations that enframe us when we play *Temple Run* or stay at the gorgeous tourist attraction its developers bankrolled through successfully harvesting, quantifying, and monetizing the attention and energies of its players.[78]

Measuring Toxicity in Gaming Cultures

In the initial journal article on which this chapter is loosely based, I puzzled through how to position myself as a feminist ethnographer at LAN events—attentive to embodiment, silences, margins, exclusions, and my own biases, commitments, and positionalities—while at the same time employing and embodying an extractive relation to study participants. While I offer this analysis as an exercise in theory-building reflexivity rather than as a "confessional," I am convinced that the framework I initially operated in, provided by predominantly white, liberal feminist theory, fell short of the project of reckoning with the ethics of relationality captured in the photograph of the model, the clan members, and me. My reflexive exercise was constrained to the figures in the frame; the question became about what I could have done differently. The analysis I offer here, by contrast, draws from anticolonial critique to consider the grounds on which we stood: the material, technical, and symbolic conditions that made the framing of the uncomfortable interaction possible to begin with. This shifts the question from "What could I have done?"—a (neo)liberal query about the consequences of individual choice that leaves the rationale for the study and my participation in it untouched—to "What was I doing there?" This query demands that I reckon more fully with the legacies and logics that framed not just the singular exploitative interaction captured on camera but also the research program, its dynamics of knowledge production, and the instrumental approach to both land and people required for and reproduced through the extraction and circulation of player data.

The verb I foregrounded in my initial account of this interaction as a means of capturing my ambivalence toward the study of masculinized gaming cultures was *to pass*. Because I can (or could) pass as a legitimate participant in any number of esports tournaments, LAN events, industry conventions, and so on due to my white, cisgender positionality, I had access to interactions and contexts that others might not have had. My presence tripped no obvious cultural sensors, as the presence of women, queer folk, and BIPOC folk routinely does in so many places of play; I could slip in, relatively undetected, to extract information about the ways men play and act when no others/Others are around. Perhaps a more fitting verb for the critique I offer here, again provided by anticolonial scholarship, is *to assimilate*. For Max Liboiron, one of the more pernicious and destructive ways that colonialism operates through contemporary scientific practices of land management is via theories of "assimilative capacity." They define this as a "term of art in both environmental science and state regulation" that holds that a given system can absorb a certain amount of pollutants before notable damage is done—that is, before contamination (the non-harmful presence of pollutants) turns into pollution.[79] Assimilative capacity is a framework—a cultural technique of epistemic enclosure—and a highly agential one: a model of how nature functions that permits tolerable levels of harm to a given ecosystem. For Liboiron, assimilative capacity is a profoundly problematic way of understanding land, even when it is deployed by environmental activists and policymakers in attempts to clean it up. Like similar threshold-based models of pollution, assimilative capacity grants polluters considerable license, and even the right, to inflict harm. By framing land as both resource and "a sink for future pollution," assimilative capacity furthers the capitalist and imperialist drive toward "incessant increase and expansion for settler futures"—futures in which land is only ever imagined as the rightful property of the colonizers.[80]

Expanding and carefully playing with this concept, we might use assimilative capacity to enrich our understanding of researcher agency and positionality: the capacity to be absorbed into a given field site. To apply it to my own work with and within gaming contexts constructed as enclaves for white, settler masculinity, though, I need to acknowledge that such places are never *un*contaminated, either in terms of cultural politics or relations to land. The forms of toxicity and harm toward women, LBTQIA+, and BIPOC folks that have long been pointed out by players, journalists, and scholars are not byproducts: toxicity is infrastructural to the operations of these contexts. Expressed succinctly, misogyny, homophobia, and racism are not bugs but features of so many sites of intensive gameplay.[81] Reimagining my work and the work of colleagues who have documented these conditions in terms of assimilative capacity—that is, the ability to enter into gaming contexts with the aim of documenting toxicity—invites us to critically interrogate the purposes served by continually creating and circulating stories of the identity-based violence, harassment, and marginalization routinely committed in and through digital gaming cultures.

If it is useful to theorize the embodied work of ethnographic sense-making as media instrumentation, as I offer in the initial *MedieKultur* article, then perhaps the media instrument that best serves as a metaphor for assimilative capacity and toxicity in research on gaming cultures is the Geiger counter: a tool intended to sense and communicate levels of contamination accrued in and emitted by damaged and damaging bodies on land rendered dangerous (if not inhospitable) by the ravages of settler capitalist technoscience. This instrumentation has been a productive model for research on gender and gaming. Some of the most highly regarded and well-cited research in this area, as well as much of my own previous work, operates to a large extent through recounting instances of gender-based harm and processing them through the frameworks of liberal feminism. This scholarship remains foundational to our understanding of gaming's inequities, and yet, these inequities persist. Commenting on the persistence of oppression even as social scientific research continues to document it, Indigenous scholar and activist Eve Tuck describes research aimed at cataloging oppression as "damage-based research," which she defines as "research that operates, even benevolently, from a theory of change that establishes harm or injury in order to achieve reparation."[82] In this vein, approaching gaming cultures with our feminist Geiger counters in hand yields powerful (and publishable) results but perhaps does little to alleviate damage. As an alternative for understanding how research might prompt social change, Tuck proposes a "desire-based" framework that acknowledges the existence of harm but proceeds by imagining and articulating how conditions might be different, more hospitable and sustaining, for those involved. I am grateful for this distinction, and I believe it is an apt description for the kinds of games research I most admire: research that is tied to efforts at transforming the material conditions of those most often at the margins of gaming cultures, including (but not limited to) Indigenous players and communities, and that materially supports those otherwise locked out of the pleasures and rewards afforded by making and playing games within communities in which they can belong.[83]

The rest of the chapters in this book take a slightly different tack than the desire-based alternatives Tuck espouses. They report on research that neither catalogs harm (for instance, by documenting problematic representations in games or toxic language and practices of masculine players) nor follows the kinds of interventionist approaches of the work I just cited. Rather, each chapter is an attempt to center the *grounds* of gaming— understood as material land, whether in homes (chap. 2), LAN events (chap. 3), university campuses (chap. 4), or games industry conventions (chap. 5), and as discursive terrains. I accept that my own assimilative capacity—my ability to move in and through these sites—remains an ambivalent precondition of the insights I offer in subsequent chapters. As I have shown here, this capacity is as tied to legacies of settler capitalism and its extractive logics as it is to patriarchal gender hierarchies. But at least now you know where I stand. The direction I take in the remaining chapters is to move past stories of gender-based damage—beyond the figures in the frame, in their casually misogynist and utterly routine compositions—and inquire instead about the place-making practices of play and the formations of white masculinity infrastructural to them.

NOTES

1. This project is reported on more fully in other work: Taylor et al., "Public Displays of Play," and Taylor, "I'd Rather Be a Cyborg Than a Gamerbro." As I discuss in greater detail later in this chapter, the account that follows has been borrowed, with some minor revisions and with the journal editors' approval, from the second of these articles.

2. Haraway, "Situated Knowledges," 581.

3. Haraway, "Situated Knowledges," 581.

4. "Casual" is a loaded term in game studies, particularly in regard to gender; see Cote, *Gaming Sexism*; Anable, *Playing with Feelings*. For those who travel hours to play video games intensively for days and nights on end, the term typically refers to gaming that is not supported by corporate sponsorship or associated with an organized tournament or league.

5. Taylor and Witkowski, "This Is How We Play It," 5.

6. The use of promotional models, or "booth babes," at gaming events has received considerable critique in games and technology journalism and, to a lesser extent, in academic work. See Thompson, "Weird Things You Learn as a 'Booth Babe'"; Cornfeld, "Babes in Tech Land"; Taylor, Jenson, and de Castell, "Cheerleaders/Booth Babes/*Halo* Hoes."

7. Taylor, "I'd Rather Be a Cyborg Than a Gamerbro," 19.

8. paperson, *A Third University Is Possible*, 11; Denoon, *Settler Capitalism*; Liboiron, *Pollution Is Colonialism*, 13.

9. Tuck and Yang, "Decolonization Is Not a Metaphor," 31; Liboiron, *Pollution Is Colonialism*, 16.

10. See, for instance, Bulut, *A Precarious Game*; Dyer-Witheford and Peuter, *Games of Empire*; Joseph, "Discourse of Digital Dispossession"; Rodgers, "Into the Social Factory"; Woodcock, *Marx at the Arcade*.

11. TallBear, "Standing with and Speaking as Faith," 4.

12. This is a (bad) allusion to Trinh Min-ha's *Framer Framed*.

13. Bulut, *A Precarious Game*; Trammell, *Repairing Play*.

14. Phillips, *Gamer Trouble*; Cote, *Gaming Sexism*; Condis, *Gaming Masculinity*; Paul, *Toxic Meritocracy of Video Games*.

15. As a counterpoint to the framing of the promotional model I helped reproduce, please consider reading a *Vice* article that presents a collection of quotations from promotional models about their labor. The piece performs a useful inversion of how promotional models are frequently framed: it foregrounds their voice and knowledge rather than their appearance. See Thompson, "Weird Things You Learn as a 'Booth Babe.'"

16. Sontag, *On Photography*, 3.

17. Barad, "Posthumanist Performativity," 818.

18. Kittler, *Optical Media*, 59.

19. Kittler, *Optical Media*, 61.

20. Norman McLaren, as quoted in Johnston, *Pulses of Abstraction*, 3.

21. Johnston, *Pulses of Abstraction*, 23.

22. The fact that "frame per second" shares the same acronym as "first person shooters" ought to excite those of us interested in the deep historical interconnectedness of optical media and military technologies and the ways games manifest and extend these connections. See Elam, "Automated"; Crogan, *Gameplay Mode*.

23. I am thinking specifically of *Super Smash Bros* (*Smash*) players, who frequently prefer to play on cathode-ray tube (CRT) televisions rather than more modern LCD screens owing to the additional processing time of high-resolution monitors. For the hyperprecise choreography of moves and counters in *Smash* franchise games, not to mention other games played competitively, even a single-digit delay in FPS can

render a game unplayable. This is why *Smash* players can be seen lugging clunky CRTs to tournaments: to reduce their reaction time by fractions of a second. I am indebted to Bryce Stout for this insight; see Stout, "Smashing Some Bros," 79.

24. A frame is also a physical artifact for displaying visual media. When we want to display and preserve a picture, drawing, or painting, we usually frame it, and a host of options becomes available: with matte or without? Glass pane, acrylic, or none? Wood, metal, or plastic? Framing thus is not only an act of selecting and excluding what is captured and what is not but also a series of curatorial decisions around the means of staging representations—a set of techniques for both highlighting an image (or elements of it) and incorporating it into its surroundings (or making it stand out). As physical artifacts, frames mediate the boundary between a given representation and the world around it.

25. Goffman, *Presentation of Self in Everyday Life*, 8.

26. Goffman, *Frame Analysis*, 37.

27. Note, too, that Goffman refers to the moment-to-moment mess of sociality as "strips," further deepening the sense that the social order is mediatized.

28. Scheufele and Tewksbury, "Framing, Agenda Setting, and Priming"; Cacciatore, Scheufele, and Iyengar, "End of Framing as We Know It . . . and the Future of Media Effects."

29. Feste, "Frame Theory," 16.

30. See, for instance, Consalvo, "There Is No Magic Circle," 413; Deterding, "Modes of Play," 18; Tobin, "Time and Space in Play," 131.

31. Linderoth, "Effort of Being in a Fictional World"; Fine, *Shared Fantasy*.

32. Linderoth, "Effort of Being in a Fictional World," 489. Though I agree wholeheartedly with Linderoth that the normative understanding of immersion as the "default game experience" needs to be updated, our understanding of how immersion happens differs widely, as evident in my treatment of the concept in chapter 2.

33. Lin and Sun, "Role of Onlookers in Arcade Gaming," 126.

34. Though I am not citing Heidegger directly here, I am indebted to Liboiron's rationale for how and why they draw on Heidegger's works, given his deeply problematic affiliations. They write: "I cite Heidegger to demonstrate that even anti-Semitic, white supremacist, Nazi, canonized European thinkers not only are well aware of colonial land relations but also can see them with great clarity and nuance." Further, Liboiron argues that Heidegger's paradox—both a luminous philosopher and a Nazi—works against the tendency to view awareness as the first step toward change in settler-Indigenous relations. They ask instead, What if settlers knowing did not change anything? For them, Heidegger's example is demonstrable proof that awareness need not lead to action. I am grateful for Liboiron's keen grasp and exercise of citational politics, though I fall well short of their example. Liboiron, *Pollution Is Colonialism*, 65.

35. Liboiron, *Pollution Is Colonialism*, 62.

36. Liboiron, *Pollution Is Colonialism*, 63. Liboiron uses "land" to refer to geographical territory, that which is most commonly treated as resource in settler technoscience, and "Land" to refer to the set of spiritual and ethical relations Indigenous peoples have with physical land.

37. Kinsella, "Heidegger and Being at the Hanford Reservation," 197.

38. Blomley, "Law, Property, and the Geography of Violence," 128.

39. Kinsella, "Heidegger and Being at the Hanford Reservation," 206.

40. As with the fieldwork story that starts this chapter, I will be borrowing the description of the project from Taylor, "I'd Rather Be a Cyborg Than a Gamerbro."

41. Liboiron, *Pollution Is Colonialism*, 26.

42. El-Nasr, Drachen, and Canossa, *Game Analytics*.

43. Williams has since established a data analytics consulting firm, Ninja Metrics—a suitably Orientalist name, perhaps, for a business built on the capacity to observe and extract without detection.

44. Huh and Williams, "Dude Looks Like a Lady"; Chee, Taylor, and de Castell, "Re-mediating Research Ethics."

45. In my own prior work, I draw attention to how university-based *League of Legends* players navigate the uneven and shifting surveillant regime of collegiate esports. Taylor, "Numbers Game."

46. Hsu, "Inside the Largest Virtual Psychology Lab in the World"; Strom, "For Riot Games, Big Data Is Serious Business."

47. Sarkar, "Valve Hires Economist to Assist with Linking Its Virtual Economies."

48. Kerr, *Global Games*, 108.

49. Kerr, *Global Games*, 106; Whitson, "New Spirit of Capitalism in the Game Industry," 793.

50. Kerr, De Paoli, and Keatinge, "Surveillant Assemblages of Governance in Massively Multiplayer Online Games," 330.

51. Andrejevic, "Ubiquitous Computing and the Digital Enclosure Movement," 107.

52. Couldry and Mejias, *Costs of Connection*.

53. Couldry and Mejias, *Costs of Connection*, 89.

54. Couldry and Mejias, *Costs of Connection*, 85.

55. Couldry and Mejias, *Costs of Connection*, 92.

56. Couldry and Mejias, *Costs of Connection*, 45.

57. Couldry and Mejias, *Costs of Connection*, 45–46.

58. Couldry and Mejias, *Costs of Connection*, 46.

59. Liboiron, *Pollution Is Colonialism*, 65.

60. Connell, "Periphery and Metropole in the History of Sociology," 74.

61. It is worth noting that the contemporary production of academic knowledge follows similar global patterns: in a metareview of collaborations between European and North American scholars and scholars from formerly colonized countries, the

former tend to have the status of first or sole author while the latter are either coauthors or are relegated to nonauthor fieldworkers and local consultants. Dahdouh-Guebas et al., "Neo-colonial Science by the Most Industrialised upon the Least Developed Countries in Peer-Reviewed Publishing," 338.

62. Kalpagam, *Rule by Numbers*; Kakkar, "'Education, Empire and the Heterogeneity of Investigative Modalities'"; Connell, "Periphery and Metropole in the History of Sociology." I am grateful to Gayas Eapen for directing me to the rich work of scholars in India who study the histories and politics of information in colonial contexts.

63. Rivera, "Digital Enclosure and the Elimination of the Oceti Sakowin"; Benjamin, *Race after Technology*; Browne, *Dark Matters*.

64. Liboiron, *Pollution Is Colonialism*, 71.

65. Dyer-Witheford and Peuter, *Games of Empire*, 224.

66. Monserrate, "Cloud Is Material."

67. Hogan, "Big Data Ecologies," 652.

68. Hogan, "Big Data Ecologies," 636. I am grateful to Chris Ingraham, in his work on LEGO's green initiatives, for pointing out the vast incongruity between capitalist and environmentalist notions of sustainability. Ingraham, "Fake Plastic Trees."

69. Of all the odd metrics associated with gaming's big data analytics, this is one of my favorites. How many fridges worth of game devices do *you* have?

70. Mills et al., "Toward Greener Gaming," 172. I discuss the platformization of digital gaming (and of communicative action more generally) in chapter 4.

71. Murray, "Work of Postcolonial Game Studies in the Play of Culture"; de Wildt et al., "(Re-)Orienting the Video Game Avatar"; Mukherjee, *Videogames and Postcolonialism*; Patterson, *Open World Empire*.

72. The anticolonialist analysis of *Temple Run* presented here is expanded on in an article in *Eludamos*. Taylor, "Reimagining a Future for Game Studies, from the Ground Up."

73. Murray, *On Video Games*, 222.

74. visitRaleigh, "Raleigh's Heights House Hotel Named among World's Best New Hotels."

75. Mattson, *Evolution of Raleigh's African-American Neighborhoods in the 19th and 20th Centuries*, 25.

76. Bulut, *A Precarious Game*, 79; Kerr, *Global Games*, 157.

77. Towns, *On Black Media Philosophy*.

78. Stark hierarchies of race and class are often jarringly visible in places like Raleigh. Down the other side of the hill from Heights House, almost visible from the boutique hotel, is the Raleigh Central Prison. Housing both prison industries and the state's execution chamber, it is one of the many carceral sites where Black inmates (who are vastly overrepresented in prisons compared to the overall state

demographics) are put to work as cheap labor and, not infrequently, put to death. Smith and Linn, "Central Prison"; Editor, "From Plantation to Prison."

79. Liboiron, *Pollution Is Colonialism*, 39–40.

80. Liboiron, *Pollution Is Colonialism*, 64.

81. Taylor, "Kinaesthetic Masculinity and the Prehistory of Esports"; Ask and Svendsen, "Sexual Harassment in Online Games."

82. Tuck, "Suspending Damage," 413.

83. Fisher and Harvey, "Intervention for Inclusivity"; Schoemann and Asad, "Design for the Margins"; LaPensée and Lewis, "Skins: Designing Games with First Nations Youth"; Richard and Gray, "Gendered Play, Racialized Reality."

2

CIRCLES

It All Starts at Home

"Live in Your World. Play in Ours."

This slogan for the first two generations of Sony PlayStation console captured a certain turn-of-the-millennium discourse: the fantasy that new digital technologies, particularly games, could not only offer new sorts of experiences, pleasures, and communication but could also *transport* us to new places and modes of being. For a time, both popular culture and academia fixated on the potential for emerging networked, computational media to take us elsewhere, from science fiction visions of almost all-encompassing virtual worlds (William Gibson's cyberspace, Neal Stephenson's avatars, the Wachowski sisters' matrix) to academic fixations on the capacities of ludic and networked technologies to let us leave the real world behind.[1] As discussed in the introduction, many in the then-nascent field of game studies suggested (and still do) that games offer players a sense, often seductive and problematic, of transportation from real life and into gameworlds that is abetted by "flow," the "magic circle," and "immersion."[2] Both popular and academic accounts of digital play abound with metaphors of being transported, leaving behind, and escaping—of going somewhere other than here.

This work has been vigorously criticized for its binary ontologies (real vs. virtual, physical vs. immaterial, and as pertains to networked media, online vs. offline) and for its reliance on psychologistic, technologically reductive, and formalist ways of conceptualizing digital play. Mia Consalvo asserts that "there is no magic circle"; rather than occupying a space apart, digital games are enmeshed within (and constituted by) numerous cultural,

political, economic, technological, and legal milieus.[3] Stefanie Boluk and
Patrick LeMieux, following the lead of game designer and instructor Eric
Zimmerman, wonder whether anyone "actually believes" in the concept or
if it is rather a pervasive straw man in game studies, claiming that "the desire
for the magic circle wields far more power than many want to admit."[4] T. L.
Taylor's breakthrough *Play between Worlds* offers an ethnographic apprecia-
tion for how massively multiplayer online games (MMOGs), often held up as
the paradigmatic vehicle for cyberspatial transportation, are situated in and
constituted through everyday/everynight realities.[5] Bart Simon similarly
argues for an insistence on the contexts in which play takes place as a means
of recapturing an understanding of the mundane, intimate realities of digital
play—an understanding that mitigates the unhelpful stereotype of the gaming "flaneur" as an untethered and mercurial traveler of and through digital
worlds.[6] In the sociological sensibility Simon urges for, alive also in Taylor's
work (among others), traveling is ultimately a limited trope for making sense
of digital play. These scholars urge us to resist conflating the look and feel
of being elsewhere that games can provide with *actually* being elsewhere;
following their lead, scholars operating in a broadly materialist tradition of
media studies have begun considering the ways that the physical conditions
of play allow for (or do not allow for) this sense of transportation.[7] This shifts
us from wondering whether anyone actually believes magic circles are real
and invites us to acknowledge that for many players, the phenomenological
experience of immersion in fantasy worlds is *real enough*. Rather than going
around in circles debating the existence (or not) of magic, we can ask what
sorts of apparatuses and conditions *provide* for these subjective experiences
of material escape and virtual immersion.

This chapter acknowledges that the primary (for many of players, the
first and most consistent) sites of intensive play—and, by extension, the
experiences, practices, and subjectivities that accompany it—are domestic
contexts. These sites are made possible by particular configurations of gaming technologies in the home, regardless of what form that home may take.
My examination of domestic play in this chapter works from the premise
that the kinds of masculine subjectivities associated with sustained investment in games and gaming cultures are first and foremost facilitated, indeed
constructed, through the kinds of domestic arrangements designed to enable certain players to be immersed, to "play in other worlds while living in
theirs" (invoking the slogan for Sony's PlayStation consoles in the 1990s).

Immersion, in the account offered here, is an effect of spatial and temporal relations that, in Canada and the United States at least, has historically privileged white, cisgender men and boys.

The question guiding this chapter is straightforward: what kind of space—literally—does gaming take up in our homes? Once we begin to answer this question, we can ask what patterns of gender- and race-based privilege and marginalization are associated with spatial (and temporal) arrangements of games, game-related gear, furniture, and so on. To get at this question, I devised a qualitative study in which I worked with a graduate student to collect and analyze images of gaming setups posted on NeoGAF, an influential gaming-related online forum. As with scholars looking at domestic arrangements of Twitch streamers, it was my hope that peering into the basements, rec rooms, bedrooms, and dens of masculine gaming enthusiasts would give insight into the coconstitutive relationships between gendered subjectivity and media in domestic space.[8]

But Are They Man Caves?

The empirical study I draw from in this chapter was carried out with Katreena Alder, who was at the time a graduate student in the Communication, Rhetoric, and Digital Media (CRDM) program at North Carolina State University (NCSU).[9] The image of the man cave loomed large as we embarked on this study, as indeed it does in the broader cultural imagination; it is, currently, the most ubiquitous way we have of expressing our understanding of particular arrangements between white masculinity, domestic spaces, and domesticated (or domesticating) technologies. Man caves may vary according to geography, class, race, sexuality, and so on, but the reason given for their existence, the *need* for them, largely transcends these variances: as a cultural logic, the man cave represents a desire on the part of masculine subjects to find an escape within (mostly) heteronormative domestic space. While research on man caves is in its infancy, an interview with Tristan Bridges, a sociologist of masculinities, helps shed some light. Bridges notes two aspects of contemporary man caves based on interviews he has done with both straight- and queer-identified man cave denizens.[10] The first is that man caves are ostensibly built to accommodate many people, but in the day-to-day reality of the men Bridges spoke with, they are used almost exclusively in solitary ways by the owner. Their second defining aspect is that they are conceptualized as spaces in which the man or men of the house can find refuge from the allegedly feminizing influence of other domestic spaces—often spaces of domestic labor and social reproduction. Man caves, in Bridges's analysis, are cultural techniques for escaping the work of domestic care.[11]

That said, theorizing gaming setups as man caves may not be the most useful way to understand them. What little research there is concerning man caves suggests that they typically occupy entire rooms (garages, attics, basements, and so on), whereas the gaming setups we looked at vary widely in how much and what kinds of space they take up. More importantly, man caves are often less associated with gaming than with pursuits like hunting, sports spectatorship, car repair and car fandom, card play, and high-fidelity audio—many if not all of which arguably predate digital gaming and connect forms of masculinized leisure based in more mechanical or physical competencies and pleasures. Most obviously, users on the gaming forums we studied simply did not refer to "man caves" when describing their setups. This suggests that gaming setups afford a different kind of spatial subjectivization than what is associated with man caves, something not linked to forms of leisure organized around overtly physical competition (or the representation thereof) but with roots in other masculinized mediascapes— the study, curiosity cabinet, stereo room, computer room, tabletop gaming room, model railroad setup.[12] For this reason, this chapter positions gaming setups as culturally adjacent to (and frequently a material component of) man caves, while taking care to account for the separate but overlapping histories, affects, practices, and subjectivities associated with different types of gaming setups. This approach lets me attend to the ways that masculinized practices of domestic place making—those that involve gaming and those that do not—are united in offering forms of technologically mediated escape to those allowed to enter and stay, while avoiding easy reductionism and collapsing the important specificity of these forms.

Domestication and Escape

Taking this more expansive view on domestic gaming setups—not seeing them as variations on the man cave but instead asking how they configure spaces and times of digital play within the home and exploring what the politics of those configurations might be—means that these setups are arguably situated within multiple, overlapping histories of media domestication. A full accounting of these histories is well beyond the scope of this chapter (and could, indeed, occupy several books), but it is necessary to acknowledge the research to which I am most immediately indebted: academic work that documents the ways lifestyle magazines helped situate various media within the home, whether high-fidelity audio and television post World War II or game consoles in the 1990s and early 2000s. This vibrant trajectory of scholarship draws from multiple disciplines, including human geography, architecture, and media studies, to examine how the advertisements and editorials found in lifestyle magazines such as *McCall's* and *Better Homes and Garden* in the 1940s and 50s, *High Fidelity* and *HiFi Review* over the same period, and *PlayStation Magazine* in the 1990s and early 2000s envisioned and articulated the ideal ways new media should be incorporated into the home.[13]

In the case of the television in the 1950s and the Nintendo Wii in the mid-2000s, incorporating these media into the home meant placing the respective media prominently in the family's shared space (living room, den, TV room), enjoying the domestic bonding these media supposedly made possible. Lynn Spigel, considering women's lifestyle magazines of the late 1940s and early 1950s, notes how the television was advertised as a "lubricant" that could bring family members into more harmonious realignment—long before most families could even afford one.[14] According to Spigel, these magazines offered *spatial* solutions to the challenges of postwar life. Traumatized men returning from war to take up white-collar jobs could find reprieve in the garage; women compelled into house care and child rearing after wartime employment could fashion a quiet and unobtrusive nook for themselves. In this spatial imaginary, the centrally located television set was sold as "the new family hearth through which love and affection might be rekindled."[15] Deborah Chambers makes similar observations regarding advertising for the Nintendo Wii in women's lifestyle magazines of the 2000s, albeit under drastically different conditions than the introduction of the mid-twentieth-century television set. Rather than ameliorating the traumatic effects of postwar transition to suburban life, the Nintendo Wii was marketed as a device that could reengage family members around a singular form of screen-based entertainment at a time when devices proliferated and content was increasingly subdivided into niche markets. The Wii, with its family-friendly aesthetic and games as well as its spatial demands, could compel family members to put down their individual screens and once again come together. If the television was a spatial and technological cure for the ills of postwar suburbia, the Wii was a cure for the ills of hyperindividuated media consumption.[16]

The postwar television and postindustrial Nintendo Wii were thus marketed as technologies that could bring families together, both physically and affectively. In contrast, accounts of high-fidelity stereo advertisements in the 1950s and PlayStation consoles in the early 2010s explore how these media were advertised as technologies of masculine *escape* rather than (and in defiance of) domestic cohesion. Keir Keightley offers a parallel account to Lynn Spigel's, analyzing the discourses at work in high-fidelity magazine editorials and advertisements of the 1950s. These magazines encouraged (white, male) readers to surround themselves in sound through the barely domesticated technology of high-fidelity audio equipment. According to Keightley, magazines like *High Fidelity* framed domestic life in antagonistic terms for its audience of postwar, suburban men—as a war, fought with media, for the masculine self-worth of its readers. On one side was the television, with its emasculating passivity and its location in the feminized space of the hearth, and on the other side, the military machinery of stereo equipment, the operation of which connected men not only to the aesthetic pleasures of music made by men, for men, but also to histories of DIY engineering and technical fabrication. The hi-fi stereo was marketed as an apparatus for escape— immersion—into the soundscapes it offered. It could not only shut out the (ever shrewish, perpetually aggrieved) wife but also shut her up.[17] Likewise, Bernadette Flynn's research on domestic gaming in the late 2000s, which combines textual analysis of advertisements with ethnographic observation of families' media use in their homes, notes how one PlayStation 2 advertisement depicts a bombed-out living room, the games' enactments of spectacular violence so immediate that they carry over into the real world. Flynn claims, "It seems that the dreams of bodily liberation and visceral engagement (for the men to whom the advertisements speak) can only be manifest through violently destroying the icons of domesticity."[18] Like the discourses articulated in the pages of 1950s stereo magazines, this advertisement imagined domestic space as a literal battleground, the male player reclaiming domestic space via the militarized media apparatus of the PlayStation console. Aaron Trammell's work on the "networks of privilege" formed through early tabletop gaming and model

railroad communities constitutes a vital link between these masculine leisure practices and whiteness. As discussed in the introduction, Trammell
shows how tabletop gaming and its precursors took root in the garages, basements, and sheds of suburban America, enclaves for white families decamp-
ing from urban centers in the 1950s and 1960s out of fears of Black uprising.
The same connection might be made for hi-fi setups during this period,
particularly given the suburban contexts of the "hi-fi man."[19]

Of course, in everyday life and away from the hypergendered texts examined by these scholars, media platforms and the spaces of their use are
highly negotiated (at least in homes shared by more than one inhabitant).
The temporal and spatial dynamics of actual domestic play has been given
some scholarly attention; in Alison Harvey's ethnographic accounts and
in the research by Jo Bryce and Jason Rutter, gaming consoles are either
located in boys' bedrooms or in communal spaces largely taken over by
male inhabitants during play time.[20] Sam Tobin, in his illuminating work
on how the Nintendo DS game system is played, discussed, and imagined by
members of the Penny Arcade online gaming community, notes how these
dominant (and dominating) patterns of media use elide other, less visible
forms of gaming on mobile platforms. In Tobin's account, Penny Arcade
forum users play DS on the toilet, at the kitchen counter, or on the couch
while their partners play on a console, "cocooned" by an array of objects to
support their play: a drink, a stylus, their phone.[21] His research emphasizes
that such configurations—say, one family member curled up on a chair playing DS while two others sit on the adjacent couch playing PlayStation—are
new technological iterations of much older configurations of domestic sociality. Of this kind of "social play with media in domestic space," he writes,
"it harkens back to the parlors, drawing rooms, and living rooms of earlier
eras, where family members sat together chatting while engaging in different
activities, such as the needle point, letter writing, and harpsichord playing
of the Regency period upper-class domesticity described in Jane Austen's
novels or the interwar period where people listened to the radio while reading the newspaper, knitting, and playing with toys."[22]

Following Tobin's lead, this chapter considers how an online gaming
community circulates descriptions and depictions of domestic play. Like his
work on the DS, I am interested in exploring what these configurations say
about our contemporary relationships to digital play and the ways gaming
technologies configure domestic space and time.

Digital Spelunking

In examining game-related forums, I depart from the kinds of approaches to documenting gaming communities that I draw from elsewhere this book, based on spending time in public, physical contexts of play such as local area network (LAN) parties (chaps. 1 and 3) and university classrooms and media studios (chap. 4). While hanging out with people in their domestic gaming sites would certainly be possible and highly productive, I am more interested in asking how a distributed community of players makes space for gaming within the home and how players display and discuss their setups with community members. I therefore am indebted to scholars who have undertaken similar work to look at the ways online gaming communities discuss and enact gender issues, including sexuality, pornography, and harassment.[23] These scholars demonstrate that online forums are a key site in the reproduction of gendered privilege and oppression in gaming culture, particularly insofar as they traffic in and sanction misogyny, racism, and homophobia and imagine straight, white, cisgender men as the culture's rightful owners, operators, and producers.

The site to which I was drawn when I began this study in summer of 2017 was NeoGAF, a long-standing and influential gaming culture site that, as of July 2018, had over eight hundred thousand message threads.[24] Though never a frequent visitor to the site, I was initially drawn to NeoGAF because of its reputation as an influential and active gaming community and for its annual "Show Us Your Gaming Setup" thread, stretching back to 2003 and continuing in 2023.[25] These threads are between one thousand and three thousand posts long, initiated in January of the given year with some variation of the basic prompt (show us your setup) and remaining open throughout the year. Users respond with photographs of their gaming gear and surrounding context, either posted directly to the site or linked to from image hosting platforms. The content, quality, and quantity of images varies quite a bit; some users post upward of a dozen pictures, from wide-angle shots of the room in which they have their gaming tech to close-ups of specific gear and media collections. Some post only one image. Images are often, though not always, accompanied by text, including technical specifications, statements about the users' upcoming plans for the space or tech, and self-deprecating claims about the quality of the gear or the cleanliness of the setup. Most posts are responses to image posts, often appreciative of either the setup as a whole or of specific gear or other details. As with most online forums, game related or not, users' genders are not specified; however, reading through these threads, it becomes clear that a majority of usernames are masculinized, and users themselves consistently use male pronouns and masculine-linked vernacular (dude, bro, guys) to refer to themselves and others. Thus, while we may not be able to make definitive claims about the gender demographic of this community, it is certainly masculinized in how users relate to each other—consistent with what we know of games-related forums and gendered histories of how publicly available print and image-based media have envisioned particular technologies (hi-fi equipment, computers) and their users as masculine. Taken together, the "Show Us Your Gaming Setup" threads constitute an archive of photographs of domestic gaming spaces, assembled and curated by members of a once vibrant and still active games community. This archive offers a productive glimpse into how leisure technologies conventionally coded as masculine—game consoles, peripherals, computers, high-fidelity audio equipment, home theaters—are envisioned and enacted by a community that exerted considerable influence in games culture over much of the time these threads were being populated.

Far from offering an unmediated glimpse into users' gaming setups (as if unmediated observation is ever possible), NeoGAF itself shapes what is presentable and knowable about users' gaming setups in ways that are worth acknowledging. The site is notable for requiring users to link their account to an email provided by their ISP, workplace, or education—meaning neither free email services like Gmail nor stand-alone accounts can be used to register. Each new registration is reviewed and approved (or not) by site administrators. The site's terms of service emphasize that its moderation is "not by democracy," and moderators are given broad leeway in ensuring what the terms of service call "civil, evidence-based discussion" with zero tolerance for "sexual, racial, or ethnic slurs."[26] In 2014, the outright ban on gamergate-related discussion made it clear that the site's moderators were active and engaged; as Adam Rosenberg wrote, covering the site's misadventures for *Mashable*, "NeoGAF was, by and large, a safe space to geek out without worrying about racists and gamergate trolls."[27] This is in stark contrast to Reddit, which launched around the same time: registration for the "front page of the Internet" is much more open, and for years its more hands-off governance made it (notoriously) a haven for groups organized around bigotry and toxicity.[28] Most NeoGAF gaming setup threads begin with links to previous years' threads, and in some cases, pictures of what moderators deemed particularly noteworthy setups from the year before. This, together with the site's relatively stringent registration and moderation policies, means that users who posted to the threads analyzed were likely already enculturated into what kinds of images, and what kinds of responses, were permissible and welcome.

Katreena Alder and I stored all the images from the first thirty posts with functioning image links from two different years' forum threads: 2007 and 2015.[29] Though users are required to log in to post images and comments, the threads themselves are visible to nonregistered users—which is to say, they are public. That said, we took care to omit usernames from the images we stored, and none of the images I share and discuss in this chapter contain information by which a reader might identify the original user (unless the reader is, or knows, the setup's owner). Following an open coding protocol, we generated a coding scheme through analysis and discussion of the first five posts on each year's thread.[30] We coded multiple posts collaboratively to refine our coding scheme, after which point Katreena coded the remaining images on her own over the course of two months, checking in with me on a weekly basis to address any issues with how to code particular images.

We chose images from the annual 2007 and 2015 threads because each coincided with the widespread adoption of what were then the newest generation of consoles (the Xbox 360 was released in late 2005, with PS3 and Wii following in late 2006; both the Xbox One and PS4 were released in late 2013). As each successive console generation attempts to become an integral home media platform rather than mere game device, we were interested to see how users responded to the commercial pressure to place consoles at the center of domestic life; in this, we followed the lead of Bernadette Flynn in exploring the ways that users quite literally *make room* for game consoles that are increasingly clamoring to become more central to the "socio/spatial dynamics of the home."[31] At the same time, we were attuned to the multiple ways that other gaming platforms, such as desktop and laptop computers, tabletop games, mobile devices, and even arcade cabinets, are arranged in domestic spaces—spaces that are, in turn, reconfigured around these technologies.

Our coding scheme began with cataloging the number and types of gaming platforms (laptop or desktop computer, mobile, console), screens (computer monitor, TV, projector), input devices (wired or wireless mice, keyboards, game pads, specialized controllers), and audio systems (speakers, headsets). We also included straightforward descriptors of the physical attributes and features of each photographed space. Was it illuminated by natural light, overhead lighting, lamps, or the camera's flash? Were stairs visible, and did they lead up or down? What sorts of furniture supported and surrounded the setup (desk, home theater console, milk cartons, built-in shelves), and what else was stored alongside it (toys, collectibles, photographs)? Were the walls decorated, and with what? Did the setup involve couches, bean-bag cushions, office chairs, and recliners? Once we had coded for these obvious attributes, we loosely followed the tenets of open coding and identified themes based on how certain codes coalesced. We began to ask of each setup whether it seemed built for one user or multiple users; whether it seemed situated in a house or an apartment; whether it was arranged in a mainly vertical (stack) or horizontal (sprawl) orientation; to what extent and in what ways the setup seemed staged for the photograph; how many times the poster took close-up shots and of what; and what sorts of organization and attempts at orderliness were visible. After this round of coding, we had a rich and compelling dataset from which to begin generating a deeper understanding of the practices and politics associated with these setups. And yet, at this point, nothing was jumping out at me as a potential hook, a fulcrum for analysis. The data was well organized and rigorously coded, but I did not know how to read it.

Man(cave) in the Mirror

Around the time Katreena and I were sifting through this archive, not surprisingly, I began to pay more attention to my own gaming setup in our house in Raleigh (where my family was at the time), such as it was. When not reassembled on the kitchen counter for the occasional mancounter, it occupied a small corner of the third floor of our house, which was used as a guest room when friends or family stayed and consisted of a modernist wooden desk supporting two small monitors, my desktop PC (a custom-built gaming rig, which was showing its age by 2018), and my PlayStation 4. When I sat at the desk, I was to the side of the couch and television; during the times, several nights a week, when my partner and I were both up there, I would sit close to the desk so that I did not block her view of the television, and the two speakers that flanked the monitors would be turned off. Pushed against the wall was the computer tower, a large but nondescript matte black slab of plastic and computer hardware. On top of the computer tower was a white plastic box with a faux-wood lid, and on either side of the lid were open slots. The purpose of the box was to house excess cords, though I used it mostly to store game controllers. Around the time of the study, my partner and I decided to move the setup from our bedroom to the third floor in order to make more space in our bedroom. After the move, it took me some time to get around to managing the many cords involved, an endeavor complicated by the fact that I was semiregularly moving the setup to the kitchen and back for mancounter evenings. My partner despises cords; I see them as an inevitable side effect of my leisure activities. In what was otherwise a relatively harmonious arrangement of our shared tastes—modest black hardware arranged between modernist furniture in an unobtrusive part of the house that nonetheless let us be together while engaging in separate media entertainments—the wires quite literally stuck out.

This realization prompted me to return to the coding scheme we had developed and begin coding for whether and where, in each setup depicted in the images, we saw visible evidence of wire management techniques (such as clips, boxes, tethers, whole wall panels), where wires were visible with no apparent attempt at managing them, and where we saw no wires at all. We applied the following codes: *wire management: visible* for when wires were in the photograph but showed clear signs of organization; *wire management: invisible* for when no wires were visible in the photograph, despite the presence of wired technologies in the image; and *no wire management* for when wires were visible and unorganized.

The Cords That Bind

Wires are compelling yet utterly banal media technologies. As the tendrils of our networked infrastructures for connectivity and computation, they remain largely invisible, unworthy of our attention, except when they become tangled or are chewed, yanked, and tripped over, at which point they become nuisances if not outright hazards. For all their banality, they are physical conduits of power and connection and have stitched us into globalized networks of electrical current and data since the Industrial Revolution, when endless miles of "singing wires" were strung alongside canals, railroads, and rivers for the production of telegraph infrastructures.[32] At one point, wires were imagined as the "nerves" of Western imperialism; over the course of our gradual shift toward a "dematerialized," ethereal view of communications media, however, wires have "seemed to vanish from view."[33]

Many contemporary perspectives on networked media take an almost antagonistic stance toward wires and the messy physicality they represent and to which they continue to bind us. For the tech gurus of MIT and Silicon Valley such as Nicholas Negroponte (ironically, one of the founders of *Wired* magazine), wires only trip us up in our march toward unfettered mobility; they are umbilical cords tethering our hypermediated present to our slow, clunky, industrial past. Adrian Mackenzie, stating that "wirelessness struggles against wires," remarks on the simultaneous ubiquity and invisibility of wires at a time when tech industries and consumers are investing heavily in wireless devices.[34] As Mackenzie notes, we are surrounded by and reliant on more wires than ever, but they are, increasingly, disappearing from sight: going microscopic, forming the thousands of pathways of conductivity in every chipset, or underground, buried beneath our feet and underwater, snaking in and out of the rural data centers that power the cloud, as considered in chapter 1. Closer to home, wires are shoved behind wall panels, special wire boxes, and so on. Indeed, on the subreddit "r/cableporn," users upload and comment on before and after pictures of their attempts to both organize masses of wires and render them invisible.[35]

Wires and their (in)visibility in domestic settings carry powerful class-related connotations. Bart Simon, writing of the case modding community in the early 2000s, describes computer modders as arraigned against an aesthetic of "invisible" computing that, in his view, is epitomized by Apple products (and perhaps more recently by flat-screen TVs that are indistinguishable from a framed painting when turned off): computational technologies that are barely there, that blend seamlessly into the chic, modernist decor of the hip, upper middle-class home.[36] As scholar-artist Joanna Zylinska writes, wires are "intrusions into the oft minimalist or functionalist arrangements of living or work spaces, a material reminder of the excess of the everyday that cannot be swept away."[37] Wires make a conspicuous appearance in the editorials Keightley cites, in which audiophiles—looking for connections to masculinities rooted in mechanical fabrication and self-reliance—revel in the amount and visibility of wires connecting their hi-fi equipment.[38]

Such connotations were certainly in play in my own domestic negotiations with my partner around whether and how to manage the wires that too frequently hung, semicontained, from our home office desk. And, as I argue below, they are abundantly evident in how and when wires show up in the images of gaming setups we looked at. After coding for "wire management" and examining which codes clustered around the three different configurations of wires, it became clear that we were on to something: in our dataset, approaches to wire management (or lack thereof) gestured to a whole host of other consistent differences between gaming setups in these threads. Once we began to follow the wires, we identified three different takes on how contemporary gaming setups are constructed—and, by extension, how different masculine subjects are constituted through material and spatial relations between bodies, technologies, and domestic settings. It turns out that wires are powerful place-making technologies in our domestic mediascapes. In the following sections, I show examples and give a broad description of each configuration before considering what different kinds of practices, politics, and subjectivities may be associated with it. For reasons I explain in more detail below, I label these three types of setup *hearth, cabinet,* and *bunker.*

Hearth

Hearths are the type of setup associated with *wire management: invisible*—setups in which wires have been tucked out of sight. The name given to these setups is an explicit nod to Lynn Spigel and Bernadette Flynn's work on the 1950s television and 2000s game console, respectively, in which they consider the ways these communication technologies remediated the fireplace and, later, the radio. In our dataset, hearth users' posts often include multiple images of their setups, showing the whole space from several different perspectives or focusing on certain features: movie and game collections, a storage technique, or a new piece of gear, for instance. These setups appear to be spaces of shared and negotiated media use among multiple members of a household, as indicated by couches, multiple chairs, large spaces, and multiple game consoles. Game controllers and DVD storage boxes are often arranged alongside other artifacts, such as toys, musical instruments, books, and photographs, speaking to spaces that can be used for gaming but also as construction toy sites, reading nooks, home theaters, and so on—perhaps at the same time by multiple family members. These are typically large spaces, with media and furniture arranged horizontally; the setup might stretch the width of a wall in a sizable family room (as in fig. 2.1) or

Figure 2.1. An example of a gaming hearth from the 2015 NeoGAF thread. Screenshot taken by author.

a spacious, well-lit corner (as in fig. 2.2). Gaming hearths are often beside windows, and their adjacent walls are often adorned by framed paintings. These characteristics suggest a prime location in the home, whether the den or basement of a suburban house or the central area of an apartment or condominium.

Extrapolating from these shared commonalities, it is possible to see hearths as spaces of togetherness and shared, as well as negotiated, media use. While none of the NeoGAF images we coded include actual people in them, it is not hard when looking at these pictures to imagine a couple curled up on the couch with their pet watching a movie or a parent playing Xbox while children play with toys on the floor. The television is the focal point of these spaces, and in that way, they are continuations of the domestic arrangements Lynn Spigel finds in the pages of 1950s housekeeping magazines. The television remains at the center of family life as that which facilitates time spent together.

Figure 2.2. An example of a gaming hearth from the 2015 NeoGAF thread. Screenshot taken by author.

Bunker

At the other end of the spectrum of wire management and associated setups are bunkers, images in which our code for *no wire management* indicated broader patterns of similarities between setups. In photographs of gaming bunkers, wires are everywhere, and there is little to no attempt on the part of the user to manage their unruliness, much less their visibility. Wires appear in all their tangled glory, dangling in great knots from the back of a desk, stretched across the floor to reach a wall socket, curling to form dust-covered nests on tops of shelves. These are spaces of singular (and individual) use; there are very few couches visible in the photographs, and often no more than a single chair. Furniture often consists of an old or inexpensive office desk and swivel chair and, occasionally, armchair. They are often setups primarily intended for desktop computers (fig. 2.3), though most bunkers involve configurations of multiple monitors and gaming platforms. The

Figure 2.3. An example of a gaming bunker from the 2015 NeoGAF thread. Screenshot taken by author.

pictures of these gaming bunkers place the technology front and center, with the post often consisting of only one photograph of the setup or of multiple close-up photographs of particular gear. Not only are there wires everywhere, but these spaces also often appear unkempt. In several posts, used bowls, plates, and cups are visible, suggesting meals eaten at a desk while watching or playing (and not cleaned up prior to the photograph).

The pictures of these spaces often show stairs leading up or down (see fig. 2.3), with low or slanted ceilings, indicating a location at the top or bottom of a building—a converted attic or basement of a house, perhaps, or a basement apartment. Walls are either bare or hung with unframed prints from Western or Japanese comics, video games, and superhero, sci-fi, and fantasy movies. There is often little to no natural light and little in the way of desk lamps or standing lamps; as a result, the pictures themselves are often of poor quality. Across all these posts, there are few attempts at what was tagged in our coding scheme as *staging*—meeting certain standards of photographic production (well lit, tidied) to make the space appear more orderly and inviting than it might otherwise be. Additionally, bunker users

Figure 2.4. An example of a gaming bunker from the 2007 NeoGAF thread, described by one user as "ghetto geek." Screenshot taken by author.

most often posted only one image of their setup, typically shot to foreground the gaming and computer technology.

In a post from 2007 (fig. 2.4), a laptop, modem, speakers, and peripherals sit on top of a glass desk, wires running all over and books and papers stacked haphazardly underneath. The setup's owner writes the following:

My ps3 sits on top of 2 hawaiian punch mix boxes to keep it off of my old as hell surround sound system until I can find a shelf thing that I like. The receiver gets extremely hot after long hours of gaming, it's ridiculous.

and yes, I use a magazine as a mouse pad.

edit: ignore all the terrible jpg artifacts on the walls

edit2: holy crap, I didn't realize how messy all those wires were, I'm gonna have to start saving bread bag ties: lol

The first reply commends this user's thrift and emphasis on technology: "I mean no disrespect when I say that some of the things you mention are great of examples of 'ghetto geek.' Good stuff." Not unlike either the 1950s audiophiles who proudly display the bare wires that power their hi-fi setups or the case modders who deliberately draw attention to their souped-up computer towers, inhabitants of bunkers seem to embrace (albeit, perhaps ironically) their wires-out, hardware-first aesthetic.

The term "bunker" is meant to indicate a space centered solely around digital play and the technology that supports it. Bunkers are, of course, fortified enclosures intended for (most often male) soldiers and other military personnel, usually high ranking, to withstand bombardment.[39] They are also sites where militarized media are used intensively: technologies of surveillance, communication, and coordination, of extended vision, pattern recognition, and threat assessment, which are close cousins to contemporary gaming technologies. Not surprisingly, in these posts and elsewhere in online discussions of gaming setups, PCs are frequently described as battle stations.[40] The militarization here is metaphorical, certainly, but also consistent in key ways with the historical role of bunkers; as I argue below, gaming bunkers are designed to allow a certain masculine subject to continue to exert agency, from his fortified location, in a world he views as increasingly hostile.[41]

Cabinet

If the bunker represents, as one user put it, a kind of "ghetto geek" (and I certainly acknowledge the problematic invocation of institutionalized, race-based poverty that such a term invokes), the third category of setups displayed on NeoGAF we arrived at by following the wires might be regarded as "geek chic," following Bart Simon.[42] These are setups that prominently display digital media alongside related popular cultural artifacts—LEGO sets, figurines, movie props—in spaces that appear (like the bunker) to be constructed by and for a single user. In these spaces, wires are adeptly managed though left visible. Frequently, users take images of the cord management techniques themselves, in ways that parallel more wire-focused online forums like r/cableporn. They appear in ordered braids or rows, partially but not wholly blocked by modernist or industrialist office furniture, part of the scenery as much as neatly stacked figurines, physical storage media, and other artifacts of cultural currency in gaming, geekdom, and fandom. In these setups, artful compartmentalization abounds, with different categories of curated material housed in discrete, box-shaped displays. Like gaming bunkers, these spaces often indicate solo use: a room in which all four walls are crammed with artifacts and technologies with only a single

Figure 2.5. An example of a gaming cabinet from the 2015 NeoGAF thread. Screenshot taken by author.

office chair visible or a studio apartment with a bed at the center of a media nexus (fig. 2.5). Unlike the bunkers, however, they are often immaculately staged; these are spaces meant not just for consuming audiovisual media but to be themselves framed and visually consumed. Curiously, cabinets are far more prevalent in the 2015 thread than in the one from 2007.

As applied to these arrangements, "cabinet" refers not to the piece of furniture or even the housings for arcade games.[43] Rather, invoking a longer history of the term, it refers to the rooms used by wealthy men of Renaissance Europe to take pleasure in and show off their amassed wealth—books, paintings, tapestries, sculptures, and other media of the time, collected from around the world and curated for private enjoyment rather than public edification (fig. 2.6).[44] These "cabinets of curiosity" ("wunderkammer," as they were coined in German), displayed objects gathered from all over and were thought to enable a sense of immersion and "inquisitive voyaging" within a carefully constructed and enclosed world. They prefigure by a few centuries late twentieth and early twenty-first-century notions of networked media offering transportation to virtual worlds, trafficked by internet scholars

Figure 2.6. *Cardinal Albrecht of Brandenburg as Saint Jerome* by Lucas Cranach the Elder, 1526. Credit: Wikiart.

and sci-fi authors.[45] The cabinet, in both its Renaissance and contemporary formulations, is a space dedicated to consuming and *curating* media; this curation reflects the cultural and economic capital, the tastes, of its owner. Further connecting these gaming setups to their Renaissance precursors are overt displays of Orientalism, emphasizing their role as enclaves of not only masculinity but also whiteness: trappings and curios from "exotic" cultures, the presence of which indicates a privileged and centralized position in the given era's globalized media and transportation infrastructures. These are places of play and display, or more accurately, places where the practices of play and display and their associated pleasures and labors are conflated. The cabinet is not only where the user curates the ludic artifacts of his many subcultural interests and investments but also where this curation is itself a pleasurable and productive practice of rearrangement. Display *is* play.[46]

Figure 2.7. A gaming cabinet showing the pleasures of ludic curation, from the 2015 NeoGAF thread. Screenshot taken by author.

Likewise, these spaces not only *house* technologies of immersion; they *are* technologies of immersion.

Alongside this conflation of curation and play is another set of conflations. In the hearth, media technologies recede into the background (with the exception of the television, which is, of course, the center of the hearth itself). In bunkers, conversely, the focus is explicitly on the machinery for play; all other aesthetic considerations, from furniture to lighting to decor, are either underattended or employed in service of the technical apparatus. Both types of setup reconstruct a dualism between technology and decor, functionalism and aesthetics, domestic sociality and isolation. Cabinets, on the other hand, are spaces in which the lines between the two are blurred; the machinery and its visible placement *among* pop cultural and subcultural artifacts demonstrates, and indeed emphasizes, the aesthetic qualities of the gear, as shown through pictures of headphones, controllers, and mobile devices all carefully positioned among other physical media collections, toys, collectibles, and curios (fig. 2.7).

Our Setups, Our Selves

As outlined in the introduction, Paul B. Preciado describes how *Playboy* articulated a new kind of masculine subject through, in large part, reconstructing domestic space as a media nexus for the surveillance and seduction of women. Their work provides a compelling synthesis of Foucauldian media studies with the cultural geographer's insight that subjectivities are formed *in place*.[47] As Preciado writes, "[Hugh Hefner] had somehow understood that in order to sculpt a new masculine subjectivity, one had to design a habitat: to create a space and invent a series of practices and uses of the domestic that could function as *technohabits* of the male body."[48] I am less interested here in exploring possible connections between the postwar bachelor pad and the gaming setups mapped out above as I am with Preciado's project of connecting media arrangements in the home to (re)constructions of white masculinity. Following Preciado's lead, I want to ask what kinds of subjectivities are sculpted by the domestic arrangements documented and discussed in the NeoGAF posts. Table 2.1 provides a brief but evocative overview of how I see these spaces working in terms of contributing to certain relations, experiences, and forms of subjectivity. The gaming hearth, cabinet, and bunker are ways of describing *actual* gaming setups, but they also serve as "diagrams of power": logics for arranging bodies and technologies in space and time that produce certain effects, energies, and relations of privilege and oppression—that is, politics.[49] In what follows, I focus analysis more on the bunker and cabinet, as the hearth is relatively known territory. In its configuration, with the television at the center and abundant markers of shared use, it is a continuation of the forms of media-centric domestic intimacy, negotiation, and proximity sketched by Lynn Spigel, Bernadette Flynn, and Deborah Chambers. The masculine subject most associated with hearth-like gaming setups is the suburban patriarch: the tired dad (perhaps of children, perhaps of dogs or cats) who games when he can, maybe pulling out the Xbox to play a few games of FIFA with his neighbor over beers after everyone else has gone to bed. Or perhaps he is a childless condo owner who finds time to play when his partner is at work or out with friends. In either case, gaming is one part of a broader array of domestic media practices centered around the screen; the platforms and controllers recede into the background when games are not in use, the wires tucked out of sight.

Table 2.1. Comparing three types of setup.

	Hearth	Bunker	Cabinet
Purpose	(Re)produce domestic cohesion	Survive in a hostile world; preserve established hierarchies	Display cultural status
Role of media	Bonding; shared narratives and experiences	Extended vision and control	Aesthetic self-realization
Disposition	Comfortable	Defensive	Curatorial

The hearth is, in some respects, conservative, not in terms of political leanings but in terms of its function to preserve forms of domestic mediated intimacy required for capitalist models of family life—stretching back decades, in terms of the role of the television in functioning (if even only symbolically) as the family glue, or centuries, if we consider the historical role of the hearth. As the site where the man of the house (occasionally) plays, the hearth is connected also to much older forms of domestic gender politics in which keeping the house clean is part of women's unpaid work and a vital, if deliberately downplayed, engine of capitalist social reproduction.[50] In such setups, the gendered place-making practices impelled by wires and their management suggests that keeping the hearth tidy falls squarely under the purview of historically feminized housework.

Escape Pods

Unlike gaming hearths, both the bunker and cabinet are constructed as single-use spaces. Sociality, if and when it happens, unfolds primarily online. In some corners of media studies and in popular theorizations of media, an ontological hierarchy and attendant moralism continues to paint online sociality as somehow diminished in comparison to face-to-face interactions. Such hierarchies are important to avoid, and I am indebted to a generation of invaluable scholarship, mostly from feminist traditions of media ethnography, that see online and offline dimensions of experience as fundamentally inextricable.[51] Indeed, if anything, this scholarship confirms that online sociality is always *material*, facilitated as it is by the contexts and infrastructures that enable online connectivity. Seen in this light, I want to suggest that the bunker and the cabinet—both of which seem designed for gameplay that is *physically* solitary, at least temporarily—are apparatuses of *networked* belonging. With their masses of wires (managed or not) linking modems, routers, screens, keyboards, and so on and their furniture arranged for sustained attention to screens, both bunker and cabinet facilitate the kinds of sociality we associate with networked games and online forums—many (though certainly not all) of which have long been unsafe spaces for women, queer folk, and racial or ethnic minorities.[52]

While the bunker and the cabinet may offer a staging ground for socializing in networked games and online communities, they constitute a sort of escape or exit from the forms of social reproduction associated with domestic life. Current work on man caves shows that, like earlier forms of masculine media in the home, these spaces act as enclosures in which men can escape the kinds of care that go on in other parts of the home (pet care, childcare, partner care, the work associated with feminized spaces like laundry rooms, living rooms, etc.). As Keightley notes, immersion in music became a kind of selling point for what hi-fi equipment could offer the 1950s white, suburban family guy, whose rugged masculinity was threatened by the feminizing passivity of the television and domesticity of the suburban home. Surrounded by unruly wires and military machinery, the 1950s hi-fi enthusiast *immersed* himself in music—most often (as the logic goes with mainstream games) created by men, for men. In doing so, he escaped from his wife and family. Immersion, as articulated here, is not some psychological state of transportation; it is first and foremost the product of a material media apparatus designed explicitly to shut women out or shut them up, to provide the man with a media exit. Thus, while immersion may be experienced as a state of transportation, it has historically been accomplished in domestic contexts as a technologically facilitated disappearing act, a project of assembling a barely domesticated military media apparatus in order to provide users (most frequently, white men) with an escape from the feminized home and its responsibilities. In paying attention to the gendered dynamics of who gets to shut out whom in domestic spaces, whether through music or games, we can see how immersion is an effect of persistent exclusions and inequalities in access to material architectures and media apparatuses.

I want to take a bit of a leap here and posit that the solitary spaces of gaming embodied by the bunker and the cabinet might very well serve as escape pods, not just from the feminized work of maintaining the home (as with the audiophile setups of the 1950s) but from feminization, and *feminism*, more generally. It is certainly a stretch and an ethical violation to suggest that the photographs of the very real bunkers and cabinets we analyzed are all inhabited by reactionary misogynists. Nonetheless, it might be useful to imagine what we would encounter if we spelunked through the gaming set-ups of gamergaters, incels, red pillers, and other denizens of the manosphere. As a theory-building exercise, I want to focus on two specific masculine mediascapes that attracted attention in the early 2020s: one is a cabinet and the other, a bunker. These belong to well-known figures in gaming culture and the manosphere, respectively. The first is the gaming and broadcasting room of top *Fortnite* streamer Tyler "Ninja" Blevins, and the second is the basement belonging to the mother of Roosh Valizadeh, former "pick-up artist" guru turned alt-right personality.

A Dojo for the Ninja

Tyler Blevins is a white man, in his late twenties as of this writing, more widely known by his Twitch handle, "Ninja." In summer of 2019, he announced that he would be leaving Twitch to broadcast exclusively on Mixer, Microsoft's streaming service; he returned to Twitch in 2020. Though the terms of Blevins's contract with Microsoft were undisclosed, some live streaming industry insiders suggest he could have been offered USD 6–8 million given the size of his Twitch audience (fourteen million subscribers, the streaming platform's largest) and 2018 earnings (around USD 10 million).[53] Red Bull began sponsoring Blevins in 2018, and in the fall of that year, months before his departure from Twitch, they unveiled a special collaboration: an "ultimate streaming room" dubbed Ninja's "dojo," ostensibly designed by Blevins and bankrolled by Red Bull.[54] The promotional video, entitled "Step into Ninja's Ultimate Stream Room!" is a sight to behold: in an opening scene that could be from any home makeover or interior design program on HGTV, Blevins opens the door to his new digs and exclaims "Oh my god!" We are then treated to a stylized flashback in which Blevins is shown at a drafting table busily working on the room's design, and as he sketches, facets of the room become three-dimensional models springing into animated life. In the video, Blevins goes on to introduce himself, explaining what makes him unique as a streamer ("a mixture of high tier

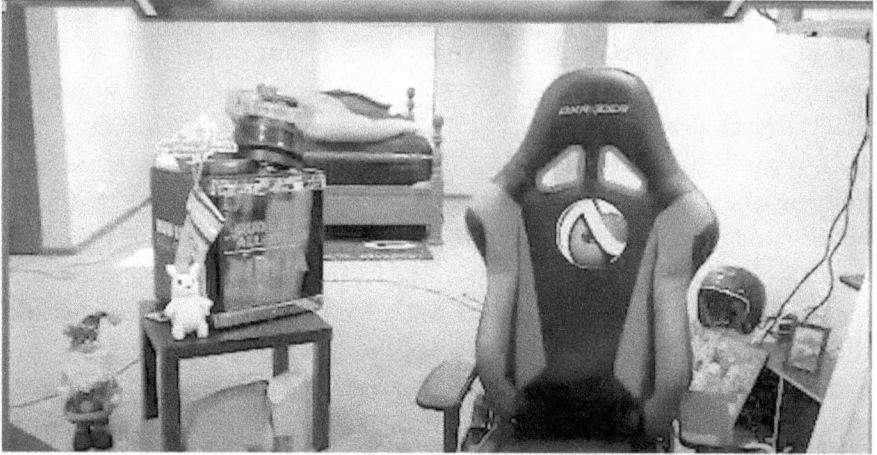

Figure 2.8. A shot of Ninja's early bunker-ish setup. Screenshot taken by author.

gameplay and shenanigans"), cut in with footage from earlier streams of him jumping up and down in his chair, yelling, and narrating his actions in voices half parodying and half emulating the bombastic tones of esports color commentators. Blevins tells us about his start as a streamer in 2012, again interspersing earlier footage—this time of his initial setup, as he describes beginning his career with very limited resources. From the footage, the apparatus Blevins initially used looks like any of the bunker-style setups we analyzed in our NeoGAF study: bare floors and walls, strictly functional desk, tangled masses of cords threading around game packaging, food wrappers, and clothing (fig. 2.8). We learn from the video that he has "always struggled" to get the best equipment and was particularly frustrated with the poor sound quality and reverb coming off from his basement.

The premise of the video is a bit hard to believe—it moves from clips of Blevins's recent ascent to multimillionaire superstardom (streaming with music and pro sports celebrities, landing on the cover of *ESPN* magazine) to Blevins's claim that his current setup "is terrible." Somehow, despite all the success, Blevins still has not managed to upgrade his gear. Fortunately, Red Bull is there to complete the rags to riches story, to complete one man's journey from bare-bones bunker to cutting-edge cabinet. As the video goes on, we see more of the stylized representation of Blevins's design process as he selects features of his room that include—in true gaming cabinet fashion— a seamless blend of the functional (noise-dampening wall panels) and the

Figure 2.9. Ninja in his Red Bull cabinet. Screenshot taken by author.

ornamental (a samurai sword on a stand). Halfway through the video, the room makeover begins in earnest. As Blevins's voiceover tells us how little care he gave to his previous setup beyond bare functionality (how bunkerish it was), we see a montage of many men at work, ripping up rugs, sawing, drilling, consulting each other, making decisive hand motions, and nodding. We are then treated to the full reveal, with several close-ups of Blevins's face, in slow motion, as he runs his hand along the clean, hard surfaces of the dojo, gazes up proudly at the trophies ringing the upper walls, and tightens his Red Bull headband. The camera pans slowly around the dojo with visual overlays pointing out the state-of-the-art technology in a kind of updated take on the lists of tech specs that "Show Us Your Setup" users frequently post with their photographs. No wires are visible save for those running directly from the monitors. Blevins shows us several features of the room custom designed around his streaming brand, including a lighting console that can change the room's hues to match various events in *Fortnite* and a "boogie" button that drops down a disco ball and blares dance music—the room itself capable of taking part in Blevins's trademark shenanigans. In the penultimate shot, he holds out his arms in gratitude, framed by the curios, trophies, and devices that surround his setup (fig. 2.9).

There is much we might unpack in this video of Ninja's new high-tech cabinet: the Orientalist motif (connecting not only to Western gaming culture's strands of otaku-dom but also to Renaissance cabinets stocked with prizes from early colonialist conquests); the unlikely premise of an incredibly wealthy professional streamer finally being given the setup he deserves through the grace and promotional savvy of Red Bull; and the aesthetic of the room itself, a mix of recording studio, night club, and internet café. It is a space that is unmistakably masculine and unavoidably white. Like Hugh Hefner's bachelor pad, it is a media habitat constructed for, reflected in, and constitutive of its inhabitant. This is no high-minded abstraction. It is a point driven home by Blevins's logo splattered across his multiscreen display wall, his own stylized anime head with crest of hair rising above a headband. But the video is also notable for an absence: there are no women in it save for a single, brief shot of Ninja and his wife, Jessica Blevins, posing together on the red carpet of the ESPY Awards.

Women are everywhere in esports, but you would not know it from attending tournaments or looking at player rosters.[55] They are most often behind the scenes or on the margins: in paid roles as managers and organizers, in unpaid roles as event volunteers, girlfriends, mothers. Jessica Blevins is by no means invisible, maintaining an active social media presence (as Jghosty), but she is known through these channels primarily as "Ninja's wife and manager." Notably, she has been a Twitch streamer herself, first posting videos of gameplay and then getting into "IRL" (in real life) streams, a genre in which streamers share mundane aspects of domestic life—specifically, in her case, cooking. She has since focused solely on managing her husband's career and looking after their home. In a profile in Businessinsider.com, Jessica Blevins gives an account of their typical day: she wakes up early to care for their dogs and handle emails and telephone calls; he sleeps later due to his nocturnal streaming sessions. During the day, while he streams, she looks after the house and business ("getting groceries, taking care of their dogs, and handling more phone calls and emails").[56] They take a break together in the late afternoon until early evening, when he starts streaming again until late at night. For a gendered labor arrangement that has produced the poster boy for a cutting-edge new media industry, it is decidedly conservative: husband goes to work (in his home streaming studio), wife supports him behind the scenes. Though the work is different, this is precisely the same arrangement Bulut describes in his ethnographic interviews with women whose husbands and male partners work in game development.[57] Of course, such arrangements go back much further. Public/private, masculine/feminine, visible/invisible, paid/unpaid—the binaries characterizing gendered labor under capitalism since at least the Victorian era remain in place.[58] The only binary that is disrupted here, arguably, is the one between "going to work" and "staying home," as both work from home. Again, here is where the Red Bull video of Ninja's new streaming room carries out its most notable achievement. Amid all the shots of Blevins sketching his dojo into existence, conferring with serious tradesmen in black polo shirts, and just being Ninja in his new dojo, there are no women. Red Bull has not only upgraded his setup but also fashioned an aesthetic and technical separation between the Blevins's home and Ninja's work. The dojo might be just downstairs, but for all intents and purposes, Blevins leaves his house, with all its zones and modes of feminized care, to go to work.[59]

Paul B. Preciado notes that the revolution Hugh Hefner enacted within heteronormative white masculinity was to move it inside: to demonstrate that patriarchy's central project of gender domination could be accomplished in a silk robe instead of a starched collar, from within the confines of a stylishly appointed media habitat designed for surveilling, capturing, framing, and endlessly reproducing the female form. Subsequent decades have seen the rise first of service-based economies and now of neoliberal gig economies, in which we can do what we love for a living so long as we are always ready to do it, often with little security or long-term prospects.[60] Particularly in the wake of the COVID-19 pandemic, working from home is no longer revolutionary or liberating—far from it. Live streaming is arguably a high-water mark in this decades-long shift to home-based work. As T. L. Taylor adeptly illustrates, Twitch is (or, perhaps, was) a platform connecting our gaming setups in our own bedrooms and dens to audiences and places outside of them.[61] But streamers like Blevins and other high-profile figures who (very publicly) design and implement glitzy new streaming setups rooms are reversing this trend: turning the bedroom or den into a professional media studio.[62] Notably, this professionalization—at least in Blevins's highly visible and culturally influential case—proceeds, in part, by walling women out while still relying on their labor.

The conversion of part of the Blevins's home into the ultimate streaming room not only carries out an aesthetic and technical separation between his domain and hers; it enacts physical and political economic divisions as well. Tyler Blevins has repeatedly drawn criticism for not having female-identified guests on his streams or costreaming with female-identified streamers. For someone with a career that has been substantially bolstered through playing *Fortnite* with people more famous than him (most notably, the hip-hop artist Drake), Blevins's lack of female guests is interpreted as an unwillingness to use his substantial platform to lift up female colleagues. In a social media post in the summer of 2018, he justified his actions by claiming that he refrains from inviting women on his stream out of respect for his marriage. According to Blevins, the internet is a factory of misinformation and rumor; if he were to have women on his stream, people might get the wrong idea. His wife's emotional well-being and reputation, and those of any female streamers he would host, would be put at risk.[63] Note the paternalistic judo flip: turning an acknowledgment of the harmful conditions often associated with streaming while female into a justification against supporting women streamers' visibility, popularity, and normalization.[64] As a paradigmatic contemporary gaming cabinet, Blevins's Red Bull dojo illustrates the mechanisms through which this kind of gaming setup carries out its gender politics. The paternalistic condescension is hardwired, as much a design feature as the cutting-edge tech, curated collections of gamer and otaku paraphernalia, carefully managed wires, and sleek lines. It is built from the ground up to reflect, embody, and extend the hip, tech-savvy white masculine inhabitant who is at the top of his game and who certainly appreciates the work of his mother/wife/girlfriend/manager but knows that she—or any other woman—is best left out for her own protection.

Bunkers versus Feminism

If the contemporary cabinet is a mechanism for designing women out of the domestic and increasingly professionalized gaming setup (ostensibly, for their own good), the bunker presents a more overtly hostile gender politics. In the analysis I present here, it is discursively and materially linked to the "manosphere," a loose amalgam of pick-up artists (PUAs), men's rights activists (MRAs), incels, alt-right meme makers, gamergaters, and anti-SJW trolls.[65] Former sites like r/thedonald, r/kotakuinaction (a gamergate subreddit), r/Braincels (a popular incel subreddit), 4chan, and 8chan (preferred site for mass shooters to post their racist manifestos) were all part of the early connective tissue of the manosphere. We certainly do not know for certain what the actual setups of the manosphere's denizens look like; here, again, I am shifting from an empirical claim to a theoretical one. But based on this glimpse into gaming setups, the bunker, with its singular focus on the functionality of the technology, has none of the curatorial flair and markers of cultural and economic capital of the cabinet, nor does it have the signs of shared domesticity of the hearth, with all of its indications of technical and aesthetic compromise for the sake of domestic harmony. Instead, it is a communications array erected for particular kinds of work: protecting games culture, and increasingly culture at large, from interventions by feminists, critical race theorists, and social justice warriors. It is not an apparatus for facilitating temporary forms of ludic escape; in significant ways, its user has already left.

Ninja's Red Bull dojo is a paradigmatic expression of how the contemporary cabinet works; the one-time basement dwelling of Roosh Valizadeh, antifeminist media personality, is the equivalent for the bunker. It is an unornamented, functionalist setup from which to launch salvos at the purported enemies of heteromasculinity. Valizadeh, or "Roosh V," has had momentary bouts of public attention as a mouthpiece for the PUA and MRA communities. He self-published a series of books under the name *Bang*, offering tips for how to seduce women in various countries; authored blog posts outlining a worldview based on reactionary gender hierarchies, including a rationale for legalizing rape on private property (which he later characterized as a joke); and, in 2019, turned to Christianity and renounced his PUA ties, though certainly not his belief in biological determinism or his insistence that feminism is ruining civilization. In early 2016, the British tabloid *Daily Mail* photographed Valizadeh at the door to his mother's house in Maryland, where he was reportedly living in the basement.[66] Despite the ensuing media buzz, we were not afforded actual views into Roosh V's mother's basement, the domestic setting in which he composed so many screeds against feminism, political correctness, and social justice advocates and in favor of legalized rape and gender oppression based on myths of biological destiny. Unlike Ninja, he did not have sponsors to provide his bunker with a well-documented makeover featured in a slick YouTube video, so we do not have much empirical material to work with as far as making claims about his media setup. At most, we have glimpses from some of his earlier video blogs (like "Why Men Shouldn't Use Shampoo") that show a dark, sparsely decorated corner of a room, which may or may not be part of a larger bunker-style arrangement.

Though we may not have up-close looks at this space, we do have an insightful theorization of the contemporary masculinity Valizadeh espouses and embodies and its relationships to technology, feminism, and place. This account is provided by Sarah Sharma; she begins with the discovery of Roosh V bunkering in his mother's basement. Sharma writes that "the troll in Mommy's basement is no joke; he is emerging cultural and political figure" and that "Mommy's basement" and its analog in tech industry workplaces "is an increasingly significant incubator for conservative ideas."[67] She goes on to provide a stunning critique of a contemporary heteromasculine subjectivity that sees itself as increasingly threatened by #metoo, political correctness, and female empowerment, to which the man responds by *exiting*—from the arena of sexual reproduction (in the case of the "sexodus"), from a liberal consensus around gender equality, from social interaction beyond the safe communities of networked games and networked misogyny. Abetting this male fantasy of exit is a masculine technoculture deeply invested in tech-driven disruptions that capture and redistribute the conventional work of feminized and, particularly, maternal care (putting food on our table, doing our groceries, driving us around) to gig workers, transforming traditionally unpaid labor into poorly paid, piecemeal labor. Within the dual transformations Sharma discusses, *place* plays a crucial role. In her account, "Mommy's basement" is not simply a fitting leitmotif but a cultural logic distributed across any number of male-dominated sites of technological production: "peek inside the workspaces of most successful tech companies," she writes, "and you will find ping-pong tables, napping pods, and bottomless snacks. That is, these spaces have a striking resemblance to Mommy's basement."[68] These are physical sites in which men are at work on technological fixes for a world they see as overtaken by feminism on one hand and troublingly reliant on female labor on the other. That these places are toxic and unsafe for women and other gender minorities is well documented and perhaps not surprising given their history as male-dominated industries and given the economic, technological, and political project these industries generally support: dispensing of Mommy by redistributing her labor throughout the gig economy.

If Mommy's basement, in its myriad arrangements throughout the tech industry, is where this work takes place, the bunker is where its denizens play and socialize. In the NeoGAF data I draw on here, bunkers occupy either the top floor or basement of a building, above or below spaces of shared domesticity (if they exist) but always separate from them. As a setup, a bunker is physically removed from spaces of domestic labor; as a diagram of power, it is a place of exit specifically from the demands of negotiation, compromise, and care. Mommy—or her proxies—make it possible, but she is not welcome, nor is she particularly safe. Like the tech coming out of Mommy's basement, the forms of sociality and leisure associated with the bunker are premised on fixing a world run amok with feminism, political correctness, and social justice warriors. The manosphere serves as the online home for many movements and ideologies, but fundamentally, it is an articulation of the white male fantasy of exit that Sharma artfully sketches: an escape from political correctness, from progressive politics, from having to give a shit about anyone or anything but yourself and those of your race, sexuality, gender, and ideology. In this sense, the manosphere is the product of bunkers and their inhabitants networked together; if the manosphere has an interior design aesthetic, it is the bunker. The bunker, in turn, is the media apparatus from which to coordinate salvos against feminism—attacks which include, of course, threats to actual people.[69] The bunker is a diagram of domestic power for a subject who perceives the world as increasingly hostile and filled with people who want to take away his toys, stop him from having fun, and deny him his status as the natural inheritor of reason and technology (including, and especially, games). He digs in accordingly, and from his fortified position behind his sparsely ornamented, maximally functional, wired and wire-filled setup, he fires back.

Magic Circles and Other Geometries of Escape

As alluded to at the outset of this chapter, the concept of the magic circle has a long and fraught history in studies of digital play. It comes originally from Johann Huizinga, a cultural historian who used the term, fleetingly, to refer to the conceptual, temporal, and material arrangements through which games are set apart from everyday life. The term was picked up and developed by game design practitioners and educators Katie Tebinkas and Eric Zimmerman, who used it as a hermeneutic for understanding the ways game rules create temporary boundaries within which different sets of rules unfold, and by Edward Castronova, an economist who took the term to mean that networked, online games are bounded, discrete systems, both economically and psychologically. It was soon critiqued by scholars (particularly those working within traditions of feminist and ethnographic research) as an unproductive invocation of the dichotomy between online and offline experiences, one that never held up to empirical scrutiny in the first place.[70] In fact, as recounted by Stefanie Boluk and Patrick LeMieux, Zimmerman himself renounced the term, claiming that the fantasy of escape it invokes is nothing more than an attempt to dodge the cultural politics of play—what amounts to a "magic circle jerk."[71]

In a bid to reboot the concept, Jaakko Stenros navigates between the "strong boundary hypothesis" put forward by Tebinkas and Zimmerman (precipitated, philosophically, in the work of Roger Caillois, who saw any encroachment on games by "the real world" as corrosive to play) on one hand and an insistence on lack of distinction between games and everyday life on the other.[72] For Stenros, the concept retains utility as a way of highlighting the social, psychological, and cultural work of boundary-maintaining that players (and designers) willingly enter in order to momentarily suspend the interpersonal, institutional, and ideological conditions that characterize everyday life. I am greatly appreciative of Stenros's efforts to save the magic circle from conceptual obscurity and of his rationale for doing so: one of the primary allures (and promises) of games is temporary reprieve everyday cares—the chance to navigate a world that is fair and rewards attention, practice, and skill, whether a marathon session of *Dungeons and Dragons* with one's friends, a Wednesday night mancounter with beer and *Battlefield*, or a quick level of *Donut County* on your phone. This allure is worth holding on to and expanding, conceptually and politically.

And yet, the critique of the magic circle leveled by feminist ethnographers is also worth maintaining and extending. This critique views the magic circle as a limiting metaphor that fails to account for the social, cultural, and economic contexts in which play unfolds. I want to conclude this chapter by revising how we conceptualize the magic circle, albeit in a different way than Stenros or Boluk and LeMieux do: I want to insist on the existence of magic circles while at the same time rearranging our understanding of what the circle consists of, particularly in domestic contexts, and attending to the processes and cultural practices through which it is made and sustained. I envision magic circles as the result of *place-making* practices. In the materialist understanding of digital play I insist on throughout this book, the boundaries that make play possible are always, first and foremost, physical. Play *takes place* whether it is physical or digital, on a tennis court or in a gaming bunker, and, to return to the insights provided by Doreen Massey, places, as concatenations of relations fixed in space and time, have politics.

Imagined as a magic circle, digital play is conceptualized as an escape from the cares and confinements of everyday life. The magic circle I am interested in here is not the game but the setup that runs the game; ludic escape is made possible first and foremost through the arrangement of technologies and bodies in space and time, only secondarily through code and all its potentials for perceptual transportation provided the proper material conditions. Immersion is not a condition promised by a game's alchemical mix of rules, mechanics, and representations but an effect, primarily, of spatial and temporal arrangements borne out of privilege. After all, it is hard to become immersed, to lose yourself in the magic of the circle, when the baby is crying, the dog is barking, the pot is boiling, or someone trips over a wire—at least when you are the one tasked with dealing with it. Paying attention to the gendered dynamics of domestic space, particularly as represented by the cabinet and the bunker, demonstrates that ludic escape is an effect of persistent exclusions and inequalities in who has access to the material architectures of immersion. Returning to the high-end audio setups of the postwar 1950s and 1960s, depicted as ways for the male audiophile to escape the feminized suburban home and drown out his wife, the cabinet and bunker are inheritors and refinements, under new technological, social, and political conditions, of the high-tech domestic mediascape as an apparatus of masculine exit.

The question that Boluk and LeMieux pose, abetted by Eric Zimmerman's critique of the "magic circle jerk," is whether anyone "actually believes" in the magic circle. It is a provocative prompt, launching acute analysis of the vehemently misogynist and antifeminist discourse that circulates in games culture. They show how this reactionary discourse is premised on the belief that gaming constitutes a space apart and is therefore apolitical (unless spoiled by feminist killjoys, that is).[73] The direction I am pointing here attempts to ground this persistent belief in magic in the material conditions that make it possible; the very idea that games represent a space apart is precisely made possible by the kinds of material apparatuses explored in this chapter and the experiences of domestic and social exit they provide. There is certainly magic in these arrangements, but it is not the mystical and transcendental magic of fantastic worlds created *ex nihilo* through the "lusory attitudes" of participants.[74] Rather, it is a dull and disillusioning parlor trick that has persisted across generations of domestic media arrangements in predominantly white, middle-class homes: the sleight of hand that erases the presence of women and historically feminized forms of labor and care from places that could not exist without them.

NOTES

1. Stone, *War of Desire and Technology at the Close of the Mechanical Age.*

2. Csikszentmihalyi, *Flow*; Sherry, "Flow and Media Enjoyment"; Huizinga, *Homo Ludens*; Stenros, "In Defence of a Magic Circle"; Calleja, *In-Game*; Ermi and Mäyrä, "Fundamental Components of the Gameplay Experience."

3. Consalvo, "There Is No Magic Circle," 408.

4. Boluk and LeMieux, *Metagaming*, 284.

5. Taylor, *Play between Worlds.*

6. Simon, "Beyond Cyberspatial Flaneurie," 62.

7. Apperley, "Digital Gaming, Social Inclusion, and the Right to Play"; Harvey, *Gender, Age, and Digital Games in the Domestic Context*; Tobin, *Portable Play in Everyday Life.*

8. Ruberg and Lark, "Livestreaming from the Bedroom"; Tran, "Twitch Spouse."

9. Parts of this study have also been reported on in Sarah Sharma and Rianka Singh's edited volume *Re-understanding Media: Feminist Extensions of Marshall McLuhan* and are reused here (with considerable modification) by permission of the publisher, Duke University Press (www.dukeupress.edu). Taylor, "Hardwired."

10. Thus far, man caves seem to have been mostly studied in terms of how they are represented in film and television. Rodino-Colocino, DeCarvalho, and Heresco, "Neo-orthodox Masculinities on Man Caves."

11. Smith, "This Guy Studies Man Caves for a Living; Here's What He's Learned."

12. Williams and Tobin, "Practice of Oldhammer"; Trammell, *Privilege of Play.*

13. Spigel, *Make Room for TV*; Keightley, "'Turn It down!' She Shrieked"; Flynn, "Geography of the Digital Hearth."

14. Spigel, *Make Room for TV*, 241.

15. Spigel, *Make Room for TV*, 239.

16. Chambers, "'Wii Play as a Family,'" 71.

17. Keightley, "'Turn It down!' She Shrieked," 150.

18. Flynn, "Geography of the Digital Hearth," 560.

19. Smith-Biwer, "Hi-Fi Man," 20.

20. Harvey, *Gender, Age, and Digital Games in the Domestic Context*; Bryce and Rutter, "Gendering of Computer Gaming."

21. Tobin, *Portable Play in Everyday Life*, 92.

22. Tobin, *Portable Play in Everyday Life*, 75.

23. Condis, *Gaming Masculinity*; Cote, *Gaming Sexism*; Massanari, "#Gamergate and the Fappening"; Salter and Blodgett, "Hypermasculinity & Dickwolves."

24. This figure is dwarfed by the size of Reddit and its various games-related forums but is nonetheless substantial for a relatively niche gaming site.

25. In fact, 2023 marks the twentieth anniversary of the tradition (https://www.neogaf.com/threads/show-us-your-gaming-setup-2023-edition-20th-anniversary-thread.1648973/).

26. Tesseract et al., "Terms of Service."

27. Rosenberg, "NeoGAF Is Back Online, but It's Turned into an Undead Nazi Version of Its Former Self."

28. Massanari, "#Gamergate and the Fappening," 343.

29. Many of the image hosting services on which users initially posted images were no longer active at the time of our study.

30. Glaser and Strauss, *Discovery of Grounded Theory.*

31. Flynn, "Geography of the Digital Hearth," 552.

32. Bollmer, *Inhuman Networks,* 54.

33. Bollmer, *Inhuman Networks,* 56.

34. Mackenzie, *Wirelessness,* 65.

35. For pointing me to this subreddit, I am grateful to Shane Russell, whose job at a home theater installation company has, over time, morphed from hooking up home theater systems to implementing pervasive but invisible networks of smart devices in rich people's homes.

36. Simon, "Geek Chic," 180.

37. Zylinska, "Vanishing Object of Technology," 2.

38. Keightley, "'Turn It down!' She Shrieked," 163. For more recent work connecting wires and masculinity, see Smith-Biwer, "Hi-Fi Man."

39. Virilio, *Bunker Archaeology.*

40. Crogan, *Gameplay Mode*; Elam, "Automated."

41. It is also worth noting that *actual* bunkers seem to be surging in popularity again, particularly among wealthy, white, and masculine "preppers": in the violent, racialized imaginaries they conjure regarding the need for bunkers and other technologies of escape, it is possible to see contemporary bunker building as an extension and mutation of white flight. I am grateful to Robyn Hope for this connection. See also Garrett, *Bunker*; Kelly, *Apocalypse Man.*

42. Simon, "Geek Chic," 175.

43. For those interested in arcade cabinets, Raiford Guins and Samuel Tobin offer separate considerations of histories and aesthetics. While we use "cabinet" differently, I share with them a desire to include the material artifacts and contexts of digital play in our assessments of its social and cultural significance. Guins, *Atari Design*; Tobin, "Cocktail Cabinets."

44. Stafford and Trepak, *Devices of Wonder.*

45. Williamson, "Exploration," 104.

46. Heljakka and Harviainen, "From Displays and Dioramas to Doll Dramas," 364.

47. Preciado, *Pornotopia.*

48. Preciado, *Pornotopia,* 180.

49. Foucault, *Discipline and Punish,* 171.

50. Frederici, *Wages against Housework*; Sharma, "Going to Work in Mommy's Basement"; Willis, *A Primer for Daily Life.*

51. Baym, *Personal Connections in the Digital Age*; Taylor, *Play between Worlds.*

52. Brock, *Distributed Blackness*; Richard and Gray, "Gendered Play, Racialized Reality."

53. Viana, "How Much Money Has Mixer Paid Ninja to Stream on Its Platform?"

54. Red Bull Gaming, *Step into Ninja's Ultimate Stream Room!*

55. This is explored in more depth in chapters 3 and 4.

56. Smith, "Meet Jessica Blevins, the 26-Year-Old Wife and Manager of the Most Popular Video-Game Player in the World Right Now."

57. Bulut, *A Precarious Game*, 109–16.

58. Welter, "Cult of True Womanhood," 151.

59. I am indebted here to Bo Ruberg and Daniel Lask's insight that women who live stream more frequently display their bedrooms than men and that live streams by men, particularly involving gaming, deliberately avoid the feminizing connotations of intimacy and care associated with bedrooms. Ruberg and Lark, "Livestreaming from the Bedroom," 683.

60. Pasquale, "Two Narratives of Platform Capitalism"; Rosenblat, *Uberland*.

61. Taylor, *Watch Me Play*, 69.

62. Woodcock and Johnson, "Affective Labor and Performance of Live Streaming on Twitch.Tv," 819.

63. Frank, "Ninja Explains His Choice Not to Stream with Female Gamers."

64. Taylor, *Watch Me Play*; Uszkoreit, "With Great Power Comes Great Responsibility"; Ruberg and Cullen, "Feeling for an Audience"; Skardzius, "I Stream, You Stream, We All Stream."

65. Ging, "Alphas, Betas, and Incels"; Marwick and Caplan, "Drinking Male Tears."

66. Bhatia, "Daryush 'Roosh' Valizadeh at Center of International 'Pro-rape' Storm Pictured."

67. Sharma, "Going to Work in Mommy's Basement."

68. Sharma, "Going to Work in Mommy's Basement."

69. Chess and Shaw, "A Conspiracy of Fishes, or, How We Learned to Stop Worrying about #Gamergate and Embrace Hegemonic Masculinity," 210.

70. Consalvo, "There Is No Magic Circle"; Taylor, *Play between Worlds*; Castronova, *Synthetic Worlds*; Tekinbas and Zimmerman, *Rules of Play*.

71. Boluk and LeMieux, *Metagaming*, 282.

72. Stenros, "In Defence of a Magic Circle," 154.

73. Boluk and LeMieux, *Metagaming*, 283.

74. Suits, *Grasshopper*, 50.

3

GRIDS

LAN Parties and the Infrastructural Grounds of Gaming

Grids All the Way Down

The grid, like the magic circle that figured so prominently in the previous chapter, is a key figure in early imaginings of digital gaming and computation more broadly. If cyberspace is a territory, as so many science fiction writers and media theorists imagine, the grid is its topography: geometrically precise, mathematically ordered, repeatable, and endlessly scalable. Frequently envisioned as a lattice of neon lines giving definition to a dark void, it has been a recurring motif in science fiction for at least the last forty years, from the punk cyberfeminist artwork of VNS Matrix to the cascading lines of flittering green symbols in *The Matrix*. But long before the grid colonized imaginings of computational space, it colonized our terrestrial experiences. Bernhard Siegert concisely captures much of this history, sketching out the ways grids were deployed to dominate space across multiple domains: in the visual techniques of Renaissance art, as a medium for the construction of more accurate representations; as a technique for controlling physical territories (and their inhabitants), from ancient Greek city states to colonial settlements in South America to the "brutal and violent" diagramming of the American West in its genocidal expansion; and as a means for transforming architecture into a computational enterprise.[1] For Siegert, the grid is a powerful cultural technique for managing entities, big or small, human or not; once on a grid, anything can be "turned into data that can be stored for subsequent retrieval by the correct addresses that logically and temporally precede them."[2] Project a plane of intersecting lines, ascribe addresses to those intersections, and prescribe individual units their own separate address, and the unit, whether a byte, a building, or a body, now has a fixed location and presence that can be recorded. The power of the grid lies in its capacity to map a symbolic and quantifiable order onto physical space, and its deployment as a means for assigning entities their proper location and tracking their movement has multiplied across domains of human experience, from video games to city planning and cultural theory to workplace organization.[3]

Chapter 2 reconceptualized the magic circle and the related and equally contentious notion of immersion in spatial terms, as an effect not of psychological transportation (at least, not primarily) but of material and technological apparatuses designed to shut out the rest of the world and isolate the apparatus that offers domestic escape, through games and related practices, for the historically white, masculine figure. This chapter does something similar with regard to the grid, approaching it not as a spatial motif for our virtual travels but as a cultural technique that shapes the technical and material conditions of the places in which we play and, by extension, their patterns of access and exclusion—specifically, as a logic for arranging (and connecting) multiple players. The grids I am primarily concerned with here are infrastructural rather than virtual: they are networks that provide power and connectivity to gaming apparatuses and spatial arrangements that put players in place in public gaming settings.

Almost any moment of digital gameplay is dependent on infrastructures of power and connectivity. We have to work fairly hard to think of digital gaming experiences that are not directly tethered to electrical grids (via the much-maligned electrical wire, discussed in chap. 2) and the internet— maybe an old Game Boy powered by AA batteries or the Playdate, a hand-cranked gaming device designed to directly invoke classic Nintendo handheld devices? But these experiences are deliberate outliers, nostalgic throwbacks to a less obviously connected time. Given this utter dependence on, first, electrical power and, second, online connectivity, particularly with the increasing ubiquity of networked game modes, streaming, and constant patches making *non*connection rare if not impossible, such infrastructures are pervasive but largely invisible to us. They are discernible primarily when they do not work or do not work optimally.

This is one of the first rules of infrastructure: when it is working properly, it is beneath notice.[4] When infrastructure breaks, fixing it is most often beyond our agency, whether the cause is a fallen tree down the street or the cascading malfunctions of faulty software and deteriorating relays responsible for knocking out power for tens of millions, as happened in 2003 while I was a graduate student in Toronto.[5] Infrastructure is distributed and complex, most of the time well beyond our immediate attention or ability to do anything about it, yet urgent in its effects. Contemporary infrastructures are vast and interconnected but almost always built on the bones of older networks. They are also, more often than not, managed through powerful and monopolistic or oligarchic concentrations of capital and technical expertise. Infrastructures are responsible for much of what we consider modern convenience and for the "sense of stability in daily life" that some of us, particularly white folks living in affluent neighborhoods (and, in the United States and Canada, on Indigenous lands) in the Global North, have the privilege to enjoy; our dependence on them and the entities that manage them is absolute.[6]

Within this arrangement of utter dependency and near invisibility, the grid features prevalently as a technique for controlling the infrastructural distribution of resources. Power meters, IP addresses, and mailing addresses are all instruments that connect our use of infrastructural resources—what Lauren Berlant calls "the lifeworld of structure"—to modes of surveillance and governance.[7] The grid is the cultural technique by which most modern infrastructures are organized. Living in, on, with, and through grids is thus an inescapable condition of modern life. Even the choice to live "off the grid," if such a thing is indeed possible, is made legible by one's absence from key infrastructures. When considering gaming, the grid is not just a technique for constructing and mapping virtual space, allowing the game's code to determine which asset should appear where and when. It is through the work of various grid-based infrastructures that players are provided with (ideally) uninterrupted flows of electrical power and network connectivity, not to mention conditions less immediate to gaming but no less felt, such as heating or air conditioning, adequate plumbing for "biobreaks," and so on. Grids all the way down—yet for all their fundamental importance, these infrastructural arrangements are beneath the attention of most game studies scholarship to this point, with some key exceptions.

When the Power Goes Out (an Anecdotal Aside)

On an atypically hot and sunny day in Vancouver in the summer of 2011, I attended my first and last Keyboard Toss. Dozens of people were gathered in the back lot of an event space belonging to the Great Northern Way Campus in East Vancouver. I was there with two colleagues to hang out at a local area network (LAN) event (LANcouver, the seventh of its name), observing and talking to people about their video gameplay.[8] But the power had gone out; no electricity was running to the computers, modems, lighting, and so on. At some point that first morning, when around one hundred attendees showed up with computers and started plugging them into the Bring Your Own Computer (BYOC) section of the event space, a transformer blew. The organizers, sensing that people might disperse and not come back without something to do, rigged up an ad hoc competition involving bursts of power—of the physical rather than electrical kind. Hauling cardboard boxes of old computer parts onto the back lot, they explained the rules to the assembled group: stand behind the designated line and see how far you can throw a keyboard, over your head and with two hands, like a soccer throw-in. I never learned how exactly they obtained so many disposable keyboards so quickly, nor why this equipment was much more readily available than, say, the expertise required to quickly fix (or prevent) the power outage. But the sideshow worked; several attendees lined up excitedly (and sometimes repeatedly) to hurl bulky input devices while the rest of us stood by and cheered on particularly long throws and destructive landings. Other scenes stand out from this fieldwork—my first sustained observation of *Warhammer* tabletop play, my sense of bewilderment watching an elite *Smash Bros* competition—but the memory of standing with other sweaty LAN attendees-turned-spectators as keyboard after keyboard arced a few meters into the air before crashing to the ground in hundreds of plastic and metal fragments has stuck most.

A few years earlier, during my dissertation fieldwork, I had my first lesson in the central importance of infrastructure to gaming—of electrical infrastructure, precisely. The grassroots esports organization I was following used tongue-in-cheek military jargon and imagery for its regular Xbox LAN events, including the names the two organizers gave themselves. "General Error," employed at the time as a human resources manager for the provincial government, was responsible for drumming up publicity, managing tournaments, and occasionally intervening to police player behavior. "General Electric" was an electrical contractor, and his job during events was to make sure all of the Xbox 360 consoles were plugged in and connected and that nothing caught fire. At the time, steeped in my humanist ethnographic training, I regarded Error's job as far more consequential, but reflecting back on this arrangement, particularly through the lens of the Keyboard Toss and other instances of infrastructure not working as gamers expect it to, their pairing—managing humans (Error) and technical infrastructure (Electric)—seems a perfect metaphor for the core competencies and components involved in running public gaming events.

This chapter brings infrastructure into the open by considering instances where it is most contingent and temporary and where its operations and grid-based logics are most apparent: LAN parties. Specifically, this chapter revisits LAN parties I attended in the past, reframing observations and interactions gathered from ethnographic fieldwork in terms offered by critical infrastructure studies. This is work I conducted over a period of eight years (2008 to 2016) at LAN events in Canada (Toronto and Vancouver), the United States (Raleigh), the United Kingdom (Telford and Newbury), and Sweden (Jönköping). In foregrounding infrastructures and their operations, this chapter is indebted to and helps extend existing work on LANs and on playing in public more generally.[9] Prior work on LANs provides rich and nuanced accounts of the communicative practices of attendees. But while LAN attendees make the occasional appearance in this chapter, I am more concerned with tracing the histories and contemporary conditions of the places in which these events unfold. Fieldwork narratives, where they do show up, are presented in a nonlinear and fragmented way. Likewise, I decenter the humanistic questions that initially guided this work (how do people play together at LANs? What else do they do? What sorts of activities characterize these events?) and ask, instead, What work did infrastructures perform? How did networks of connectivity, power, and transportation shape the forms of sociality and communicative practice I observed? In terms of cultural politics specifically, how might we understand infrastructures and their grid-based logics as *the grounds*, materially and technologically, for the subjectivities, performances, and practices that figure so prominently at these events? In what ways do infrastructural arrangements *power* gaming's gender and racial hierarchies, as enacted and reinforced (and occasionally, subverted) at the LAN parties I visited?

Killing Time

In their landmark consideration of infrastructures, Susan Leigh Star and Karen Ruhleder encourage us to think about infrastructure in temporal terms, to ask not just "what" is an infrastructure, but "when."[10] Under what conditions does the circulation and uneven distribution of vital resources become apparent to us—such as when access to running water becomes a matter of life and death, in much more acute and immediate terms?[11] Nicole Starosielski, in her consideration of underwater sea cables as media infrastructure, recasts Star and Ruhleder's attention to temporalities in terms more germane to media studies scholars, asking "*when* particular systems are infrastructural for mediation and how these systems differentially shape the dissemination of media culture."[12] Managing time seems to be an acute matter of concern for communication infrastructures throughout their geographical and historical variations, whether Roman roads, indigenous waterways, intercontinental telegraph cables, or contemporary fiber-optic networks, and especially for infrastructures responsible for distributing gaming content. There is a long-standing obsession on the part of the gaming industry with the technological manipulation of time.[13] The "when" of media infrastructures—the ways speed and slowness are manifested at different points in the grid and the uneven distribution of power and connectivity resulting in lag or long loading times—can help us make better sense of this perpetual concern. PC gamers overclock their computers to squeeze more performance out of them, accelerating internal processes to the point of breaking. *Super Smash* players drag heavy CRT televisions to face-to-face tournaments because flat-screen televisions introduce two extra frames of lag, to say nothing of the latency introduced by online play and its effects on the precise inputs required for elite play.[14] Speedrunners, looking to take fragments of seconds off official runs through long, long hours of study and practice, catalog and seek to mitigate against the molecular but discernible effects the location, humidity, and temperature of their physical play contexts have on playthroughs.[15] And as recounted in Graham Candy's brief but illuminating example of *Counter-Strike*, serious competitive game players often purchase space on game servers, form social networks, and solicit match requests with other players based on physical proximity to each other and to major clusters of server farms, geographical proximity shaving milliseconds off potential lag.[16] The more investment, the more *time* (not to mention effort and capital) one puts into certain forms of play (action and combat driven, often competitive), the more speed and efficiency come to matter, literally. In cultures of intensive and competitive gaming, these and related concerns over speed manifest a technological imperative in which players pursue a seamless techno-organic circuit, an intimate communion with technical apparatuses of play in which any delay should ideally disappear. Such is Paul Virilio's vision of machinic warfare, in which human perception itself is automated in order to diminish any delay between action, perception, and reaction.[17] These experiences of and obsessions with speed (paradoxically cultivated through endless hours of leisure time) among players with high degrees of temporal and infrastructural privilege are made possible by centuries of infrastructural development and by the inequitable distribution of information and power (electrical, cultural, and economic).[18]

Experiences of time, as Sarah Sharma powerfully illustrates, are always relational. Who has time, who is running out of time, who can make time for others are expressive and productive of power: what Sharma terms "chronopolitics."[19] It is not surprising that in gameplay and production—with concerns over greater response time, faster machines, accelerated publishing schedules, and so on—we see pronounced chronopolitical inequalities. Crunch time, the deliberate overclocking of human game workers, is an obvious and well-documented temporal disparity, in which game development companies risk the mental, emotional, and physical well-being of developers so that players can have the game as soon as possible.[20] The ludopolitical relationship here is clear-cut: they work longer, harder, and faster so that we can play sooner.[21] The other temporal relations at work when serious players invest dozens of hours of leisure time a week to gaming—answering the question, Whose time are we playing with when we game?—are perhaps less obvious. We do have some good ideas, though: feminist sociologists and ethnographers have long documented the gender disparities in leisure time, as the burden for learning and carrying out the work of social and domestic reproduction falls on female-identified members of a household.[22] Gaming amplifies these patterns through a self-perpetuating cycle in which games requiring intensive time investment are marketed to men and boys, who with their temporal privileges can then claim more sustained access to games and their attendant practices, play apparatuses, competencies, and subjectivities (as documented in chap. 2), thereby sedimenting the sets of conditions around which games are made for men and boys. The gendered feedback loop behind the play and production of games is thus both chronopolitical and ludopolitical; the long-favored subject of the AAA games industry is characterized by not only masculine pleasures and preferences but also access to spaces and *times* of prolonged play. Games for women, historically, are designed for short bursts of play and even make time management a particular and persistent theme; make productive use of the short time you have to play at managing time better.[23] Likewise, Sam Tobin's work on the Nintendo DS shows how and why this consummate portable game console found such purchase among nontraditional gaming audiences (particularly young girls and women): it did not take up space, certainly, but furthermore, its saving and pausing features meant it could be played in short snippets and put down at a moment's notice.[24]

While a more comprehensive reckoning of gaming's chronopolitics is beyond the scope of this chapter, such relations of temporal privilege and exploitation form a backdrop to my consideration of LAN parties and other sites of intensive but temporary gaming: campus gaming events, esports tournaments, and so on. LANs, which are, from a technical perspective, grids of electrical and informational circulation temporarily but expressly constructed for the purpose of networked play, allow players to surpass the temporal and spatial constraints of their regular gaming setups—including their normal access to electricity and internet. Attendees travel, often great distances and with clunky machinery in tow, in order to *kill time*, both in the sense of socializing with friends and in the sense of erasing the temporal bottlenecks they normally encounter in gaming. In my conversations with attendees, reasons for coming to LANs were often framed in social-spatial terms; players wanted to fraternize face-to-face with friends they only normally interacted with in networked games. But just as often, reasons were framed in temporal-technical terms. Attendees put a lot of time and effort into coming to a place—a localized and temporary gaming infrastructure— that fixed lag, slow loading times, and other issues caused by signals having to travel long distances over congested infrastructures.

In the account I present below, I attend to the infrastructural operations and histories of a series of large-scale gaming events I attended in England, in order to understand how infrastructural arrangements matter, greatly, to the cultural politics of LANs: who can participate and how. Over the four events I attended between 2009 and 2012 as part of the long-running Insomnia series, the first two were held in Newbury, while the last two were held in Telford. I focus on the Telford events here precisely because the reasoning behind the organizers' shift in locations between 2010 and 2011 was explicitly infrastructural—the Telford location allowed for more power and connectivity, cheaper. What follows is a telescoping look at the interconnected series of grids, the infrastructural "stack" that forms the technical conditions for these LAN events and their attendant cultural expressions.[25] I examine how and when infrastructure comes to matter by examining first the city of Telford; then the Telford International Centre (TIC), where the events were held; and last, the organization that ran the LAN events my colleagues and I attended.

Telford: Because of Infrastructure

Telford is located in Shropshire County, in the Midlands area of England, adjacent to Wales. I went to Telford twice, to the forty-third and forty-fourth installments of the Insomnia series of LAN parties, in August and November 2011. Both times, I was accompanied by colleagues with whom I split the work of ethnographic observation and extractive data processing I discuss in chapter 1. These were my third and fourth visits, respectively, to this LAN series; as I shared in chapter 1, the first two I attended, solo, were held at a horse racing track in Newbury. I was told by one of the organizers that they had changed venues to a location deemed less desirable because it provided more robust networking capabilities—that is, because of infrastructure.

It turns out that "because of infrastructure" could be the slogan for Telford itself. As part of the "new town" movement, Telford was designed via top-down urban planning expressive of a faith in postwar cybernetic logics. Its namesake, Thomas Telford, was an infrastructure builder, a Scottish engineer dubbed the "father of civil engineering" who served as purveyor of public works for Shropshire in the late eighteenth century, during which time the area was a vital source of coal and iron for the industrialization of Britain and its far-flung imperial projects.[26] The town's name thus connects it to the area's historical roots as both an incubator for techniques of industrial infrastructure building and a site of extraction for the very resources used to carry them out. Originally designated as the Dawley New Town in 1963, it was established to take in the spillover from Birmingham, located about forty kilometers away. Dawley New Town was renamed Telford in 1968, once it expanded to take in further neighboring communities.[27] Before that time, the region was "a curious mosaic of industrial revolution housing, agricultural land, and pit heaps" rather than a "contiguous urban mass."[28] Like other new towns in Britain and continental Europe, it supplanted existing infrastructures, buildings, and related histories. In this case, a Norman chapel dating from the twelfth century, which had likely served as a resting spot at a crossroads for tradespeople and workers in the heavily wooded area, was torn down to make way for the town's large shopping complex.[29]

By 1972 (a year before the first department stores opened in its new, modern shopping center), urban planners had identified a number of barriers to the town's growth and vitality despite concerted investment by various levels of government. The area's history of intensive resource extraction during the Industrial Revolution, marked by "centuries of shallow coal, ironstone, and clay mining and quarrying," had led to "an unattractive environment in which to live and work."[30] The slow state of road development linking the town to the regional highway network exacerbated the area's long-standing geographical and cultural isolation and garnered it a reputation as a no-man's-land in eastern Shropshire between Birmingham and the Welsh border.[31] Taken together, these factors made it difficult to entice industrial firms to relocate to the area, leading to high unemployment and concerns over economic stagnation. Because of infrastructure, the new town—named after a famed infrastructuralist—got off to a rocky start. Telford's design, with its spread-out housing developments reflecting a "policy of dispersal rather than concentration," epitomizes the new town movement's prioritization of efficiency, mobility, consumerism, and rational compartmentalization over historically situated modes of living.[32] While Telford does not appear particularly grid-like on a top-down map, it reflects a logic of segmentation and repetition, a logic replicated in the design of tightly packed, homogeneous, inexpensive single-family homes intended to entice young families.

A City without a Center

These are the histories of land management that shaped my experience of Telford: the first, of unchecked extraction during the Industrial Revolution, and the second, centuries later, of botched if well-intentioned efforts to reform the area according to the cybernetic principles of urban planning. For my colleagues and I conducting fieldwork at Insomnia 43 (in August 2011) and 44 (November of the same year), these histories coalesced to create a palpable sense of dislocation and alienation that we felt and talked about with each other numerous times during both of the three-day LAN events. To be sure, this sense of dislocation was also temporal and spatial, not to mention deeply personal and subjective. I was jetlagged for the entirety of both events, having come from a time zone five hours behind Telford. At the same time, my jetlag weirdly synchronized my own diurnal cycle to the temporal rhythm of the nocturnal LAN events, in which activity often did not pick up until late afternoon and went into the wee hours of the morning. Much like an airport or casino, large LAN events exist on their own time, separate from the temporal routines of normal work and leisure. This, indeed, is part of their allure: for many attendees we talked to, dislocation from the spatial and temporal conditions of everyday life (with all their attendant obligations) was a feature, not a bug. For the duration of both events, I felt out of time, as desynchronized from the normative temporality of middle-class life in the Midlands as the rest of the LAN attendees. This sense of temporal decalibration was reinforced by our walks after our fieldwork from the LAN center back to the hotel, just over a kilometer away, usually between one and three a.m., when the streets of Telford were all but deserted. As it so happens, these were the times I felt particularly awake and attentive. Jetlagged, buzzing from fieldwork and too much caffeine, primed for observation, I was at my most alert when Telford was at its most quiescent.

Not surprisingly, these walks between the LAN site and our hotel—particularly on my first visit, when I was accompanied by a colleague who is a British expat—formed my most memorable impressions of Telford. On our way from the hotel to the International Centre during daytime, the quickest and safest route was to cut through the shopping center, wending our way along its wide interior walkways rather than traversing the sidewalk-less streets that seemed to dominate the area surrounding the LAN venue. On our way back, with the shopping mall shuttered for the night, we would walk along these dark streets, nearly emptied of cars. The shopping center was also the source of most of our off-site meals (those not purchased from the food stalls at the LAN venue): Costa for coffee and water, McDonald's for lunch. On our walks around the environs of the shopping mall and the LAN venue, we found very few eateries that were not a part of a broader entertainment or shopping complex, and certainly none that were open past the early evening, save for McDonald's. "There's no pub," my expat colleague would lament every time we took meals together and had to decide where to go. We heard the same refrain from several LAN attendees I had encountered in earlier Insomnia events in Newbury (which did have a pub, close to the venue), who grumbled about the new site. "Telford is shit," they told me when I ran into them on the first day of Insomnia 43, the first event in the new town. For these working-class and middle-class white men—most in their late twenties or early thirties—the lack of a pub meant that Telford simply had no center, no identity or attraction as a *place*. Residents of Telford we talked to one evening, walking along a quieter street on a break from fieldwork, shared similar sentiments. The man and woman we encountered were, like us, looking for a place to eat. She said she had lived in Telford for four years but had not bothered to learn the area because, in her words, "there's not much to learn"; my expat colleague joked that we should all pile in a cab and head to nearby Shrewsbury in search of a "real pub," and we went on our separate ways.

Third Places

I focus on pubs (or the lack thereof) since they occupy a significant position in British culture and history. They are places of gathering, fraternizing, collaborating, gaming, and drinking and are constitutive of a certain mode of belonging typically and historically reserved for white men. They are regarded, often in halcyon terms by members of those groups, as the proper center of a certain kind of British town life, one that is under threat from suburbanization, immigration, corporatization, Americanization, and so on.[33] Pubs also occupy a central place in certain kinds of sociological imagination as material instantiations of a class-inclusive public sphere ("pub" itself being shorthand for "public house") seen as either threatened or utterly transformed by digital media and the political economies of late-stage capitalism. Held up as paradigmatic instances of "third spaces," sites for socialization and civic participation outside of work and home, pubs are theorized by American sociologist Ray Oldenburg as crucial sites of socially egalitarian community building and vital resources for civic regeneration, alongside barber shops, bowling alleys, and coffeehouses.[34] Central to Oldenburg's influential theorization of third places is a trenchant critique of the alienation wrought by a suburban mode of life that shuts us out from meaningful forms of civic participation outside of home and work. This critique operates out of an epistemology that all too often universalizes a white, heteronormative, middle-class subject position while ignoring the patterns of exclusion that have long characterized the kinds of locales and experiences associated with third places.[35]

Notably, during the mid-2000s, the notion of third spaces became a fashionable way to describe networked role-playing games, most frequently in ways that left patterns of access and inclusion unproblematized.[36] Like other spatial metaphors for networked games (and for the internet more generally), the work imagining massively multiplayer online games (MMOGs) as third places elides the fact that play and its attendant activities are always physically situated—and that there are multiple and overlapping reasons why many do not find networked play particularly hospitable or even accessible. Moreover, and particularly following the gamergate hate campaign, accounts of networked gaming as a new site of civic regeneration and social bonding *must* reckon with the fact that it has frequently been linked to *anti*social, reactionary, exclusionary movements and to powerfully negative forms of community building and belonging.[37] The socially egalitarian premise/promise behind many accounts of third places is thus frequently and profoundly limited, and neither pubs nor networked video games are exceptions—places of belonging for all so long as you are white, straight, and (cis) male or, at the very least, accompanied by someone who is.

For many of the men involved in the LAN research, and notably the study participants I spent time with across multiple iterations of Insomnia events (including the earlier Multiplay events I attended in Newbury, as reported in chap. 1), Telford really did not have a center, culturally or geographically: no site of fraternization or belonging outside of the LAN, so foundational to their class, gender, and race-based experiences of British life and British place-making. The sense was that they traveled to the LAN, not to Telford. Telford was just a space they moved through to access the temporary center of their gaming communities and practices. It is difficult to determine whether the exclusion of a pub in the cybernetic visions of Telford as a new town was by accident or by design, but its effect, for my companion and many study participants at least, was to underscore Telford's broader, pervasive sense of spatial dislocation: a city without a recognizable center that had quite literally torn down its past and paved over it, situated in the no-man's-land of eastern Shropshire.

A Center without a City

There is an irony in the claim and sensation that Telford has no center, given that we were there attending an event at the TIC, the large event space on the other side of the mall from our hotel. But what is TIC at the center *of*? Such venues are not intended to be centers in the way a pub is—a local meeting place, a structure for serving and instantiating a community associated with a particular locale (historically defined by walking distance)—however exclusionary such publics might be in practice. Newbury, the town that had hosted these LAN events before they moved to Telford starting with Insomnia 42, had a pub; the pub's trivia nights and Sunday roasts were popular draws for LAN attendees, including the lads who later opined that "Telford is shit" for its location and its lack of good places to get away from the LAN. But the Newbury LAN venue itself, a horse racing track, was a very particular kind of gathering place, as discussed in chapter 1. For Multiplay, the company responsible for organizing Insomnia, converting the Newbury venue from one sort of gaming context (horse racing track), with its own cultures, audiences, and practices, to another (LAN party) created a slew of spatial idiosyncrasies. Private booths for VIP horse racing spectators became premium rooms for networked gaming clans and esports teams willing to pay extra for the privacy of a closed door and a view of the empty horse track. During the day, attendees strolled the perimeter of the track or found spots to doze among the tiers of shaded viewing balconies. Inside areas were covered in worn carpet flecked with beverage stains. Low ceilings made some areas stiflingly hot, their ventilation equipped to deal with television-based spectatorship rather than hundreds of high-end gaming machines running, overclocked, for eighteen hours a day. Smells hung thick: beer, energy drinks, fried food, candies, the sedentary bodies processing it all. The lack of a dedicated stage area inside the venue made it difficult for organizers to showcase tournament finals and other marquee events. From the organizers' standpoint, the Newbury venue was simply too much of a certain kind of *place* to be a good site for a LAN: too many imprints of its use as a horse racing track. It was not modular enough and certainly not infrastructural enough.

The TIC, on the other hand, is an ideal venue for a LAN from this logistic perspective: it is suited to arranging thousands of powerful gaming machines into a grid that can be flooded with reliable and cheap connectivity and power. Convention centers like the TIC are not properly city centers in the ways of pubs or other local gathering places. Rather, they are meant to be temporary nodes for whatever geographically distributed community or organization pays for space and resources for a limited time.

They become centers for people in the same way that a server is a center for data: a structure defined not by its contents but by its nodal location in a larger grid and capacity to temporarily store and process entities as they circulate among globally distributed networks. From one moment to the next, a server might become a node in the distribution of Facebook posts, *Counter-Strike* kills, cat videos, pornography; likewise, albeit in the more cumbersome spatial and temporal scales of human mobilities, a convention center like the TIC might become a node for streetwear designers and retailers, alpaca enthusiasts, bedding makers, cheerleading teams, and so on, depending on the weekend.[38] It is a center in temporal and infrastructural terms rather than proximal and sociocultural ones, defined by mobility and modularity rather than by rootedness in a particular shared way of life for people living within its radius. Anecdotally, the only residents we spoke to during our stays who knew what was going on at the TIC the weekends of Insomnia events, who felt connected in some way to the center of Telford, worked in the service industry—hotel staff, McDonald's employees, taxi drivers. The TIC was the temporary center of intensive gaming culture in England for a few Insomnia events, just as it was the temporary center of British alpaca producers and enthusiasts at a different time. Its significance as a *place* is not in the sedimentation of experiences defined by shared locality and demographics—as per Doreen Massey's elegant definition of space as "simultaneity of stories-so-far."[39] Rather, a space such as the TIC attains significance through its capacity to *erase* traces of recent use and recombine its structural features for the next round of visitors. In the words of media theorists, it is a technology that can be reset and reformatted for the next function, the next community, the next group that comes from far and wide to temporarily gather—less a place and more a container technology for the processing of social and economic relations.[40]

In his work on Walmart's approach to architecture, Jesse LeCavalier offers the term "logistification": the elevation of logistics, the "science of managing things in space and time," to a mode of governance.[41] According to LeCavalier, Walmart's buildings—its supercenters but also its warehouses, shipping terminals, and server farms—are best thought of not as solitary structures but as interconnected elements of a network designed above all else for the lag-free circulation of consumer goods. Walmart "imagines its architecture in increasingly infrastructural and temporal terms: redundant, repeatable, and abstract"; the corporation's internal communications refer to single stores as "formats," virtually indistinguishable from any other instance of the "prototype."[42] Each store connected to the Walmart infrastructure is a media apparatus, a machine for the "processing, storage, and display" of *stuff* arriving from multiple points in its global network.[43] Logistification entails the subordination of all other concerns (such as choices in the design of buildings, worker well-being, selection of new sites) to the most time- and capital-efficient calibration of infrastructure. Walmart, via its half century of experimentation in logistification, remakes physical territory into a grid, a vast latticework of buildings, servers, people, scanners, bar codes, trucks, and so on, optimized for the distribution of cheap commodities through technologies of spatial and temporal manipulation. Of course, LeCavalier is discussing the operations of a single corporate entity, however powerful and broadly distributed. But his insights about the logistification of our built environments, in which buildings are configured as giant nodes for processing, storing, and distributing temporary contents, hold true for other "non-places" such as convention centers, airports, and so on.[44] Once inside the TIC, one could be anywhere, at any time of day or night; unlike the Newbury venue, where rows of windows looking out on the horse racing track served as constant reminders of the world outside and its diurnal rhythms (not to mention its awkward reconfiguration from a spectatorial venue to a LAN), the TIC halls in which Insomnia events took place had no windows. The center's promotional material is instructive here. It expressly emphasizes infrastructure over other considerations: little mention is made of Telford other than referring to its "hugely accessible location" without "the hustle and bustle" of a large city.[45] Fitting that the international center of Telford, a city named after an infrastructure builder and constructed according to decentralized spatial logics, should emphasize how easy it is to get to from other places rather than the place it occupies—a center without a city, in a city without a center.

A quick sketch of the TIC's architectural features bears out this infrastructural understanding of the venue. The ground floor of the TIC features three massive halls (Halls 1 and 2 are larger and of identical size, and Hall 3 is slightly smaller), pale concrete floors extending to each corner. Modularity is built into the core structural features of the center: walls separating the halls can be retracted such that the halls can be combined, "providing the opportunity to create a brilliant exhibition space."[46] In each hall, the slightly peaked ceiling is held up by a grid of metal ribs and cross beams

Figure 3.1. An image of one of the TIC event halls from the venue's promotional materials. Credit: Telford International Centre.

from which are strung braces of evenly spaced lights, speakers, and security cameras, suspended end points for infrastructures of illumination, communication, and surveillance. Each hall boasts access to "a dedicated off-road loading area" for moving contents in and out. The visual effect of the halls, at least in promotional images in which they are shown unoccupied, is of repeatable, abstract geometric forms in a palette of grays, blacks, and whites, constituting a space that is cavernous and Cartesian (see fig. 3.1). The halls look like they would be easy, or at least cheap, to recreate digitally with a three-dimensional game engine: a limited palette of textures, shapes, and colors copied and pasted repeatedly to create scale. It is no wonder that the space should hold such appeal for organizers as a LAN venue. There are no idiosyncrasies of form, light, and texture, simply an "infrastructural version of architecture" in which to enact a massive but temporary gaming grid.[47]

Infrastructure Culture

During Insomnia event days, of course, the halls were very different than they appear in promotional materials. They were alive with vast and intricate choreographies of machines, humans, furniture, peripherals, knapsacks and suitcases, the din of chatter punctuated by shouts of joy, surprise, and frustration, regular announcements over the loudspeakers, and the detritus of temporary human habitation. Entering the TIC main hall for the first day of Insomnia 43, my colleagues and I were overwhelmed. It was our first time at a LAN event of this scale, and we did not know where to look, where to go, what to do, how to act. There was so much going on and so much to take in. When we approached the check-in station and chatted with the organizers, they seemed just as bewildered by the turnout, which they told us later was the largest ever for an Insomnia event: around twenty-three hundred BYOC attendees. Tables were pushed together to form rows of twenty-five stations a side, rows on rows forming a grid, with multiple grids in each of the three halls. At each station were an electrical power bar and a LAN cable, lattices of power and connectivity giving order to the physical layout of computers, humans, and assorted peripherals and paraphernalia.

The activities that constitute large-scale LANs like the ones in Telford have been documented extensively elsewhere, but I will give a brief overview here of their heterogeneity and dynamism. These events are never just playing video games for multiple days and nights in a row. The much larger DreamHack gaming festival in Jönköping, for instance, turns its BYOC event halls into electronic dance parties at night, while at Insomnia, there are nightly trivia contests and other pub-based or parlor games. There is shopping—sections of the event floor, often along one side of a hall or occupying an entire building, in which vendors of food, computer peripherals, geek lifestyle and fandom paraphernalia, and board games come out in droves to set up mini shopping malls and food courts. There are contests and workshops, autograph sessions and talks, meetups and hookups. There is steady foot traffic in, out, and around the venue; there are separate sleeping quarters, but inevitably, people sprawl in various stages of repose in the BYOC areas (usually in the morning) under desks, along walls, or at their chairs. As I discuss below, esports tournaments were becoming a regular fixture at these events even in the early 2010s, complete with stages, broadcasting apparatuses, and spectator areas.

Even the central figure of the LAN—the player (most often, at Insomnia and other LANs I have been to, straight white men in their late teens to early thirties) seated at his high-end, custom-built computer—is never just playing video games. Attendees can be boisterous and rowdy or relatively silent, depending on the time of day or night. Seated, they watch videos, chat on IRC, check social media, listen to music, download or install games, recalibrate their machines, snack and drink. They cluster in knots around a particular station, sit intently at their own machines with headphones on, or chat animatedly with row mates. They fiddle with remote-controlled toys, stack empty energy drink cans in intricate pyramids on their desks, surreptitiously write work emails. Networked communication in various forms and layers goes viral, fast: memes circulate, mutate, and recirculate at shocking speed, catchphrases and snippets of songs get shouted and are completed or repeated as they travel from row to row and section to section, old or obscure games initially draw a few onlookers and are soon played by large swaths of attendees. For my colleagues and me, spending most of our days walking up and down rows of BYOC attendees, the virality of communication seemed a feature of the TIC layout. Compared to Newbury, where different rooms and floors were largely cordoned off from each other and players mostly stayed in their sections, the massive, open grids of the TIC LAN facilitated the rapid spread of ludic place-making artifacts and practices.

Given this heterogeneity, it is difficult to characterize large-scale LANs as having a singular, definitive culture. The DreamHack and Insomnia events I went to, for instance, had markedly different communities, activities, and vibes: the former felt like a giant video game theme park by day and geek rave by night, catering primarily to teens and players in their early twenties, while the latter often felt like a pub (ironically and suitably, given Telford's lack of one). Moreover, as I have discussed in this chapter, Insomnia events themselves varied greatly from one venue to the next, with geographic, infrastructural, and architectural conditions shaping the kinds of cultural expressions possible in different venues. Given this heterogeneity, I am not making the case that the prevalence of grids as a cultural technique, whether in the organization of LAN attendees, the TIC, or the cybernetic organization of Telford itself, had a direct and consistent *ideological* effect on participants. Attendees were not somehow more grid-like in disposition, affect, or activity, whatever that would look like. The LAN attendees we met with and observed were creative, funny, weird, unpredictable, and complex, even as most of their activities were broadly intelligible through the lens of what contemporary research regards as conventional expressions of masculinized and exclusionary video gaming cultures.[48] The effects of grids were more subtle and have to do with how they interfaced, materially and discursively, with other apparatuses of technocultural production. I now turn to two of these effects.

Bring Your Own Bunker

Set in a new town historically defined by infrastructural capacities (and limitations), within a venue for which the main selling point is its recombinatory spatial possibilities rather than its sense of place, Insomnia's LAN events in Telford prioritized access to infrastructures above all else. Few other place-making potentials got in the way of ensuring attendees' direct access to ample power and connectivity: not cultural attractions in the surrounding town or region, not idiosyncrasies in the venue's layout as in the Newbury site, not efforts at bringing in more diverse crowds through a greater range of gaming-related cultural practices (cosplay, board gaming), as in Dream-Hack and innumerable smaller, more niche gaming events. The effect was to attract participants for whom the valorization of power and connectivity are key expressions of their investments in gaming culture—having a custom-built gaming rig, being a member of a top-tier raiding guild or professional esports team. To apply the theorization laid out in chapter 2, what I notice looking back on both the BYOC areas and the patterning of dispositions and practices emerging from their arrangement is the prevalence of *bunkers*: a matrix of gaming setups designed for stable and unfettered access to the grids that feed serious, power- and connection-hungry leisure. Some of what went into producing rows and columns of bunkers was the logistic constraint of traveling to a LAN. In addition to your computer, it is often not practical to lug other, more communal gaming platforms—not to mention suitcases full of whatever tchotchkes, wall hangings, and knickknacks decorate your home cabinets or hearths—halfway across England for a weekend. And there would be no place to put them once there.

In chapter 2, I followed the wires into and through NeoGAF users' homes to find out what the management of wires and their (in)visibility might say about gendered patterns of privilege associated with different kinds of gaming setups. At Insomnia, where access to a robust infrastructure was the main draw, wire management took on a whole new order of importance. There was certainly no hiding wires amid the rows of utilitarian chairs and tables, but there was an etiquette to managing your wires in a way that did not compromise your row neighbors' arrangements, such as by taking up one of their electrical outlets, pulling on other attendees' wires or knocking them out of sockets while trying to set up or rearrange your station, and so on. We discovered this in a most unfortunate way on our first day at Insomnia 44, when I used a colleague's universal power adapter to connect my North American power bar, and every station in our row lost power. We learned soon after, from one of the organizers who came trotting over to assist our disgruntled neighbors, that I had blown a fuse, which had in turn blown others connected by daisy-chaining, a method that increases the scalability of a circuit but introduces acute vulnerabilities, as I had so effectively demonstrated. General Electric would have been very embarrassed. My lack of care around wires caused dozens of attendees to lose power and connectivity— access to the infrastructures that grounded the event, technically and culturally. Some were very good-natured about the gaffe and even expressed interest (and later participated) in our research study; others did not look at us or talk to us for the remainder of the event.

The logistic, technical, and cultural conditions of the BYOC turned it into a grid of bunkers, rows and columns of custom computer setups prioritized for robust pulls from the ample internet and electricity provided by the venue, each with its assigned network address and power outlets. This arrangement formed the grounds for much of what we observed of players, collectively expressive of thousands of bunkers daisy-chained together in semipublic: the virality of memes around themes of scatology and violence; a strong preference for computationally demanding and/or network-intensive games of conquest, whether solo (*Skyrim*) or networked (*Counter-Strike*); the casual misogyny and homophobia of banter between attendees; desktop images featuring seminude women; a disregard for public standards of hygiene and cleanliness, perhaps suggestive of the politics around domestic labor ported over along with computers and peripherals from attendees' own home contexts. These expressions are by no means inevitable or characteristic of all large LANs I have been to. A trip to DreamHack in Jönköping, Sweden, in the summer of 2016 was eye-opening in this regard.[49] The BYOC halls at DreamHack were substantially larger than those at the Insomnia events I had attended and relied just as much on the technical and physical organization of BYOC stations into grids. But where Insomnia prioritized infrastructural access above all else, inviting a prevalence of bunkers, DreamHack attendees were encouraged to participate in traditions and practices that mitigated against such effects. Not only was there simply more to do, in line with DreamHack's marketing as a "digital culture festival" and in contrast to Insomnia's positioning (for a time) as a BYOC LAN party with some other stuff on the side, but it is also tradition at DreamHack for attendees to decorate their stations. For my companions and I at DreamHack in summer of 2016, this meant a complicated apparatus of duct tape, PVC pipes, strings, and holiday lights from which were suspended pictures of the artist Prince; our station became a sparkly purple shrine to the recently deceased artist. Moreover, I was told by my DreamHack companions that at the winter version of the event, many attendees bedecked their stations in pillows, blankets, and Christmas-themed lighting and knickknacks. The collective effect was to incorporate a significant degree of cabinet- and hearth-based modes of place making into the DreamHack BYOC area. Perhaps not surprisingly, the crowd at DreamHack—even among attendees to the BYOC area—seemed more diverse, particularly with regard to gender and age.

In contrast, the bunker culture of Insomnia operated to make events less hospitable for women, and the majority of female attendees we saw were friends or romantic partners there with larger groups of men. But while female attendees were few and far between, Insomnia events involved a considerable amount of women's labor. This labor could be highly visible, as with the young women who worked as promotional models for particular tech brands, visiting the LAN at certain times and days to hand out swag and take photographs with attendees.[50] It could also be virtually invisible, as in the case of the women who operated the food stalls and cleaned the bathrooms. Late one night at Insomnia 43, a colleague and I had a chance to chat with a middle-aged woman who worked on the TIC's cleaning staff. She said that the LAN attendees were "generally nice boys" but that the mess they left each night (particularly in the bathrooms) was among the worst she had seen from TIC events. When we asked what sort of acknowledgment she received from attendees, she said she received an occasional "thanks" or "good job," but her labor seemed otherwise unnoticed and unremarked. Near the end of our conversation, she mentioned that as nice as the boys were, her and her other middle-aged colleagues made sure that none of their younger colleagues were assigned to the event, as that would be "courting disaster." This is a chilling reminder of the ways in which the culture of many male-dominated gaming contexts can create spaces and experiences that are powerfully unsafe for women—particularly those who occupy otherwise invisible or subordinate roles.[51] The account of this TIC employee is also illustrative of the ways in which the politics of the bunker—young men's cultural and technical immersion in practices centered around sustained gaming supported by the invisible and unacknowledged "Mommy" labor of precarious and vulnerable workers (to return to Sarah Sharma's theorization)—are all too easily recreated in semipublic contexts.[52]

No One Puts Baby in a Corner

The second effect of the overt prioritization of infrastructure arose out of Multiplay's efforts at making Insomnia more visible in the emerging global network of live streamed esports. On the first day of Insomnia 43, while we were milling around the reception area waiting to register, we were shepherded by a young woman with a walkie-talkie across half a hall to meet our main contact. He had his hands full coordinating the construction of a large broadcasting stage (replete with lighting system, cameras, and audiovisual production terminals), which he called his "baby." Set against the long wall of Hall 2, the stage and its attendant recording and production technologies faced a dedicated viewing area of around five hundred seats but were visible from almost anywhere in the LAN. By comparison, the stage at the Newbury horse racing track was much more ad hoc, situated in the main foyer with seating for around one hundred and only visible to attendees either in the foyer itself or in adjacent halls on the same floor. The Newbury stage felt like an afterthought—a sideshow, visibly separate from the primary draw of BYOC gaming. Indeed, the most action I observed on the Newbury stage was on the last day of the event, when the organizers tossed swag from the stage out to a few hundred gathered participants. In contrast, the "baby" delivered to the floor of the TIC did more than just provide a prominent stage for Insomnia's esports tournaments: it signified Insomnia's commitment to amplifying its tournament broadcasts, to becoming a player in the surging market for live streamed esports during the early 2010s. It was a boom time for an esports industry that had, over the previous decades, been largely unsuccessful at cultivating mass audiences for televised competitive gaming, at least outside of South Korea and some parts of northern Europe. In the early 2010s, with Twitch, the exploding popularity of League of Legends (LoL), and ongoing enthusiasm for Starcraft 2, esports became a much more feasible (though not yet profitable) televisual commodity. Insomnia's

apparent goal—beginning in earnest with the arrival of the "baby" to Insomnia 43—was to use its LAN events as a large production studio for live
streamed esports so that the LAN could become a temporary center not just
for gaming enthusiasts from around England but for the growing attention
economy of esports. Up to this point, the conventional relationship between
LAN events and esports, at least as I understood it, was that you would go to
a LAN to hang out with your gaming friends, play for a weekend, and maybe
check out a couple of esports matches while there. The "baby," and the palpable excitement it elicited from Insomnia organizers, marked the start of
a cultural, technological, and economic inversion in how I understood this
relationship. In a shift I would see to greater effect when attending a Major
League Gaming (MLG) event in Raleigh in 2012, Insomnia's BYOC attendees effectively became part of the televisual esports commodity produced
at the event and live streamed all over the world. Within this arrangement,
attendees were not just physically present; they became "audienced," their
presence serving as readily captured visual evidence of the allure of Insomnia's esports brand.[53] For attendees, hanging out and playing games remained the main draw of the LAN, but for Multiplay organizers, beginning
in earnest with Insomnia 43, the LAN existed as a way to gather a crowd
to their recordings of esports tournaments, one that would add substance
to broadcasts. This inversion—this decentering of the LAN in relation to
esports—was made possible (and lucrative) by the rise of inexpensive and
accessible internet-based video transmission and by an emerging platform
economy that could capitalize on these new technical and infrastructural
conditions.[54]

On the last night of the event (Insomnia 44) later that fall, we joined a
few organizers, including "baby's" daddy, for a round of drinks. As we all
sat at two tables pushed together in the shadow of the stage, the organizers
appeared exhausted yet jubilant. They had just learned that their live stream
of the weekend's events had attracted a total audience of 2.2 million views.
This was more viewers than a concurrent event in the United States, the
2011 MLG Providence Championships, the culminating event for MLG's
yearlong *Halo: Reach* and *Starcraft* tournaments. Insomnia had beaten what
was then one of the dominant esports organizations and content producers
at its own game, a feat that eclipsed the successful conclusion of an event
that had gathered over two thousand people to the TIC. What seemed to
matter most for Insomnia was not the local grid set up for players but the

globe-spanning infrastructure delivering esports content to viewers, who could then—through the grid-based surveillant apparatus of IP addresses, page visit counts, and more—be counted and reported on as an esports audience greater than MLG's.

Shifting LANscapes

This moment of exultation among Insomnia organizers is one of my lasting memories from this fieldwork. It came at the end of the last Insomnia event I attended and on the cusp of a major upheaval in my own life, as I was hired onto my first tenure-track job in early 2012 (three months after Insomnia 44), effectively drawing to a close the period of intensive LAN fieldwork carried out for my postdoctoral research. Both Multiplay and Insomnia underwent profound transformations in the years between Insomnia 44 and 2019, when this chapter was first drafted. Multiplay, the organization that founded Insomnia events, was sold to GAME in 2015; GAME is a UK-based chain of retail game stores, similar to GameStop in the United States and Canada. Player1 Events, the event management subsidiary of GAME, took over the Insomnia event series. GAME, in turn, was purchased by Frasers Group in 2019, a massive conglomerate of UK-based sporting goods and lifestyle stores. Player1 Events still manages the Insomnia series, which moved to Birmingham, England's second-largest city. Multiplay was then sold to Unity Technologies in 2017. Unity makes video game authoring assets (in particular, the Unity engine) that are increasingly deployed as content creation tools in film, television, and automotive industries. As a subsidiary of Unity Technologies, Multiplay runs a hosting service for networked games. Promotional material on Multiplay's website declares that "for over 20 years Multiplay has ensured gamers have the best possible experience while gaming online," effectively collapsing the company's decades-long experience running LAN events into its current operations hosting game servers. According to this narrative, the organization has always been about "managed infrastructures" for connecting gamers, whether in localized (non)places like the TIC or globally distributed via the Internet.[55]

In these shifts, we see at work many of the processes that transformed our economic, technological, and cultural landscape in the intervening decade between when this fieldwork was carried out and the writing of this chapter. First, the Insomnia event series is now a subsidiary of a subsidiary, subsumed under the corporate operations and portfolio of a lifestyle and clothing retail giant. It was purchased by a games retailer right around when it started producing esports content that could compete on a global stage. This says much about the value and location of esports in our contemporary landscape; outside of venture capital (more readily available in the United States), acquisition by either professional sports organizations or sports lifestyle brands seems to be one of the few ways for esports organizations to become financially stable. Including esports in their portfolio is seen as a way for large corporations to reach a key consumer demographic—a return, albeit on a larger scale, to the origins of esports as promotional experience advertising.[56] Second, the ongoing prioritization of esports production over other features of contemporary LAN events ought to be read as part of a shift toward the increasing corporatization and financialization of LAN events themselves, which in the early and mid-2000s at least still had a somewhat subcultural feel. DreamHack's history is particularly instructive in this regard: what began as a hacker community is now operated as an ancillary of German esports giant ESL, which itself was bought by the Saudi Arabian government in 2022. In just over twenty years, DreamHack transformed from a vital hub in the open source and demo community to one more, relatively minor, entry in the massive investment portfolio of a petrostate intent on "sportswashing" its public image through the acquisition of professional sports organizations.[57] And after a series of twists and turns, Multiplay is now a subsidiary of a company that produces the software assets on which games run. It went from producing LAN events for dozens of players to producing LAN events for thousands of players to producing LAN events measured by number of globally dispersed esports viewers to running server farms for networked games. In the analysis I present here, and indeed by its own admission, Multiplay always *has* been in the business of infrastructure, of operating grids for the processing of communicative action. Whether measured in terms of people or page views or electrical power, the logistic work of making digital play possible is conceptualized, by those most intimate with its operations, as managing grids.

Ground Truths

LAN events play significant roles in the reproduction of communities, discourses, and subjectivities associated with intensive gameplay. These roles are by no means stable or culturally, historically, and geographically homogeneous; I imagine that recent Insomnia events do not have the same feel as the ones I went to, nor, as I pointed out, can I compare my visits to Insomnia and DreamHack without noting their different scale and demographics and the different practices and performances enacted. But as rich and insightful as studies of LANs have been, they have tended to focus on the *figures* of the LAN—the attendees (mostly white men) who show up with their computers, socialize, fraternize, play, and so on. Often overlooked are the grounds on which these figures play. Here, ground takes on multiple meanings. As noted in the introduction, Marshall McLuhan invokes the figure and ground motif to toy with our perceptions of what matters most when considering the cultural significance of media. The "figure" tends to be what is on the screen or on the page, the representational content of the medium, whereas the "ground" denotes the sociotechnical milieu in which such contents circulate and become possible.[58] While I draw from this motif in other chapters, it is particularly germane to the analysis present here. I have attempted to explain the significance of LANs by decentering the content—the people who attend them—and instead attending to the physical, geographical, architectural conditions that exert tremendous, if frequently invisible, agency on who participates and how. But as Sarah Sharma argues, a reflexive and responsible invocation of McLuhan's theories must contend with the inability (even reticence) in McLuhan's original works to engage with the relations of power and intersecting hierarchies of race, gender, class, nationality, and so on that media systems too frequently help reproduce.[59] Building on gaming's relation to land and its colonial histories presented in chapter 1, the grounds of the LANs I consider in this chapter are profoundly intertwined with the white masculine subjectivities and practices that figure so prominently, insofar as infrastructural conditions of these events are very effective at reproducing the practices and politics of certain domestic gaming arrangements.

Ground also has numerous connotations to space, our experiences of space, and how those experiences are managed. This is the domain of geography, architecture, and urban planning and concerns the purposeful arrangement of bodies in (and in relation to) structures and cities. Attention to the grounds of LAN events, and to what I learned from walking the grounds, afforded me a productive and, up to this point, underexplored perspective on how to *locate* gaming events. I mean this geographically as well as culturally and politically. Attention to the grounds of gaming events affords the realization that like all LAN events, the Insomnia LANs I attended were constituted through temporary organization of a localized infrastructure for intensive gaming in venues capable (for the most part) of supplying ample electricity and connectivity by linking up to more far-reaching networks. But while all LANs are infrastructures, the considerations I offer here, first of the history and geography of Telford as a new town set among the reclaimed rubble of the Industrial Revolution and second of the modular, logistic architecture the TIC, help characterize the particular arrangement of Insomnia events at the TIC as *infrastructuralist*—that is, prioritizing access to power and connectivity over all other considerations. No other placemaking potentials got in the way of plugging in and powering on. As a result, we got grids of bunkers, with all their bared wires, conditions of spatiotemporal, technical, and cultural privilege, and accompanying expressions of white technomasculinity. We can expect similar figures to emerge from similarly infrastructuralist grounds: that is, when grids are not the backdrop of a LAN event but its main draw.

The grid, as Siegert says, is a cultural technique for mapping a symbolic order based on segmentation and determinable location onto messy reality. While the grid has been used in urban planning for centuries, not to mention as a fundamental tool in the development of visual arts and sciences, it has also been a powerful technique for managing electricity since the Industrial Revolution.[60] Contrary to McLuhan's assertion that electricity has no "container"—part of his broader characterization of electricity as something that is much more "of" our era than "in" any particular thing—grids are the closest we have come to containing electrical power.[61] The grid, writes Gretchen Bakke, is a "mechanism for making, transiting, and using electricity," such that even the earliest attempts to commodify electricity proceeded via controlling the infrastructure of its distribution, not to mention the means for measuring and tracking it.[62] Historical connections between the grid and the commodification of electrical power are further explored by Canay Özden-Schilling, who articulates the metonymic relationship between what she calls the "big grid"—the network of systems for measuring, storing, and distributing electricity—and "big data."[63] According to Özden-Schilling, concerns around managing and supplying electricity "necessitated and brought about early forms of big data," understood as the recording and processing of massive amounts of information. "Big grid," and the impetus it engendered to more efficiently track and manage electrical distribution, was a key concern early on in Vannevar Bush's postwar work on computation; Özden-Schilling writes that Bush "was steeped in the culture of electric power systems" and that the "grid study" subsequently carried out by Norbert Weiner, Claude Shannon, and others "helped stimulate theories of information" that eventually led to Wiener's theory of cybernetics.[64] Cybernetics theory would in turn heavily influence the early articulation and implementation of the new town movement, further wrapping the design of towns like Telford and the later construction of built environments such as the TIC according to logics of global distribution into a shared genealogy, united by the grid.[65]

Özden-Schilling's work provides a useful glimpse into the ways the grid functions as a technique for storing and distributing multiple forms of power: not only electrical power but power to reshape cities, enforce and solicit certain behaviors, and certainly, as I assert here, impel certain kinds of subject formation. It is in this capacity that I turn to the final sense of ground, as that which tethers an electrical system to the earth. In electrical engineering—the science of managing electric power—the ground serves numerous purposes. It is a protective measure, a way for built up electricity to be safely dispersed or to trigger a fuse, as I encountered when plugging my North American power bar into the Insomnia circuit and literally being ungrounded. It is also a technique of measurement, a constant reference against which electrical values can be measured—ground zero. The ground is thus instrument and container, that which makes the infrastructural distribution of power both manageable and quantifiably knowable. In this way, the analysis I present here serves as a ground for approaching and understanding the circulation of specific gender codes and protocols at public gaming events. As I articulated in chapter 2, technomasculinity circulates as readily through domestic gaming setups as electrical power. Here, I have examined how gender codes likewise travel through globe-spanning material infrastructures, reproducing among LAN attendees similar privileged relations to space and time, and a similar reliance on and erasure of feminized labor, that characterize the most infrastructuralist arrangements of domestic gaming technologies.

NOTES

1. Siegert, *Cultural Techniques*, 115.
2. Siegert, *Cultural Techniques*, 107.
3. Grant, "Dark Side of the Grid"; Massumi, *Parables for the Virtual*; Puar, "I Would Rather Be a Cyborg Than a Goddess"; Saval, *Cubed*. Both Brian Massumi and (building on his work) Jasbir Puar problematize the tendency in social thought

to mobilize the grid as an epistemological framework for social position, where intersectionality becomes a matter of one's location at the intersection of different axes of oppression. For Puar in particular, grid-based identity and oppression fails to capture the full dynamism of Kimberlé Crenshaw's original conceptualization of intersectionality.

4. Edwards, "Infrastructure and Modernity," 194; Larkin, "Politics and Poetics of Infrastructure," 336.

5. Bennett, *Vibrant Matter*, 21; Özden-Schilling, "Chapter 9. Big Grid," 169.

6. Starosielski, "Fixed Flow," 187.

7. Avancini et al., "Energy Meters Evolution in Smart Grids"; Andrejevic, "Ubiquitous Surveillance"; Rose-Redwood, "With Numbers in Place"; Berlant, "Commons," 393.

8. This research was supported by the same project that brought me to the Insomnia LAN events discussed in chapter 1 and more extensively in this chapter.

9. Jansz and Martens, "Gaming at a LAN Event"; Jonsson and Verhagen, "Senses Working Overtime"; Swalwell, "LAN Gaming Groups"; Taylor and Witkowski, "This Is How We Play It."

10. Star and Ruhleder, "Steps toward an Ecology of Infrastructure," 112.

11. Biswas and Tortajada, "COVID-19 Heightens Water Problems around the World."

12. Starosielski, "Fixed Flow," 56.

13. Hanson, *Game Time*.

14. Stout, "Smashing Some Bros," 5.

15. Schmalzer, "Transition Games," 69.

16. Candy, "In Video Games We Trust," 136.

17. Crogan, *Gameplay Mode*; Taylor and Elam, "'People Are Robots, Too'"; Virilio, *War and Cinema*.

18. Aouragh and Chakravartty, "Infrastructures of Empire."

19. Sharma, *In the Meantime*, 6.

20. Cote and Harris, "'Weekends Became Something Other People Did,'" 162; Harvey and Shepherd, "When Passion Isn't Enough," 495.

21. Bulut, *A Precarious Game*, 121.

22. Frederici, *Wages against Housework*; Parker and Wang, "Modern Parenthood"; Sharma, *In the Meantime*; Shaw, "Family Leisure and Changing Ideologies of Parenthood."

23. Anable, *Playing with Feelings*; Chess, *Ready Player Two*.

24. Tobin, "Time and Space in Play," 136; Tobin, *Portable Play in Everyday Life*, 69.

25. Bratton, *Stack*.

26. Rolt, *Thomas Telford*, 47.

27. Simson, "Post-Romantic Landscape of Telford New Town," 2.

28. Tolley, "Telford New Town," 343.

29. Friends of Telford Town Park, "Heritage"; Shropshire Star, "Watch."

30. Tolley, "Telford New Town," 353.

31. MACE Archive, "From Dawley to Telford."

32. MACE Archive, "From Dawley to Telford"; see also Wakeman, *Practicing Utopia*; Lefebvre, "Notes on the New Town."

33. Campbell, "Glass Phallus"; Jayne, Valentine, and Holloway, "Place of Drink"; Jones, "Labour, Society and the Drink Question in Britain, 1918–1939."

34. Oldenburg, *Great Good Place*, 33.

35. Fullagar, O'Brien, and Lloyd, "Feminist Perspectives on Third Places," 29.

36. Steinkuehler and Williams, "Where Everybody Knows Your (Screen) Name," 886.

37. Chess and Shaw, "A Conspiracy of Fishes, or, How We Learned to Stop Worrying about #GamerGate and Embrace Hegemonic Masculinity"; Taylor and Voorhees, "Introduction"; Mortensen, "Anger, Fear, and Games."

38. These examples were all taken from the TIC's 2019 calendar of events.

39. Massey, *For Space*, 12.

40. I engage the notion of container technologies further in chapter 5.

41. LeCavalier, *Rule of Logistics*, 33.

42. LeCavalier, *Rule of Logistics*, 14–18.

43. LeCavalier, *Rule of Logistics*, 78.

44. Augé, *Non-places*.

45. Telford International Centre, "About—TIC."

46. Telford International Centre, "Hall 1 Specifications."

47. LeCavalier, *Rule of Logistics*, 89.

48. Taylor et al., "Public Displays of Play"; Witkowski, "Eventful Masculinities."

49. I had the good fortune of attending this event with Emma Witkowski and T. L. Taylor, two seasoned DreamHack veterans. Our trip was funded by the ReFiguring Innovation in Games (ReFiG) research grant, awarded by the Social Sciences and Humanities Research Council of Canada.

50. This includes the episode central to the reframing work in chapter 1.

51. Several such instances were documented well before (and certainly have been since) the gamergate hate campaign more broadly illuminated the rank misogyny of masculinized gaming culture. These instances are well documented in work by Amanda Cote, Megan Condis, and Amanda Phillips, among others. See Cote, *Gaming Sexism*; Condis, *Gaming Masculinity*; Phillips, *Gamer Trouble*. Chapter 5 examines efforts on the part of women and nonbinary games industry workers to mitigate against such harms at games industry events.

52. Sharma, "Going to Work in Mommy's Basement."

53. Bratich, "Amassing the Multitude," 245; Taylor, "Now You're Playing with Audience Power," 296.

54. Partin, "Bit by (Twitch) Bit," 8.

55. Williams, "About Multiplay."

56. Borowy and Jin, "Pioneering E-sport," 2255

57. Wilde, "Major Esports Host ESL Gaming Is Now Owned by Saudi Arabia"; Ingle, "Money Talks."

58. McLuhan, *Understanding Media.*

59. Sharma, "Introduction," 3.

60. Özden-Schilling, "Chapter 9. Big Grid," 165.

61. McLuhan, *Understanding Media,* 384.

62. Bakke, "Chapter 2. Electricity Is Not a Noun," 31–33.

63. Özden-Schilling, "Chapter 9. Big Grid," 162.

64. Özden-Schilling, "Chapter 9. Big Grid," 165–67.

65. Bowker, "How to Be Universal," 120; Wakeman, *Practicing Utopia.*

4

PLATFORMS

Making Space for Collegiate Esports

Spaced Out

On an early afternoon in fall 2018, I sit anxiously in the virtual reality (VR) lab in North Carolina State University (NCSU)'s D. H. Hill Library, watching the five members of NCSU's *League of Legends* (LoL) collegiate team set up a practice game. Also in the room is the library fellow tasked with running the VR lab and a PhD student with whom I am working. We are all men, and all but one of us (an Asian team member) present as white. The practice session in the VR lab is the culmination of some delicate planning between the team captain, me, the library fellow, and his bosses. At stake is whether the VR lab can work as a makeshift esports facility—a place in which the team can hold practices throughout the week, as well as play scheduled collegiate LoL games every Saturday starting later in the fall and running through February. The lab is clean and sparse, comprised of a small lobby and check-in area and a larger, classroom-sized space with eight PCs capable of running VR setups. It is on the newly renovated second floor of the library, down the hall from a graduate student lounge and adjacent to a well-appointed faculty workspace. Like all the technological resources offered by NCSU libraries, the VR lab is run by generous, knowledgeable, and open-minded staff who capably carry out the mandate of making these resources (and the training required to enjoy them safely) widely available to all members of the NCSU community. On paper and in email, the union of the VR lab and NCSU's competitive LoL team, for which I serve as faculty supervisor, seems perfect. The lab *should* provide something this team has never enjoyed, in stark contrast to an increasing number of teams it has competed against since its founding in 2015: space, or more specifically, ready access to a well-equipped space on campus in which to practice and play. The lab offers multiple high-end gaming rigs with stable and fast internet connections and has open spots available throughout the week, amenable (for the most part) to the team's demanding nightly practice schedule and formal matches on the weekend. The library staff have installed and tested LoL. The team members have arrived on time, and everyone has been pleasantly introduced.

But in practice—as *this* practice makes apparent—the match is not so perfect. It says much about the professionalism of the young men making up the LoL team that my concern over the pairing is entirely one-sided: despite LoL's reputation for toxic behavior, I am not worried about how they will behave or what sort of impression they will make on the library staff. Rather, I am worried about whether the space will accommodate their needs. The team members have all brought their own mice and keyboards, which, perhaps unsurprisingly, are posing issues for the centrally administered gaming machines. Drivers must be installed, administrator credentials must be provided, two-factor authentication must be inputted, and so on. One player's mouse fails to register altogether. This is to say nothing of the graphics and monitor settings, key bindings, and so on that must be adjusted within the LoL game client. For elite players whose competencies are expressed through and dependent on a highly specific configuration of software, hardware, and peripherals, these seemingly minor inconsistencies can lead to pronounced difficulties in executing their game and exercising their skill set.[1]

After the practice session concludes, we part ways. I receive an email from the captain, a couple days later, explaining that they appreciate the effort that I and the library fellow went through to set up the practice session, but the team feels it is just not going to work out. The captain explains that it is mostly a matter of logistics: they all live closer to the southern campus, where much of the more affordable student housing is, and bussing or carpooling to the main campus would add another hour to their daily schedules, to say nothing of the time they would likely have to spend configuring the university machines in the VR lab, geared for students and faculty to run VR applications, for their highly specific setup. The team members feel like the work involved would outweigh the benefits of playing on the more advanced machines. I feel crestfallen, like I have let them down. I assure him that they do not need to feel bad about turning down the arrangement, that it was intended as an experiment.

In the following collegiate LoL 2018–19 season, the team went on to have its greatest success yet, placing as the eighth seed in the collegiate LoL finals and getting flown out to Los Angeles, to the League Championship Series (LCS) studio located on Riot Games' lush campus. It was one of two teams among the final eight to not be supported by a collegiate esports varsity program, and the only one without a dedicated esports venue on campus.

In this chapter, I discuss key moments from my own involvement with this team and other esports activities at NCSU between early 2014 and summer 2022, when I left the university. I situate these moments within the broader trajectory of esports' intensified involvement with postsecondary institutions in the United States and Canada over the past decade. I trace shifting arrangements between the gaming, esports, and technology industries; NCSU's academic administrators, student leaders, staff, and faculty; and the school's competitive gaming communities. As I allude to in the above vignette, these arrangements come into sharp focus when we consider the *spaces* on university campuses that esports have laid claim to over a decade of investment, development, and transformation, from ad hoc arrangements in dorm rooms and classrooms to corporate-sponsored arenas in centrally located student centers.

Space is already highly significant, and highly politicized, in university life. I am following the lead of scholars studying *actual* campus space rather than referring to space in a metaphorical sense when discussing universities.[2] Efforts to make "safe spaces" on universities, particularly for those from underrepresented sexual and racial backgrounds, exist alongside the acknowledgment that university campuses host some of the *least* safe spaces, often for these same folks.[3] Struggles over the cultural and political legacies of racism, colonialism, and imperialism are frequently situated on university campuses—from tearing down the statue of Silent Sam at UNC Chapel Hill in 2018, a potent symbol of North Carolina's not-at-all-distant history of slavery, to renaming Toronto Metropolitan University in 2022 in an effort to distance the institution from its original namesake and his role in establishing the residential school system. The current political economy of universities means that more and more room in both budgets and geographical plans is given over to campus amenities, seen as vital to recruitment efforts, and lucrative science, technology, engineering, and math (STEM) fields, seen as key drivers of the technology, military, and pharmaceutical industries. Fewer resources and less space are given to underfunded programs in the liberal arts and humanities, increasingly maligned as dead weight in postsecondary education's realignment along rationales of economic performativity. These cultural and economic dynamics are layered over not-too-distant histories of spatial segregation on many American campuses and in many disciplines: particular buildings (often, but not always, those associated with technology-related fields), if not whole departments and requisite spaces on campus, in which women, Black people, and other nonwhite, nonmale subjects were not welcome. This is to say nothing of the ostensibly space-saving (and money-saving) characteristics of distance education, a trend that drastically intensified during the COVID-19 pandemic.[4] All of this means that space on most Canadian and American university campuses is contested and costly, and who gets allocated what kinds of space, for what purposes, and with what kinds of administrative, infrastructural, and technological support is *always* political. How, then, have so many universities *made space* for collegiate esports in the years between the great recession and the acute phase of the COVID pandemic (roughly 2009–22)—a time, for so many in higher education, defined by austerity, precarity, contraction, and a struggle to simply hold on to whatever resources, spatial or otherwise, we already had? And inversely, reframing the other central question guiding this book, what kinds of *place-making* do collegiate esports carry out on college campuses? What sorts of relations between space, technologies, students (current, prospective, and former), faculty, university staff, and so on do they require and help produce?

In the account below, I filter insights and experiences from nearly a decade studying, supervising, and helping organize collegiate esports on NCSU's campus. The interconnecting mesh of scholarship I draw from here includes work on the spatial politics of universities (particularly, but not limited to, those in Canada and the United States); recent efforts to institutionalize competitive gaming; the political economic realignment of universities in an era of neoliberal governance; and the exclusionary histories of STEM disciplines, with STEM being positioned as the economic engine of modern universities and, not coincidentally, the rightful home on university campuses for collegiate esports.

The geometric motif for this chapter is the *platform*, understood in its manifold complexity as both a cultural technique of connection, elevation, and visibility and a mechanism of datafication, monetization, and capture.[5] My account of collegiate esports and the spatial politics of Canadian and American universities sketches a dynamic interplay among multiple technical, economic, and cultural platforms over a period of intense (and ongoing) transformation. These platforms include software clients like LoL and other esports-focused games; a host of services like PlayVS that have sprouted up in the past few years to facilitate interscholastic gaming tournaments for a fee; universities themselves and their visions for and physical instantiations of campus-based esports spaces.[6] Uniting all of these is a concern with connecting different constituents (students, sponsors, audiences, and so on) and managing and monetizing these "multisided" connections.[7] In the analysis I present here, the intensive efforts on the part of Canadian and American universities to make space for esports on their campuses is an extension and reflection of the emerging platformization of universities. I understand platformization as "the penetration of *economic, governmental*, and *infrastructural extensions* of digital platforms" into domains in ways that render the university's cultural products—degrees, patents, courses, sports teams, and merchandise, not to mention less obviously tangible experiences—into "contingent commodities."[8] Platformized commodities are contingent, both in the sense of being "contingent on" a select few, immensely powerful digital platforms (Alphabet, Apple, Meta, Amazon, and Microsoft) and in the sense of becoming contingent, which is to say, "malleable, modular in design," and therefore capable of ongoing revision based on steady streams of usage data.[9] As I explain in detail further below, the platformized university enacts and operates through a nexus of transactional arrangements between constituents—students, donors, teaching staff, researchers, alumni, proximal industries—managed by a technocratic managerial class and mediated by an array of datafication techniques (often provided by monopolistic digital platforms), from donor databases to h-indexes to projected enrollments, national and international rankings, user satisfaction surveys, and so on.

For this managerial class, collegiate esports offer a compelling if at times befuddling plug-in to the multisided market of the contemporary university, a means of attracting new students through demonstrating commitment to (and ideally, prowess in) an increasingly popular, youth-focused media industry. That this industry has long been constituted through appeals to tech-savvy young men, often via the deliberate exclusion of others, poses a conundrum for university administrators.[10] On the one hand, catering to a markedly stratified and frequently toxic culture poses both a PR and legal problem.[11] On the other hand, collegiate esports share with STEM— positioned as the economic engine of the platformized university—a preoccupation with a certain idealized subject: the young man who is really good at computers. As it turns out, making space on campus for collegiate esports is not that hard of a sell for many universities, as they are already primed to accommodate the pursuits and proclivities of computationally proficient young men. In this way, the logic of platformization works to intensify the exclusionary histories and patterns of both STEM and esports through their deliberate intersection. As I show below, efforts to make collegiate esports more inclusive and welcoming (and by extension, sustainable) face compounded and intersecting patterns of exclusion. These patterns operate acutely at the level of physical space via the place-making practices of university power brokers, esports promoters, and students alike.

"The Best Team without a Varsity Program"

Back in late 2015 when NCSU's competitive LoL team first formed, the discursive and material positioning of esports on collegiate campuses was only beginning to be articulated. In 2014, the same year that Riot, publisher of LoL, began its intercollegiate league, Robert Morris University established the first esports *program* in North America. It was followed closely by a host of other universities, most prominently UC Irvine (UCI) in 2015. Notably, UCI conceptualized and enacted esports as a multifaceted endeavor, engaging not just players but also researchers, support staff, and a diverse range of student groups. In this, UCI was (and remains, as of 2022) a compelling model for other universities around the United States and Canada, particularly for university administrators, who perhaps see in its efforts to engage multiple audiences a paradigm for how a collegiate esports program can itself become a platform connecting multiple groups and interests. This positioning was evident in the 2018 UCI esports conference, dubbed (somewhat misleadingly) "the first academic conference on esports," and its explicit aim to offer means of connecting esports professionals and practitioners in industry and academia.[12]

It was against this backdrop of emerging institutionalization that I met NCSU's LoL team for the first time, at a local area network (LAN) event in NCSU's student center in early 2016. After a brief conversation and exchange of emails, the team invited me to sign on as faculty adviser so that it could obtain official student club status. I willingly accepted, seeing a chance to extend my then-provisional research with the LoL community on NCSU's campus, with the team's support. From our earliest exchanges, team members were acutely aware of the *power* of space, and access to space, in a university setting: the team captain at the time said that the dream for him and his teammates was to be able to walk into the student athletes' dining hall and be greeted as a fellow athlete. As I have documented elsewhere, this team took its involvement in collegiate LoL very seriously, often practicing for upward of twenty-five hours per week.[13] What is more, team members took on work that has increasingly been given over to dedicated (and often paid) support staff in universities with full-fledged programs: preparing reports on upcoming teams and matches (analyst); arranging scrimmages, coordinating tryouts, promoting and demoting players between the two tiered lineups (coach); keeping track of prize money, sponsorship opportunities, terms and conditions for various tournaments, and the team's institutional status as a student club (manager). In the six years between when they first started (2015) and the initial writing of this chapter (2021), this work became progressively more difficult. Not only did they compete against teams that had some if not all of this work outsourced to nonplayer personnel, but over the years, Riot Games has repeatedly restructured the terms of its annual collegiate LoL season around the resources and capabilities of varsity programs. In this way, Riot's own platform governance works to normalize the program model of collegiate esports, exacerbating what Bryce Stout and I refer to as the "two tiers" of collegiate esports: a marked divide between schools that have varsity programs and those (like NCSU, at the time) that try to field competitive teams through the university's student-run club system.[14] This makes the NCSU LoL team's achievements during this span (2015–21) somewhat remarkable. Team members won over $75,000 USD in scholarship money in tournaments in which the majority of their opponents were well-supported varsity programs. This track record—made possible through resourcefulness and labor—suggests that their self-characterization (stated matter-of-fact in a group interview during their

2017–18 run) as "the best collegiate esports team without a program" was not empty self-aggrandizement.

Integrated Circuit

As Stout and I learned in our interviews with collegiate esports leaders representing clubs and programs in Canada and the United States, access to a dedicated space on campus for practices, scrimmages, tryouts, and league matches is the most immediate and routinely felt distinction between programs and clubs.[15] The failed experiment in fall 2018 with NCSU's VR lab emphasized the importance to collegiate esports participants not just of *access* to infrastructure and gaming setups but of *dedicated resources* for their intensive time investments and technical specifications. Despite not having a dedicated place and time to play, the team did have access to a space on campus for running weekly meetings in which to debrief, study upcoming opponents, discuss team composition, review communication strategies, and so on—all the substantial work of participating in a highly competitive collegiate esports team outside of actually playing. Like the library's VR lab, this space, called Circuit Studio, is located on NCSU's older, main campus. While some of buildings on the main campus date back to the late nineteenth century, Ricks Hall Addition (RHA), which houses Circuit Studio, was constructed in the 1970s.[16] RHA is a building underserved by infrastructure. With only one bathroom, located on the top floor in offices exclusively reserved for another university organization, Circuit Studio's users—not to mention PhD students in the communication, rhetoric, and digital media (CRDM) program, whose cubicle-style offices adjacent to the studio predate the studio by a number of years—must go to one of the adjacent buildings to access plumbing. The space itself features a row of workstations along its east wall, a set of equipment lockers beside two flat touchscreen monitors on its south wall, two large projection screens along its north wall, and a long workbench set in a few feet from the windows along the west wall, creating a separate pathway between the main entrance to the RHA and the graduate student cubicles. As Sarah Read and Jason Swarts note in their analysis of Circuit Studio's planning and development, its opening in 2013 was less the result of "premeditated" and "tactical" moves by key stakeholders than of "accreted, opportunistic rhetorical-political alignments" between researchers, students, and other university personnel.[17] Indeed, the provision of "scarce and rarely available" space on the crowded and aging main campus was largely due to the faculty's opportunistic pitch to the IT director, and subsequently the dean of the college, to use the space as a site for digital humanities research.

It is worth dwelling on the origin story of this studio space for a moment and integrating it with the perspective on the platformized university offered above. During the mid-2010s, small private colleges and some state schools in the United States began establishing dedicated spaces on campuses for esports, providing the architectural and material foundations for varsity programs. Over the same period of time, NCSU's competitive LoL team—acutely aware of its own liminal and undersupported status in relation to many rivals—began holding regular team meetings in Circuit Studio, a space established through the rhetorical sway the digital humanities hold over university administrators concerned about humanities' paltry economic performativity relative to other fields. Humanities research has frequently been cast as nomadic and placeless, requiring very little space, material, or infrastructure, particularly compared to the laboratory-based work of the physical sciences (famously illustrated through Bruno Latour and Steve Woolgar's ethnographies of science labs).[18] In the neoliberal conceptualization of postsecondary knowledge production and its place-making practices (however undermined by the COVID-19 pandemic), humanities research can transpire wherever there is internet access or, failing that, a light to read by. According to Urszula Pawlicka-Deger, digital humanities and adjacent resource-intensive forms of production such as critical making constitute a convincing claim for humanities researchers to occupy campus space and resources at a time when the "massification" of postsecondary education under neoliberal governance makes older, established campuses like NCSU's main campus more crowded.[19] In a spatial sense, set within the political economy of university resources (increasingly tied as they are to economic performativity, real or imagined), the digital humanities have *re-placed* conventional humanities research.

The activities that the LoL club carried out in weekly meetings made robust use of Circuit Studio and its environs. The five members of the main ("alpha") team gathered every Friday evening, pushing some of the mobile desks together into the center of the room to create a meeting and dining table and spreading out bags, laptops, and takeout containers. Sometimes they came with food already in hand, and sometimes they would break halfway through to bring back dinner from numerous fast food and fast casual pizza, Mexican, and Chinese restaurants across the street from the studio. While the rest of the team would eat and chat, usually amicably, the team captain would log into one of the desktop computers using his NCSU credentials and pull up his weekly scouting report. Using the studio's stand-alone console for broadcasting different platforms (game consoles, laptops, desktops) to different screens in the room (one or both of the projectors, one or both of the touchscreen monitors), he would display the week's meeting agenda on one projector while queuing secondary texts on the other. These secondary texts could include recorded videos of matches involving either the NCSU team, previous opponents, or upcoming opponents; the website for upcoming opponents, showing roster and match outcomes; one of the many websites that pull statistical data, via LoL's API, on individual users and the ban rate of particular playable champions; and so on.[20] Meetings usually lasted at least two hours, covering a range of topics from strategies for upcoming matches (during the collegiate LoL season) to club governance and personnel to balancing school and esports.[21] Through these place-making activities, undertaken via an opportunistic arrangement between adviser and team members (I served as faculty adviser and also helped direct the studio) in a space that itself came about through opportunistic arrangements between researchers and university administrators, the studio and the team's identity were coconstituted. Keenly aware of its own lower technical and operational skill relative to top collegiate LoL teams—the "somatic attunements" required for players' microsecond executions of game mechanics—the team dedicated itself to, and prided itself on, understanding the game's "meta."[22] This term refers to a shifting set of optimal strategies centered around selecting (and preventing opponents' selection of) playable characters that either individually or in composition with other playable characters work to tip the scales of a match and make up for deficiencies in operational skill.[23] Within this binary bifurcation of expertise, it is perhaps unsurprising that the LoL team excelled in the competencies for which it had actual, physical *space* to develop. Members did not have space to play together, but they had a place to study together; they advanced remarkably far for a team without a varsity program, primarily by outstudying their opponents.

On the other side of this coconstitutive relationship, the team's regular meetings became a compelling use case for Circuit Studio, showing that the space was serving its mandate to engage in emerging forms of valuable knowledge creation with multiple constituents around the university. Proof was written up in documents for university administrators reporting on the team's technology-intensive activities and referencing scholarship my colleagues and I produced, in part, through collaborating with the team. These accounts circulated through the administrative hierarchies of the university, justifying further investments of equipment and personnel in the form of graduate research assistantships and equipment. Through these relationships, Circuit Studio itself functioned as a platform: a mechanism for connecting multiple audiences, technologies, and knowledge production practices in the pursuit of performativity and elevating these connections, making them visible to audiences within the university and beyond.

Esports at Maryville University: Elevating the Bunker

In the spring of 2019, at the conclusion of the same collegiate LoL season for which we had tried to orchestrate use of the VR lab, the NCSU team secured the eighth and final spot in collegiate LoL finals. The team was flown out to Los Angeles to Riot's LCS studio, a media production venue primarily used for professional matches. As the eighth seed, NCSU faced off against top seed and defending champion Maryville University. The team lost the best of three series two games to zero, concluding what for team members was a dream season and the most success they had enjoyed. Maryville, for its part, went on to win the tournament decisively, claiming the collegiate championship for the second year in a row and the third time in four years. Shortly after their victory, two members of Maryville were signed by the Golden Guardians, an esports organization owned by the NBA's Golden State Warriors, to join their professional LoL team. This marked another major milestone for a collegiate esports organization built (literally) from the ground up to win. I want to dwell on Maryville University's highly competitive esports program for a moment to offer it as a paradigmatic example of one notable way in which postsecondary institutions are making space for collegiate esports in the platformized university.

Maryville University is a private college outside of St. Louis, Missouri. Though it is historically a liberal arts college and emphasizes its "innovative liberal arts foundation for all our students," the school has made a concerted push into both online education and STEM fields in recent years, launching a computer science degree in 2021.[24] The esports program was established in

2015, making it one of the first in North America. In 2020, the program of-fered players a minimum $2,000 USD scholarship package, with additional scholarship money provided based on player skill as determined by LoL's extensive player metrics. During the 2020–21 season, the team was sup-ported by four paid staff. As with the members of the LoL team that season, all personnel were men. The program director, assistant director, and coach were all former professional esports players; the coach had worked with the Golden Guardians coaching team before joining Maryville. The program also had a dedicated social media content creator and videographer. As of the time of this writing, it was housed in the Esports Performance Center, which the program's website describes as "a centerpiece for the Varsity program" and "one of the premier training centers for collegiate esports." The space is further characterized by its infrastructural and technological features: "a lag less environment, top-of-the line peripherals, and the best PCs on the market" as well as a "lounge area and dining space" so players "can perform the best whenever they need to."[25] The building looks, from the outside, like a barracks—gray walls of corrugated steel with no windows. Pictures from the inside, however, give it the appearance of a kind of building-sized, esports-themed *bunker*, using the term introduced in chapter 2 to describe an aggressively functionalist aesthetic. At the same time, this esports bunker is, like many of the gaming *cabinets* I considered, intended as much for visual consumption as for prolonged periods of intensive play. Judging from the promotional photographs on its website and social media, everything in the space seems color coded with the red, white, and black of the team's logo, from players' jerseys and face masks to the walls and chairs. Like the venues chosen for the LAN events examined in chapter 3, it is a space constructed for infrastructural connections to digitally distributed audiences—a plat-form for producing esports content rather than establishing local connec-tions to other campus constituents.[26]

My ethnographic work with the NCSU LoL team showed their activities in Circuit (and elsewhere) to be heavily platform contingent: reliant on Cir-cuit itself as a physical platform, as well as on the capacities and services of giant software platforms like Google, Riot, and Riot's parent company, Ten-cent, the massive Chinese technology and entertainment company. Despite not being able to peer inside the black box of Maryville's top-ranked colle-giate esports program outside of what its dedicated content creator shows us, we can see how it is differently, though perhaps even more intensely, platform contingent. What we *do* see of its activities is entirely prescribed by the platform logics of Twitter, Facebook, and Instagram. On its highly active Twitter feed in particular, a large number of posts from the 2020–21 season were images of varsity players in some sports-related pose or another, bedecked in team jerseys against a black and red backdrop, with information about either an upcoming match or results of a recent match, sponsor logos displayed prominently. It is a program built from the ground up for the platformized university, marshaling tremendous amounts of human, infrastructural, and technical resources to produce cultural commodities that traffic in the aestheticization of the privileged subject of both esports and computer-related STEM fields: the young white or Asian man who excels at highly specialized computational skills.

Lights, Camera, Subsidies: Courting Esports on Campus

In the early fall of 2019, almost a year after the unsuccessful tryout of the VR lab and half a year after NCSU's trip to the collegiate finals and loss to Maryville, I was contacted by one of the NCSU employees responsible for developing partnerships with outside businesses. They invited me to accompany them on a tour of the campus arranged for the visiting representatives of a Europe-based esports organization. An initial telephone conversation with this colleague laid out the situation: the esports organization was looking at setting up a production facility somewhere in the eastern United States and was shopping for options. We would be touring a prospective location on Centennial Campus, which was set up in the 1980s as a dedicated home for many STEM departments (notably, the computer science school) as well as the Hunt Library, NCSU's architectural landmark that opened in 2013. As none of the NCSU personnel on the tour had knowledge of esports, I was told that my role would be to represent faculty and students and demonstrate the vibrant interest in esports at NCSU. I was one of two faculty members participating on the tour, and the only one from NCSU's College of Humanities and Social Sciences. We were joined by a handful of other stakeholders: a local esports entrepreneur, a representative from Raleigh's business bureau, and two staff members from the university's architecture office. After meeting the esports organization's representatives outside the business development office and exchanging brief pleasantries, we walked over to one of the buildings on Centennial constructed specifically for business development partnerships. These are arrangements in which local businesses (predominantly in the technology sector) are encouraged to set up shop on campus, benefiting from access to NCSU's amenities, proximity to potential recruits and hiring mechanisms like job fairs, and other forms of "locational capital."[27] Typically, NCSU does not own these buildings outright; they are owned and their leases operated by a third-party firm.

On the way to the site, the local entrepreneur explained to me what the esports organization was after: space and resources for an esports production facility that would host broadcasted tournaments for a total of twelve weeks each year. During these periods, players and support staff would stay in accommodations close to the facility. They would use the facility for training and tournament play, which would be professionally produced and live streamed. There were challenges to this arrangement. Because the organization would only be using the space for twelve weeks out of the year, it was looking for a heavily subsidized lease, hence the need to get both the university and the city of Raleigh on board. The university, for its part, needed compelling ideas for how to use the space the other forty weeks of the year, particularly since NCSU owned the building, unlike more typical arrangements. It would need to come up with activities consistent with the school's mission of community engagement and service. In other words, the multiple sides of this arrangement—city, university, local business, foreign esports organization—were pursuing a platform that could serve multiple needs, negotiating for the economic conditions on which such a platform might be based, and imagining what kind of content could make use of the platform for the majority of time each year that it was not being run as a professional esports production studio. This was a tall order. As faculty members involved in esports, my colleague and I were positioned as potential content creators: parties that could, through research and teaching, come up with uses for the space during the long off time between tournaments and in doing so help shore up an economic rationale for the city's and university's investments.

Contrary to this chapter's geometrical motif of the raised platform, the site we visited that day was sunken below ground. It occupied the basement of one of the corporate partnership buildings, and at the time of tour, it was *very* unfinished: plastic tarps laying on top of a bare dirt floor, large square concrete pillars supporting a very high ceiling, exposed pipes hanging down from steel cables, and a loading bay next to the door through which we entered. It was a brutalist, unfinished cousin of the convention center I discussed in the last chapter, a raw canvas for imagining what a university-based multimedia esports production facility could or ought to be, what sorts of place-making activities might animate it. Tellingly, on arriving at the site, the senior representative from the esports organization said that what was needed most from the space was ample access to material infrastructure—"lights and wires." The content of the space, the *stuff* that would use all that infrastructure, would be supplied by the organization and be mostly modular in function: movable dividing walls for creating casting booths, lounges, green rooms, press rooms, and so on; mobile computer desks and chairs; and of course gaming setups and broadcasting equipment.

At the time, I was very excited at the prospect of having an esports production facility that would be unused by its main tenant for most of the year. Even though the esports organization itself was not in the business of producing collegiate esports, it was difficult not to see the potential facility on campus as an obvious support structure for the LoL team and other esports groups at NCSU. The deal did not go through—the esports organization's plans scuttled, as so much else, by the pandemic—but it had the effect of putting collegiate esports on the radar of university administration, an effect I examine in more detail below. First, I want to explore what this courtship reveals about contemporary American and Canadian universities: their changing cultural function, their relationship to local industries (and to technology and media industries especially), and their capacity to serve as engines of social and economic (in)equality. What follows is an attempt to historicize this tentative courtship between university administrators, city tourism officials, faculty, and the esports industry, as we stood on the dirt floor of an unfinished and strongly infrastructuralist space and imagined its potentials. What histories was this moment a part of—and how might we understand it in a longer history of universities' gifts of land, both given and received?

Land, Space, and the Value(s) of Public Universities

Like most other American land-grant universities, NCSU was a beneficiary of the Morrill Act, signed by Abraham Lincoln in 1862 for the purpose of supplying land to educational institutions that would focus on instruction in fields of science, engineering, and (increasingly industrialized) agriculture, though not to the exclusion of "classical" liberal arts studies.[28] This massive state investment in higher education was a response to numerous factors threatening the US economy, including the abolition of slavery, and a perceived skills gap between American workers and their counterparts in more rapidly industrializing countries like Germany and Britain.[29] Universities like NCSU that were not given direct access to land on which to build were provided vouchers, or scrips, for land located in the central and western United States. In some cases, universities held on to these scrips, and in other cases, as with NCSU, the land was sold briskly, the capital that it generated used to set up endowments, pay for new buildings, and so on. The land-grant mission has become enshrined in NCSU's strategic planning, expressed as a commitment to serving the common good, engaging with and supporting local communities, and championing research that has strong practical applications, particularly in the areas of agriculture, science, technology, and engineering.[30] At the same time, however, it is crucial to acknowledge the mechanisms through which this historic transfer of wealth came about; as a collaborative study between academic researchers and the *High Country News* meticulously illustrates, the vast majority of land granted to postsecondary institutions by the Morrill Act was expropriated from Indigenous nations, "dubiously acquired" by the US government through faithless treaties and violent seizures to be then gifted to the nation's fledgling economic engines.[31] Recasting land-grant universities in this colonial history as land-*grab* universities, the authors of this report write: "Hundreds of violence-backed treaties and seizures extinguished Indigenous title to over 2 billion acres of the United States. Nearly 11 million of those acres were used to launch 52 land-grant institutions. The money has been on the books ever since, earning interest, while a dozen or more of those universities still generate revenue from unsold lands."[32]

The authors insist that their work is not meant to diminish the numerous ways that land-grant universities have enriched lives; rather, it allows us to acknowledge that such work has not come without a cost, contributing to the dispossession and brutalization of Indigenous nations. This fundamental ambivalence regarding the origins of land-grant/land-grab universities, not to mention the values they espouse and the value they offer, serves as useful context when considering the logics through which contemporary universities *make space* for certain activities and communities, including esports. As I explore below, such gifts always come with a price, particularly through the ways universities participate in a neoliberal economy that traffics heavily in structural violence against Black and Latinx communities.[33]

Acknowledging land-grab universities' historical indebtedness to the forced dislocation of Indigenous communities might allow us to become better attuned to more subtle legacies of exclusion and disenfranchisement that continue to shape their contemporary existence as engines of social and economic growth. This is particularly crucial considering current transformations in higher education, in which growth is measured primarily in terms of economic performativity—a profound shift signaled by Jean-Francois Lyotard's "report on knowledge" to the Québec Conseil des Universités, which became *The Postmodern Condition*.[34] The transformation Lyotard charted in the late 1970s is characteristic of what numerous scholars and educational activists describe as the neoliberal reconfiguration of the status of knowledge—and the function of the university—in a globalized, digitized world. Neoliberalism is the "hegemonic discourse of western nation states" that "has become dominant and effective in world economic relations as a consequence of super-power sponsorship."[35] As a social and economic set of logics, it "imposes free-market fundamentalist values on all human interactions."[36] Under neoliberalism, the subject is no longer the citizen but the consumer, a self-interested individual whose freedom is reflected and constituted through consumer choice and entrepreneurial acumen (hence the recent appropriation of "hustling" and "grinding" by hegemonic masculinities mentioned in the introduction). Jennifer Hamer and Clarence Lang further characterize neoliberalism in these terms, which I have quoted at length here in order to capture the authors' vital attention to the disparities that neoliberalism both creates and exacerbates.

> A shift from an industrial economy to one driven by speculative finance capital; market deregulation and the privatization of public goods; the corporate demand for higher profits at the expense of livable working conditions and pay for working- and middle-class people; the rolling back of social welfare protections in order to render all labor contingent and insecure; the denial of social compassion and shared civic responsibility in favor of a social Darwinist politics of disposability; growing accumulations of income and wealth among a few, facilitated by regressive tax cuts, anti-union laws, and other subsidies to the elite "1 Percent"; debilitating household debt for the "99 Percent" majority, and heightened socioeconomic class stratification; the creeping debasement of political life through the purchasing of electoral candidates and legislation; and a politics of austerity and punishment reinforced through state-sponsored surveillance and brutality.[37]

For universities, the embrace of neoliberal policies often entails (and is catalyzed by) drastic reductions in state funding; expansion on the one hand of a technocratic managerial class and on the other, of precarious and contract-based teaching positions, coupled with diminishment of tenure-track positions and attacks on the tenure system more generally; measurement of university success in terms of economic productivity, as expressed in quantifiable metrics (everything from student credit hours to citation counts); a transactional approach to the relationship between universities and students; and increasing reliance on private companies to deliver everything from plagiarism detection tools to trash disposal. Henry A. Giroux, educational philosopher, describes neoliberalism's "mantra" in relation to higher education as follows: "Higher education should serve corporate interests rather than the public good."[38]

Scholars have been alerting us to the neoliberal makeover of higher education for at least four decades. Recent work in this vein, however, suggests that key aspects of the neoliberalism of postsecondary education—namely, an emphasis on entrepreneurialism, a transactional understanding of the relationship between universities and their various constituents, and the use of statistical data to guide decision-making—are intensifying and morphing through the rise of platforms. Gary Hall describes this transformation as the "Uberfication" of the university, as academic research and instruction become at once less secure and less attainable for most workers and more subject to quantified performance metrics.[39] Hall's consideration of how academic work is being recast as precarious content creation parallels scholarship on platformization, in which increasing sectors of the economy are at once more contingent on software platforms and also more modular, quantifiable, and monetizable—more contingent on the logics and economic imperatives of platforms. In a similar vein, we can consider how postsecondary administrators (and educators) are increasingly turning to datafied systems run by for-profit platforms, covering everything from tools to help students shop for universities based on a range of quantified metrics to AI-driven grading and plagiarism detection applications to course management systems. This trend toward platform contingency was vastly intensified by the pandemic, as third-party companies raced to put out applications that could plug into or fully supplant existing course delivery systems. Under these conditions, the university is becoming a kind of metaplatform, a system capable of supporting and connecting any number of quantifiable and data-driven solutions to content creators of all kinds, from software developers to instructors to students to donors to alum to administrators, all for the purpose of creating more value.

STEMification and the Engineering of Inequality

Within the increasingly platformized university environment, STEM reigns supreme. Engineering and agricultural science were regarded as key mechanisms for economic growth in the push for industrial universities fueled by the Morrill Act and its distribution of stolen lands. In the 1980s, the Reagan administration—a key orchestrator of the West's "super-powered sponsorship" of neoliberalism—once again pushed for public schools and universities to focus on engineering and the hard sciences, along with widespread adoption of quantifiable assessments and standardized testing.[40] This push was trumpeted as a means of catching up to other nations, particularly Japan, that were overtaking the United States in key areas of the economy. More pertinently, it allowed business groups to heavily influence educational policy under the guise of educational commissions, recalibrating public education toward the goal of providing students with employable skills and thereby outsourcing much of the costs of private sector job training to taxpayers. The key difference between the emphasis in postsecondary education on engineering and technical skills in the late 1800s versus the late 1900s was the main beneficiary. Educational reforms seen as leading to the betterment of the nation and the "common man" in the Progressive Era became, in the 1980s, mechanisms for corporate cost cutting. Situated within this broader historical context, Ajay Sharma calls the more recent push for STEM education by politicians and educational policy makers (backed by corporate interests) throughout the late 2000s and early 2010s an instance of "zombie categories": the recurrence of political and economic concepts, such as market liberalism, trickle-down economics, or the nation-state, that "seem alive and important to supporters but in fact fail when matched with available evidence and current scholarship."[41] Sharma points to statistics showing that the United States is in fact overproducing STEM graduates relative to demand for positions and suggests that the recent "STEM bandwagon" is *not* about a skills gap in technical and scientific fields in the United States but about something else—principally, providing the "chemical, pharmaceutical, technology, and aerospace" industries even more sway in demanding and implementing educational reform.[42] We might find a further rationalization for what Sharma calls the "STEMification" of education in the efforts of university administrators to maximize tuition revenues. STEM fields are a big draw for international students, and at most public universities in the United States and universities in Canada, international students can be charged far more for tuition than residents. The United States may not need STEM workers, but US universities need STEM tuition revenue, particularly from international students.

As Bryce Stout and I learned from our interviews with campus esports leaders, a certain trend toward STEMification is also at work in collegiate esports, as university administrators and esports program directors find ways to sell competitive gaming to reluctant or unfamiliar university leadership. The logic here is relatively straightforward and reductive: esports is like sports, but for STEM.[43] Esports, in this view, showcase the computational virtuosity of young men competing in an ostensibly meritocratic arena.[44] Success in this arena depends on the same characteristics that make for good workers in marquee STEM fields such as software development, data analytics, and military intelligence: an ability to work effectively in groups, under intense pressure, on attentionally demanding computer-based tasks. From this perspective, esports are an aestheticization and dramatization of competencies regarded as essential to national economic superiority in much the same way other systems of para-athletic university-based competition helped showcase the kinds of skills universities could develop in support of economic or cultural imperialism.[45] We might see collegiate esports carrying out a similar function with regard to STEM-based competencies as twentieth-century debate clubs played with regard to Cold War–era diplomacy. Where debate clubs dramatized print-based literacies associated with rehearsing and weaponizing facts in rhetorical strikes against a worldview constructed as the antithesis to capitalism, esports dramatize team-based competition in computational virtuosity, played on and produced through the dominant economic engine of our time: software platforms. Esports and STEM share more than the capacity of one to act as ritualized arena for the other, however; both have been characterized by the long-standing exclusion and marginalization of women and racial minorities. The specific reasons for this are too many and too complex to list here, but they find shared histories in the deep—and deliberately forged—discursive and material connections between whiteness, masculinity, and computation.[46]

At the same time, the STEMification of esports deploys a very particular set of racial and ethnic dynamics. There is a potent racial imaginary circulating in the globalized esports industry, in which South Korean (and increasingly, Chinese) dominance in LoL at the highest levels of play is regarded as an acute threat to US-based—which is to say, white—teams and esports organizations.[47] As Matthew Jungsuk Howard notes, esports publishers have attempted to level the ethnic playing field through mechanisms like region locking—tethering player accounts to their "home" geographic region and restricting the means through which professional players can compete outside their designated region—and banning play strategies favored by South Korean teams.[48] At the same time, the United States makes it possible for esports athletes to enter the country on P-1 (athlete) visas, and in 2022, the Biden administration announced a series of changes to immigration law making it easier "to attract global talent" to STEM fields, deemed "critical to the prosperity, security, and health" of the country.[49] Many of these changes target international students in particular. The combination of esports' racial imaginary and the economic imperative of neoliberal universities sends a clear message, even if few university administrators seem willing to say the quiet part out loud: collegiate esports programs are being discursively framed as a means to attract international STEM students, particularly from China and South Korea.[50] In fact, a startup called Esports Connect International—yet another platform—purports to connect esports coaches in American universities with non-American esports players, a service it offers free to players but with an annual fee ($250 USD) for coaches.[51] Through the interplay of these logics, an old pattern reemerges. Asian labor is positioned as infrastructural to America's economic prosperity, even as it is viewed with suspicion and scorn.[52]

Dislocating Collegiate Esports

Looking back at that moment on the tarp-covered dirt floor of the would-be esports production facility on Centennial Campus, I now understand that these histories and contemporary transformations were in play. University administrators, faculty members, economic developers, and industry professionals had been pulled together by the connective potentials of economic growth to find out if we could bring esports to NCSU's campus in a way that would satisfy our individual needs and constituents (whether students, sponsors, players, or taxpayers). The grounds of our interaction were conditioned by the legacies of faithless dispossession of Indigenous lands, provided as startup capital for the land-grant university; the firm insistence, recurrent for over a century under different guises, that universities such as NCSU exist for the economic improvement of society (or of corporations, which, under neoliberalism, is the same thing) and that the surest path to prosperity is a focus on technical fields; the histories of deliberately constructed exclusions that characterize STEM fields; and the old reliance, under novel technical conditions, on the exploitation of Asian labor. Such are the grounds on which esports at NCSU *could* have been constructed. How might we locate new grounds on which to build collegiate esports? Before answering this question, I turn to the profound dislocation suffered by both the esports industry and postsecondary education due to the pandemic.

COVID-19 shuttered universities across the United States and Canada and throughout the world, and the resultant scramble toward (more) online teaching proved a tremendous boon for educational software developers—though this amounts to a drop in the bucket compared to the tremendous economic and cultural power the pandemic provided platform oligarchs, as substantial sectors of the economy become even more platform dependent.[53] In an industry for which "disruption" is a byword for financial opportunity, the pandemic has been a generation-defining disruption. For a vast number of university educators, adopting software that bundles educational interactions and pedagogical strategies into discretized, modular platforms became a more expedient option than adapting to the different temporalities, affects, and labor associated with deliberate and effective online teaching. Stay-at-home orders slowed, almost to a halt, the production of quantifiable outputs on the part of university researchers. For some whose productivity relied directly on routine access to university-based resources such as laboratories, provisions were made to allow them on campus in limited fashion. Broadly, though, the idea that much of the work associated with contemporary, digitized knowledge creation is placeless (particularly, but not exclusively, humanities research) was profoundly undermined. University workers fortunate enough to already have, and be able to maintain, stable employment had to negotiate the banal and mundane effects of social isolation, childcare and the domestic labor of virtual schooling, and heightened anxiety, all of which undercut our ability to generate value for the platformized university.

As for collegiate esports, Riot canceled its immediate tournament plans for 2019–20, as did many other collegiate and professional esports organizations. The publisher redistributed the prize money for winning each of the collegiate divisions equally to every team that had placed in the top eight of their respective divisions prior to the lockdown (including NCSU in the South division). For the LoL team at NCSU, this was a silver lining to what was already going to be a transitional time. One of its core members had graduated the year before, with the team captain—who carried out the bulk of the work of managing, compiling and analyzing data, and coaching—set to graduate in spring 2021. Riot made plans to resume the season in 2021–22, with the top thirty-two teams in the country eligible for the final tournament. Limiting its prize pool, Riot awarded money to only the top sixteen teams in the country. At the outset of the division playoffs, NCSU's new team captain informed me that the team's goal was to place in the top sixteen nationally, but despite placing in the top eight in the South division again, the team was not able to win its way into the thirty-two-team nationals bracket. No doubt the loss of some seasoned and high-ranked players contributed to this disappointing finish, but so did the lack of access to Circuit Studio, the shared space where the team normally carried out, in person, the work that had thus far defined it. Despite being a formally placeless team in the sense of having no dedicated arena on campus to train and play, members nonetheless suffered for the shuttering of the university's physical spaces during lockdown.[54] In its own indirect and localized way, the team's struggles undermined the prevailing opinion on the prospects for esports during and after the pandemic, which held that esports—being borderless, wholly digital, virtual—would thrive under pandemic conditions.

Will Partin's work on the faulty premises supporting what he calls the "continuity of competition" aligns neatly with many of the claims in this book.[55] Looking at the decision on the part of ESL ("one of the largest esports tournament organizers in the world") to move its ESL One *Dota 2* tournament from its production studios in Los Angeles to an online format, Partin shows how the new structure of the tournament—and the subsequent personnel decisions made by participating teams—reflected a concern for the acute effects of geographical (dis)location. Specifically, rather than hold an in-person tournament with teams flown in from around the world, ESL designed a "multi-region tournament in which teams from each region competed against each other," with the winners of each crowned regional champion. Partin explains that the teams were grouped not according to "Westphalian political geography of bounded nation states" but by proximity to *servers*: the media infrastructures that make networked play possible. While these servers may have "supra-national reach," they nonetheless introduce greater lag the more distance and the more nodes they have to travel; according to Partin, the "~60 millisecond latency disadvantage" experienced by, say, a North American team playing against a European team on a European server would, for elite players, constitute a "game-losing handicap." Partin recounts the decision on the part of the Swedish esports organization Ninjas in Pyjamas (NIP) to release one of its star players (Sahil "Universe" Arora, one of the most successful esports players in terms of prize winnings) from its *Dota 2* team due not to Arora's underperformance but rather to his physical location in the United States at the time of the tournament. Arora had an *infrastructural* handicap preventing him from competing on a level playing field with and against European teams.[56] As Partin shows, professional esports are about as "placeless" for inconveniently located players under lockdown orders as online instruction is for students who rely on subpar internet access, say, because they moved back with family in rural North Carolina during the pandemic or share a crowded connection and bad ISP with other residents of a student housing complex and cannot regularly go to campus.

Relocating Collegiate Esports

Beginning in 2021, against this backdrop of platform-dependent dislocation and platform-boosting disruption in esports and academia, NCSU began to take tentative steps toward a more institutionalized presence for esports on its campus. Tasked by upper administration to determine the feasibility of an esports program, an esports workgroup was formed that included multiple administrators from the university's athletics department, partnership office, and licensing department, me and a faculty member from computer science, and three colleagues who were, at the time, PhD students. Given my experience, I was regarded as the workgroup's resident expert on collegiate esports culture. When the group was in its formative stage over the course of its first few meetings, this status allowed me (in concert with my PhD student colleagues) to shape the group's baseline understanding of esports. We made sure to emphasize that collegiate esports can link to numerous academic disciplines beyond STEM; that inclusivity, equity, and labor exploitation are fundamental concerns for collegiate esports; and that the interests of for-profit platforms, both game publishers like Riot and third-party intermediaries that organize intercollegiate tournaments, do not necessarily align with the interests of collegiate esports programs and communities. In what follows, as a way of concluding this chapter, I present these considerations as articles that might constitute something as practical as a charter for collegiate esports programs, at NCSU or elsewhere. They might also serve as a manifesto outlining how to "make space" in collegiate esports, securing sustainability and autonomy in the face of the monopolistic impulses of commercial platforms and the vagaries of the esports industry.[57]

1. Success Is about Growth and Participation, not Winning

Universities such as Maryville and Harrisburg have constructed what appears to be a winning formula for fielding highly competitive esports teams: focus efforts on a small number of popular games; recruit players based primarily on quantified and individualized metrics; and dedicate space, infrastructure, and personnel to the exclusive support of the program. Central to this formula is the mobility of players and support staff between collegiate programs and professional esports. Recruiting from the professional ranks brings a certain credibility and skill level to a college program, while having collegiate players put their postsecondary education on hold in order to go pro is seen as indicative of a program's quality. Proponents of this model point to the idea that winning is the most surefire way to get reluctant faculty and staff "on the esports bandwagon."[58] There are a number of limitations and pitfalls associated with this approach, not least of which is its alignment of amateur athletic activity with the toxic and exclusionary models associated with professional esports (not to mention high-profile intercollegiate athletics). In more immediate and concrete terms, the model relies on a haphazard "talent pipeline" for esports, with little agreement among publishers, organizations, and players regarding who should foot the bill, and how, for systematically and sustainably developing skilled players.[59] As Will Partin notes, professional sports leagues like the NBA and NFL have been tremendously successful in co-opting collegiate sports, using public funding to propel the production of athletes capable of playing in their leagues. Such a model is not viable for esports both because of the geographical specificity of their model (only the United States and Canada have yet developed collegiate esports programs) and because esports players are often already at or past their prime by the time they are college aged. This explains why esports organizations are eager to push into high schools, which offer a more direct route to talent than college-aged players and their conflicting aspirations and claims on time. As it stands, however, the biggest pipeline for top esports talent remains the communities that play them, which leads to at least two fundamental challenges for any esports program—but particularly programs focused on winning above all. The first challenge, as Partin explains, is that esports are still bound by the lifecycles of video games, which can fade out of popularity quickly and are wholly owned by publishers.[60] An esports title's popularity may decline precipitously, its existing pipeline drying up faster than a collegiate program focused on a small number of titles can pivot to a new game, or a publisher might decide to charge universities a licensing fee for participating in its tournaments, staking a more direct claim on educational funding. Either scenario could provide a major setback to a collegiate program that defines success primarily in terms of ability to field very good teams in a select few games. What is more, as Bryce Stout and I observed, relying on esports communities alone to produce esports talent leaves little possibility for altering stark disparities along lines of gender, race, and ethnicity.[61] It is no accident that among the more elite collegiate esports teams, there are almost no women. For numerous reasons well documented by scholars of gender, esports, and gaming, when we leave esports communities to their own devices, they produce top talent that is almost universally male and steeped in technomasculinity, even as they insist that competitive gaming is a meritocratic domain.[62] Under such infrastructural conditions, toxicity flows through these pipelines as readily as talent and cannot be easily filtered out within the current cultures of competitive play. For universities that trumpet commitment to inclusivity and diversity—and that are legally mandated (at least in the United States, under Title IX) to provide equal opportunities and resources to men and women—the naturalized production of privilege and exclusion within the gaming communities that produce talent should give pause.

Esports programs could chip away at this toxic meritocracy by deemphasizing winning, shifting the metric of success from teams' records toward less immediately quantifiable outcomes.[63] This strategy might seem at odds with the push to legitimize collegiate esports on the basis of their connection with both college athletics and professional esports; indeed, sidestepping these connections is the point. The rush to professionalize collegiate esports—to field a winning team as expediently as possible—undermines their potential as sites for learning and positive social change. Where the vast majority of students at universities with programs like Maryville engage with their esports program primarily through social media, programs like UCI and Ohio State make efforts to meaningfully involve students in the use of their centrally located facilities and in the life of the program. Following their lead, the success of an esports program might be measured in terms of the opportunities it provides students for personal and professional development, not just as players but as analysts, nutritionists, broadcasters, event organizers, psychologists, and so on. For players specifically, the quality of a program might be measured not in terms of how skilled they are coming into a program but in their growth over the course of their involvement. This would shift focus away from recruiting and retaining players who already have a high skill ceiling and toward training and developing players who show an interest in participating. In other words, it would ground collegiate esports in values associated with learning and growth rather than winning. Doing so would make space in esports programs—at least in theory—for a greater diversity of players, particularly if making deliberate attempts to recruit players from backgrounds typically underrepresented in esports, such as through the contentious but very well-grounded efforts by organizations such as AnyKey to support esports teams and tournaments for women and nonbinary gamers.

2. Esports Are Media Productions

An oft-repeated but misleading definition of esports is that they are games played competitively. This definition ignores the constitutive role that organization and spectatorship play in the history of esports and their contemporary economies and cultures. If I sit down and play a game of LoL with other random players on the internet, I am not "doing" esports any more than I would be participating in television production through the act of telling a scripted joke or talking to myself while baking a cake. Competitive gaming *becomes* esports through the technical construction and engagement of an audience, which necessitates at the very least an infrastructure for arranging and presenting the spectacle.[64] More likely these days, it involves infrastructures for digitally recording, storing, and distributing competitive gameplay. Esports are media productions, and collegiate esports programs can become truly robust and compelling sites of connection and collaboration if they fully embrace this reality. Key examples here are the esports programs at the University of Utah and Ohio State, both of which offer internship opportunities for students interested in multimedia production.

Doubling down on the acknowledgment that esports are media productions could involve positioning communication and media arts departments as partners for esports programs, on par with STEM departments and collegiate athletics departments. Aligning esports programs more closely with communication and media arts would not only provide students with more professionalization opportunities; it would also place collegiate esports in close institutional proximity with a field that has a better track record of gender and racial inclusivity than STEM disciplines.[65] Furthermore, developing a strong infrastructure on campus for in-house esports media production might serve as an institutional and discursive bulwark against efforts on the part of game publishers and predatory third-party services to tightly control and monetize, if not monopolize, the production of esports-related content.

3. Esports Are Sites of Connection

Esports represent a vibrant, lucrative, and increasingly mainstream cultural industry. As the narratives and analyses throughout this chapter demonstrate, they pull people together, like any good platform; *how* they do this and to what effect is open not only to academic debate but also to academic intervention. Heavily professionalized programs like Maryville or Harrisburg establish connectivity by making their esports programs directly accessible to only a select few but consumable by many through social media and livestreaming platforms. Their success is highly platform contingent, both in terms of their emphasis on being very good at a select few games and of how they circulate the outcomes of their ample, if narrowly focused, investments. Their campus esports facilities remain black boxes, inaccessible and inscrutable save for what they show on social media. Programs like UCI and Ohio State are much more open by comparison, which is not to say they eschew social media or are not concerned with fielding competitive teams. Rather, their esports facilities are placed in central locations on campus and can be used during off hours by individuals or groups; UCI's arena, for instance, feels like a cybercafé or PC Bang, albeit decked out in the cheerful blue and yellow of the university logo. These programs make deliberate efforts to engage other groups on campus, from training staff and students in ways that draw on best practices of campus social justice advocacy groups to conducting outreach events aimed at generating interest in esports among underrepresented communities.[66]

In keeping with the theme of this book, it is difficult to overstate the role of space in determining how a collegiate esports program operates as a platform. Esports programs housed in central locations, or as a part of other campus-based entities with a mission to support a broad and inclusive community, such as libraries and student centers, are *physically* and *institutionally* much better positioned to develop relatively open systems of exchange and collaboration with a host of other campus communities. This platform seems more desirable, if not sustainable, for esports than a black-boxed bunker accessible for most only through Twitter or Twitch.

4. Codes of Conduct Work

If put into practice, the articles sketched out above would go a long way toward making collegiate esports a more open and welcoming space, but such changes require labor, time, and capital from multiple campus-based constituents with different priorities and aspirations for esports. In terms of immediate and concrete impacts, evidence strongly shows that a code of conduct—clearly stated and unavoidably visible—is an effective check against the kinds of toxicity that have become naturalized in many esports cultures, which current talent pipelines pipe in alongside skilled players unless otherwise checked.[67] In my research with Bryce Stout, we learned that most varsity *program* leaders do not fret too much over what their code of conduct includes, where it is posted, and how it is enforced, since they do not have the kind of diversity among players that might produce the kind of racist or misogynist aggression and resentment a code of conduct would be most effective in helping resolve.[68] On the other hand, the *club* leaders we spoke with often went out of their way to post a code of conduct prominently in both their physical and digital meeting spaces, this visibility proving an effective deterrent against the toxicity that too often accompanies competitive gameplay.

Platform Power

The articles of the part manifesto / part charter I have sketched out here are explicitly concerned with how collegiate esports might become a site to truly *do* esports differently, exercising the capacity of universities to intervene into, rather than replicate, the exclusionary, toxic, and exploitative mode of cultural production currently practiced by professional esports. For my own part, I continue to waver between cynicism and cautious optimism regarding the potential (and willingness) of universities to effect real, if localized, change in this regard. In the summer of 2022, when I left NCSU, the university organized a response to the $16 million USD in funding they were "gifted" by North Carolina's Republican-controlled state legislature to build a state-of-the-art regional home for esports on NCSU's campus.[69] The funding package included $4 million USD for an esports truck but nothing for operating expenses—that is, for the labor and equipment required to make esports happen. Despite the unfavorable circumstances, the team tasked with building the program remained committed to considerations of inclusivity and diversity in all aspects of planning, including—especially—considerations around space. The commitment and creativity of colleagues like those I had at NCSU has pushed me (back) into a mode of cautious optimism.

I want to conclude this chapter by emphasizing that the considerations outlined above, meant to curtail esports' current inclinations toward exclusion and exploitation, operate at the same time as checks against the encroaching power of digital media platforms—the power to dictate the terms by which we connect and collaborate. In a university setting, this power shapes the conditions under which we engage in teaching and learning, determining which kinds of knowledge have value and which do not. I have framed collegiate esports, and the willingness and ability of universities to make space for esports on campuses, as a site of contention over the extent and terms of this encroachment, as our dominant metaphor for universities' economic performativity moves from industrial (*engines* of economic growth) to postindustrial (*platforms* for connection). In doing so, I have cast programs like those at Maryville and Harrisburg as almost wholly in the service of platformized and corporatized modes of cultural production: from the individualized, quantified skill rankings of the young men they recruit to the social media posts through which they share their successes with the rest of the university (and the world). I have used these programs, perhaps unfairly, as foils against which we might envision a different way of connecting campus constituents through esports, one less concerned with the quantifiable expressions of success endorsed by both platform giants and the hyperquantified, heavily masculinized domains of professional esports and professional sports. In her examination of four modes of "associationalism" undertaken by national esports organizations, Emma Witkowski highlights the work of Esports Denmark to foster what she calls a "civics-oriented" esports infrastructure in which the extractive logics of the industry (including parasitic commercial services) are held in check by active regulatory involvement on the part of the state and meaningful participation from the nonprofit sector.[70] I believe it is worthwhile to consider whether, in the much different context of the United States and Canada, collegiate esports might constitute a similarly civics-oriented infrastructure for sustainable, equitable, and nonexploitative esports. Such a goal is certainly worth striving for, since after all, "the potential and power of collegiate esports is that it can do better than what we have now."[71]

This is a fitting point on which to conclude: as Rianka Singh notes, the logics of platformized governance and the politics of patriarchy and white supremacy are engaged in mutually enriching, mutually enforcing choreographies.[72] Disrupting one means disrupting both. And at least in the very localized, very contingent world of collegiate esports, we can do so by quite literally *relocating* gaming.

NOTES

1. Taylor, *Raising the Stakes*, 130.
2. Temple, "From Space to Place"; Pawlicka-Deger, "Place Matters."
3. The Roestone Collective, "Safe Space"; Allen, Fenaughty, and Cowie, "Thinking with New Materialism about 'Safe-Un-Safe' Campus Space for LGBTTIQA+ Students."
4. Doughty, "Future of Online Learning."
5. Gillespie, "Politics of 'Platforms,'" 349.
6. As with the challenges facing countless other platforms, school-based esports (both high school and university) have found it difficult to prevent the incursion of predatory and parasitic operators. PlayVS, for example, provides an infrastructure for interscholastic esports and attempted to leverage its partnerships with game publishers into a monopoly on interscholastic esports competition. This included

threatening legal action against public high school teachers who attempted to set up esports competitions without PlayVS's service. Amenabar, "Teachers Say PlayVS Wields Partnerships to Monopolize Scholastic Esports."

7. Nieborg and Poell, "Platformization of Cultural Production," 4277.

8. Nieborg and Poell, "Platformization of Cultural Production," 4276.

9. Nieborg and Poell, "Platformization of Cultural Production," 4276.

10. Taylor, "Kinaesthetic Masculinity and the Prehistory of Esports."

11. Funk, Pizzo, and Baker, "Esport Management," 12.

12. "UCI Esports Conference 2018 Schedule." As Emma Witkowski notes, the esports conference in Cologne, Germany, had been running for years by 2008. But the esports industry and esports scholars are certainly not shy when making claims about newness and firsts. Witkowski, "Growing Pains in Esports Associationalism," 147.

13. Taylor, "Numbers Game," 129.

14. Taylor and Stout, "Gender and the Two-Tiered System of Collegiate Esports," 454.

15. Taylor and Stout, "Gender and the Two-Tiered System of Collegiate Esports," 456.

16. Ricks Hall itself was completed in 1922, when NCSU was still State College, and served as an agricultural extension building.

17. Read and Swarts, "Visualizing and Tracing," 28.

18. Pawlicka-Deger, "Place Matters," 321.

19. Pawlicka-Deger, "Place Matters," 329; Whitton, "New University," 36.

20. At the start of a typical LoL match, teams not only pick the champions (the game's playable characters) each player will control but can also block opponents from selecting particular champions. The frequency with which certain champions are banned is referred to as the ban rate.

21. As Nyle Sky Kauweloa and Jennifer Winter note, work-life balance is a major concern for collegiate esports athletes. Kauweloa and Winter, "Taking College Esports Seriously," 41.

22. Ash, "Technologies of Captivation," 27.

23. Donaldson, "Mechanics and Metagame," 428.

24. Maryville Strategic Plan, "Vision & Mission."

25. Student Life, "Esports Clubs at Maryville University."

26. In early 2022, Maryville University announced that it is aiming to redevelop commercial land in St. Louis into an esports arena. The proposed venue includes seating for three thousand spectators, a residence hall, and retail space (Traub, "Maryville University to Redevelop Center for Esports Space"). Collegiate esports are becoming a machine of spatial (and economic) reconfiguration beyond university campuses.

27. Temple, "From Space to Place," 22.

28. Lee and Ahtone, "Land-Grab Universities."

29. Sharma, "STEM-Ification of Education," 238.

30. NC State University, "Pathway to the Future," 1.

31. Lee and Ahtone, "Land-Grab Universities."

32. Lee and Ahtone, "Land-Grab Universities."

33. Hamer and Lang, "Race, Structural Violence, and the Neoliberal University," 897.

34. Lyotard, *Postmodern Condition*, xxv.

35. Olssen and Peters, "Neoliberalism, Higher Education and the Knowledge Economy," 314.

36. Hamer and Lang, "Race, Structural Violence, and the Neoliberal University," 899.

37. Hamer and Lang, "Race, Structural Violence, and the Neoliberal University," 899–900.

38. Giroux, "Public Intellectuals against the Neoliberal University."

39. Hall, *Uberfication of the University*.

40. Olssen and Peters, "Neoliberalism, Higher Education and the Knowledge Economy," 314.

41. Sharma, "STEM-Ification of Education," 45.

42. Sharma, "STEM-Ification of Education," 47.

43. In contrast, a number of scholars have pointed to the rich educational potential of networked competitive play, largely in the domain of communication and collaboration. Rusk and Ståhl, "Coordinating Teamplay Using Named Locations in a Multilingual Game Environment."

44. Paul, *Toxic Meritocracy of Video Games*; Taylor and Stout, "Gender and the Two-Tiered System of Collegiate Esports," 460.

45. Marcella Szablewicz offers this insight in regard to national economic interests; see Szablewicz, *Mapping Digital Game Culture in China*.

46. See, for instance, Brock, *Distributed Blackness*; Disalvo and Bruckman, "Race and Gender in Play Practices"; Ensmenger, *Computer Boys Take Over*; Kendall, "'White and Nerdy.'"

47. Zhu, "Masculinity's New Battle Arena in International E-Sports," 242.

48. Howard, "Rendering Hallyu," 155.

49. The White House, "Biden-Harris Administration Actions to Attract STEM Talent and Strengthen Our Economy and Competitiveness."

50. As of this writing, I see this connection as primarily discursive rather than empirical. In the United States at least, collegiate esports programs have proliferated more rapidly among small, private universities than larger, public universities; private colleges often lack the infrastructure to recruit international students. But I suspect the discursive links connecting STEM, international student recruitment, and esports are certainly in play in the efforts of larger institutions, like NCSU, to implement programs.

51. Esports Connect International, "Play Esports in College."

52. Chee, *Digital Game Culture in Korea*; Fickle, *Race Card*; Howard, "Rendering Hallyu."

53. *BBC News*, "Amazon, Facebook and Apple Thriving in Lockdown."

54. Amanda Cote and her colleagues present a compelling look at these and other challenges. See Cote et al., "COVID Season."

55. Partin, "The 'E' in Sports."

56. Partin, "The 'E' in Sports."

57. Chee and Karhulahti, "Ethical and Political Contours of Institutional Promotion in Esports," 219.

58. Funk, Pizzo, and Baker, "Esport Management," 16.

59. Partin, "Esports Pipeline Problem."

60. Partin, "Esports Pipeline Problem."

61. Taylor and Stout, "Gender and the Two-Tiered System of Collegiate Esports," 462.

62. Ratan et al., "Stand by Your Man"; Witkowski, "Doing/Undoing Gender with the Girl Gamer in High-Performance Play"; Taylor, *Raising the Stakes*.

63. Paul, *Toxic Meritocracy of Video Games*.

64. Taylor, "Now You're Playing with Audience Power."

65. *Data USA*, "Communication and Media Studies." That said, it is important to acknowledge the histories of racism and misogyny that characterize contemporary communication studies, as argued by Paula Chakravartty and her coauthors (Chakravartty et al., "#CommunicationSoWhite," 272).

66. UCI Esports, "2017–2018 Inclusivity Plan."

67. AnyKey, "Diversity & Inclusion in Collegiate Esports," 15.

68. Taylor and Stout, "Gender and the Two-Tiered System of Collegiate Esports," 459.

69. Luongo, "NC State Receives $16M to Build Esports Facilities on Campus."

70. Witkowski, "Growing Pains in Esports Associationalism," 153.

71. AnyKey, "Diversity & Inclusion in Collegiate Esports," 10.

72. Singh, "Platform Feminism."

5

POCKETS

Practicing Safe Storage at Games Industry Conventions

Counting Cargo Shorts

In April 2019, just under a year before COVID-19 put a pause on any kind of conventional fieldwork, I attended the East Coast Games Conference (ECGC) in Raleigh, North Carolina, with my colleague and friend Dr. Aaron Dial. ECGC is an annual convention that brings together regional game publishers and developers, community colleges, universities, and a whole plethora of games-related or games-adjacent businesses and organizations: for-profit universities, independent game makers, live streaming consultancies, high school esports clubs. Unlike larger, more international events like the Games Developer Conference (GDC) in San Francisco, the Montréal International Games Summit (MIGS), or the Electronic Entertainment Expo (E3), run by sprawling entertainment and event companies, ECGC is run by Wake Technical Community College (Wake Tech), a Raleigh-based community college. Aaron and I attended the event to learn how it works as a particular interface between the games industry and various publics—an urgent topic considering the reckoning game publishers and development studios situated in the Global North have faced recently for incidences of sexual harassment and violence, labor unrest, and race- and gender-based marginalization.[1]

The trip to ECGC was, like a lot of fieldwork, an opportunistic arrangement, a chance for Aaron and me to collaborate on qualitative sense-making regarding a type of event with which we had different experiences. During my graduate education, I had attended a number of games industry conventions, including one trip to MIGS, two visits to GDC, and one trip to the Tokyo Game Show. At each, I was a dutiful attender of talks and collector of swag, almost completely unaware of the eddies of professional and social networking opportunities—after-parties, private meetings, off-site hotspots to eat and drink—swirling around such events. Aaron's prior experience was as an eager but critical consumer of live-streamed E3 footage, paying as much attention to the comportment and persona of key speakers ("bad-fitting jeans, a company logo T-shirt, and blazer," as he put it) as to the details of new games and game systems they were hyping. Both of our experiences were, in the McLuhanian terms I use throughout this book, focused on the informational *figures* of these events (speakers, talks, swag) rather than the *grounds*.

For our trip to ECGC, however, we shifted our focus. While we attended a few talks, we were far more drawn to the main event hall and adjacent concourses. In the purposefully generic nonplace of the Raleigh Convention Center's upper floor—the kind of endlessly reconfigurable, data-server-for-humans I discuss in chapter 3—the organizers of ECGC had set up a bazaar at the crossroads of games industry, postsecondary education, and commerce. Technology demonstrations, small esports tournaments, indie game arcades, sponsor booths, merch tables: it was a place of exchange for things, information, insights, favors, jobs. Volunteers strode or jogged purposefully from one small crisis to the next; knots of people formed, shook hands or hugged, talked excitedly and gestured to something or other, maybe swapped cards or contact information via phones, and broke apart. People clustered at some stalls, bypassing others. A constant traffic of event goers left through the main doors, frequently returning with coffee from the Starbucks across the street. It looked exhausting; it *was* exhausting. And we were just there to watch.

On the afternoon of the second day, Aaron and I sat together amid mostly empty rows of fold-out convention chairs, facing the modest esports stage occupying one end of the main gathering room. We had not been there long, or done much, but we nonetheless felt a bit fatigued from both conducting fieldwork and simply walking around a congested event space with one's attention pulled constantly in multiple directions. On the stage, currently in between sessions of tournament play, were two young men from Wake Tech playing *NBA 2K19*. Aaron and I watched them absently while chatting about school, this event, games. On our meandering list of topics was Aaron's ongoing tally of how many cargo shorts he had seen at the event (thirteen, by that point), which he described as a specifically racialized, not just gendered, article of clothing: "Black dudes don't wear cargo shorts," he said. These shorts would go on to feature prominently in the provisional account we provided of our fieldwork.[2] Alongside the Game Fuel soda cans we encountered at the Mountain Dew booth later that afternoon and the massage chairs positioned at the top of the elevators leading to the main event hall, cargo shorts were among the handful of artifacts that jumped out at us—compositional elements that, in their banal connections to bodies, places, and practices, tell us much about the material culture of games industry conventions.[3]

In the subsequent research we did on cargo shorts, we came to understand them (as have countless others, from journalists to fashion theorists to satirists) as characterized by an excessive abundance and visibility of pockets.[4] The aggressively practical large pockets grafted both internally and externally onto shorts allow the wearer to store items while on the go. Like countless other masculinized media, cargo shorts were developed for military purposes but now serve civilians as mobile storage devices for any number of portable technologies: flash drives, snack bars, "giant phones, AirPods, charging cases, and EDC multitools."[5] As media objects, they extend the body's abilities by allowing the (white, masculine) wearer to take a whole bunch of stuff around with him while keeping his hands free. As garments worn at a professional networking event, they signal that their wearer prioritizes his gear, his intimacy with technics, over his appearance; he is not letting feminizing dictates of fashion get in the way of his ability to access his gear while on the move. If the bunker's denizens had a dress code for trips into the meatspace, it would be cargo shorts.

Containing Mobility

Cargo shorts, like those Aaron tallied worn by white guys at ECGC, are a fairly recent innovation in the long history of pockets. They are nonetheless expressive of pockets' broader gender politics. Unlike other "container technologies," which Zoe Sofia argues are predominantly feminized, pockets have, for centuries, been associated with men—likely because of their affiliations with certain kinds of public mobility conventionally not afforded to women.[6] Rebecca Unsworth draws from an extensive archive of recently digitized "portraits, prints, objects, letters, books and wardrobe accounts" to locate a key inflection point in the history of pockets, in European fashion of the fifteenth century.[7] Unsworth shows how early pockets came in many forms, from removable pouches worn between layers of clothing to codpieces that doubled as storage devices (particularly among laborers and soldiers—two characteristically mobile classes of masculinized labor). In keeping with the heavily gender- and class-striated social worlds of "the long sixteenth century" in Europe, the design of pockets both reflected and reinforced social distinctions between nobility and commoners, men and women: among nobility, women's pockets were fewer and more discreet, while men's pockets were frequently placed on the outside of the garment and adorned or embellished.[8] The popularity of pockets during the Renaissance grew hand in hand (or hand in pouch) with the emergence of the bourgeoisie. The intersection of urban mobility and early consumerism required safe places to put purchases. Women needed fewer pockets, and less pocket space, because such agency was primarily the province of (well-to-do) men. Thus, for Unsworth, even at this early stage in their history, pockets become "liminal and constructed temporary extensions to the natural or clothed body" that both demarcate and construct gendered identity: pockets are technogenders.[9] These gendered and classed striations in wearable storage continue to condition our contemporary access to pockets. On the one hand, cargo shorts perhaps continue the historical legacy of codpieces—prosthetic technologies that exaggerate masculine physicality while ensuring men have more storage space on the go. On the other hand, the reticence by the fashion industry to consistently build functional pockets into clothing for women has become a meme: "Thanks! It has pockets," she says.[10] These gendered distinctions in access to rudimentary storage are powerfully demonstrated in a series of data visualizations showing the relative size of pockets in jeans designated for men versus women and the inability of pockets in popular women's garments to adequately (much less comfortably) store gender-neutral media such as smartphones.[11] Understood historically and technologically as mobile storage technologies, pockets become a spatial and material motif through which we can comprehend the persistent differences in how genders (among other hierarchies of privilege and oppression) shape our movement through the world. This is as true for contemporary game developers hobnobbing at an industry convention as it was for Renaissance nobility stuffing the day's shopping into their pouch phalluses.

In this chapter, I burrow a bit deeper into pockets, approaching them as both a spatial motif and a specific discursive-material medium—that is, a cultural technique—through which we might understand the gendered practices and politics of games industry conventions. This chapter builds on and extends the earlier work Aaron and I did at ECGC, refining the scope of the study while deploying alternate (and experimental) means of gathering data about how games industry convention attendees perceive and move through such events. This work has been carried out with the recognition that games industry conventions like GDC are frequently unsafe for women. These events are where games industry workers go to (re)connect with each other and interface with the public, but they are also, frequently, where they go to cut loose, hang out, pick up. The central focus of this chapter is to understand the work that the women and nonbinary games workers I spoke with for this project carry out to ensure their safety and the safety of their friends and colleagues. As I demonstrate, their concerns for safety arise out of the *infrastructural* conditions of such events: the ways these events serve as temporary platforms not only for connecting games industry professionals, researchers, journalists, students, and so on but also for circulating alcohol and caffeine, sexual objectification and predation, masculine entitlement and resentment. These events and their frequently inhospitable conditions have not received much attention within academic research on games industries, even as research meticulously documents the intersecting forms of marginalization, discrimination, and harassment that characterize so many game studios and other sites and forms of games-related labor.[12] But they have been talked about in other publication venues, and often by academics; in an article for games culture site *Unwinnable*, for instance, Mahli-Ann Butt discusses the anxiety and unease she felt while at GDC, where she saw so much of the masculinized culture of the games industry not only on display but in alcohol-fueled overdrive. Likewise, Stephanie Fisher's autoethnographic account of two very different GDC parties—one an after-hours, off-site dance party hosted by Microsoft, featuring female dancers in skimpy schoolgirl outfits, the other an event celebrating the achievements of women in the industry—both involved profoundly problematic, if different, connections between vulnerability, visibility, and objectification for her and her female and nonbinary colleagues.[13]

Most of the women and nonbinary folk I talked to for this research discussed games industry conventions (mainly GDC, but also ECGC, E3, and MIGS) in terms of navigating stark boundaries around what is safe and unsafe: day versus night; on-site versus off-site; alcohol-free versus alcohol-fueled; events specifically for (and run by) women and gender minorities versus events with mostly men in attendance. Across all these boundaries, mobility is both a key tactic and a key concern. Stay moving, do not stand still, but also do not go off by yourself, at least not without telling your friends where you are going. As I learned, *pockets* are central to the work of keeping themselves and each other safe. Pockets (in backpacks, pants, jackets) are used to store things your friends and colleagues might need to stay upright, relatively comfortable, safe, and connected while navigating the event for long hours each day and night—Motrin, a protein bar, hand sanitizer, a battery charger. Used in a second sense, as a diagram of power and not solely as a spatial motif, pockets become a way to understand the work of cutting less visible spaces for themselves and their colleagues out from the cultural and spatial fabric of the event: a women in games luncheon, an alcohol-free tea party. For women and gender minorities at games industry conventions, then, pockets are container technologies for the storage and circulation of *care*, operating both at the level of individual clothing and accessories and at the level of place-making practices at convention centers and off-site spaces. This core insight emerged out of a straightforward, even naive question Aaron and I developed as we adapted our initial fieldwork-based study for COVID-19 lockdowns, event cancellations, and social distancing practices: "What are the most important things you bring when you go to a games industry convention?"

Memetic Sense-Making

To address this question, we developed a short Qualtrics survey divided into two parts. The survey was intended for people who have attended at least one games industry convention. One section (which participants did last) asked for demographic and nonspecific professional information. The survey asked participants about their current relationship to the games industry; the length of time they have worked in their current position; all the games industry events they have attended; the activities they participated in while there; a ranking of which activities were most important to them; how their trip to the event was paid for; and whether they consider attending industry events a necessary part of their job. Basic demographic information included age range, gender identity, and racial identity. The survey also asked whether participants were interested in a follow-up interview.

The other section of the survey was a little more experimental and took inspiration from the world of memes. At the time we devised this part of the study, the "starter pack" meme was well circulated. The meme typically involves a handful of generic images from the web (often product images or stock photographs, their watermarks visible) labeled with the title

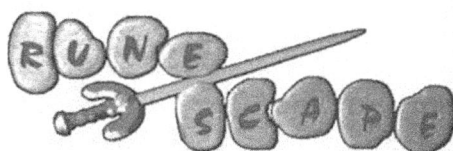

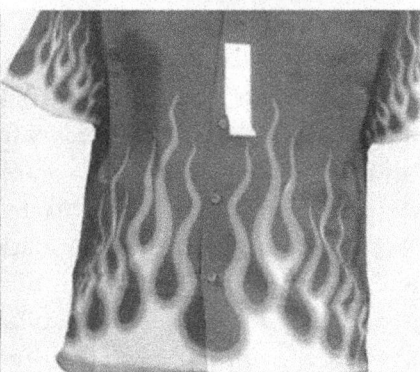

Figure 5.1. A classic example of a starter pack: "Edgy Kid from Early 2000s."
Credit: unattributed.

"[Particular Identity] Starter Pack." Starter packs have been defined as "memes consisting of one or more images accompanied by (1) titles providing commentary and/or context and (2) illustrating a prototype of a cultural artifact, member of a community, or shared experience."[14] The meme's arrangement implies that a starter pack contains the essential items not so much for a particular activity but rather for an identity, everything you need to be a certain subject. Figure 5.1, for instance, shows a starter pack for "Edgy Kid from Early 2000s": this edgy kid sports dark shades and spiky hair; wears shirts with flames; listens to obnoxious rap metal; and plays the massively multiplayer online game *RuneScape*, known (at that time) for its young and often exuberant player base.[15]

As a form of what Ryan Milner calls "memetic logic," the meme traffics both in the cultural specificity of the subject position in question and the notion that this (indeed, any) subjectivity can be accurately expressed through a small, select range of artifacts.[16] Starter packs can therefore be regarded as "the collective expression and recognition" of certain culturally legible identities.[17] The meme relies on the same kind of sense-making regarding a "pack" that Unsworth points to in discussing the historical purpose and ongoing cultural significance of pockets (indeed, "pack" and "pocket" share the same etymology): "What people stored in their pockets can also provide a sense of what they believed to be important or necessary."[18] For these reasons, the starter pack meme offered a useful framework for asking games industry workers about essential items for attendance at games industry conventions—and asking how a specific combination of generic artifacts expresses who they are in relation to these events and the games industry more generally. The starter pack portion of our survey invited participants to either upload or link to pictures of four items and provide captions for each. We opted for four to promote a selective economy of meaning and because four images are easy to visually organize, as many of classic examples of the meme attest. The survey noted that images should not contain any identifiable information. This was to ensure confidentiality and in keeping with the aesthetic of starter pack memes: a kind of expedient, unpolished bricolage where style and staging matter less than function and where the cultural specificity of a given subject position or "prototype," realized through a combination of items, matters more than individuality.[19]

Beginning in July 2021, we circulated the survey via personal networks and on Twitter. We were at a disadvantage, as neither Aaron nor I work in the games industry; we were thus entirely reliant on the few direct connections I have with industry workers and even more so on my connections to academics whose research more directly engages the games industry. Over a four-week period, the survey garnered thirty-three responses, thirteen of which were incomplete. This left us with twenty complete responses—far from a robust sample from which to make generalizable claims about people's experiences at games industry conventions, but that was never the point. Rather, the aim was to understand participants' perspectives on their experiences at games industry conventions. The twenty starter packs and accompanying background information we received, and the seven follow-up interviews we conducted, constitute a modest but nonetheless generative case study. In what follows, I offer an overview of participants' demographics and professional backgrounds. I unpack individual starter packs to show how evocative they are of certain subjectivities, before thematically grouping and discussing the kinds of artifacts included across all the starter packs collected for the study, drawing heavily on the seven follow-up interviews Aaron and I conducted.[20] Through these photo-voice exercises, participants figuratively dumped out the contents of their starter pack, sharing stories and insights about the items' uses and significance.

Demographics and Professional Backgrounds

The majority of survey respondents (twelve) were women. Four were men, three were nonbinary, and one preferred not to disclose. This spread diverges widely from the gender demographics of both the games industry and games industry conventions and is almost entirely a product of my reliance on networks of feminist scholars and game designers.[21] In terms of age, survey respondents were much more similar to the demographics of the games industry more broadly: twelve were between the ages of thirty-five and forty-four when completing the survey, seven were between twenty-five and thirty-four, and one was between fifty-five and sixty-four. Respondents overwhelmingly identified as white, with two identifying as biracial (both Asian/white) and one preferring not to say. This is consistent with the racial demographics in both academia and the games industry.[22] In terms of current professions, almost half of respondents (nine) listed "game developer." Six identified as instructors/educators, three as games researchers/analysts, and of the two "other" positions, one indicated they are a student, and the other wrote that they direct a nonprofit organization for women in games. These categories do not capture important details regarding porous boundaries and frequent circulation between positions, however, like the fact that one of the educators had recently left the games industry after several decades, another respondent had just left academia to launch a game studio, and another teaches in the game design program at their university and accompanies their students to ECGC to showcase their games. Despite fluctuations between "game developer" and "instructor/educator," the majority of respondents (fifteen) had occupied their current role for more than five years at the time they took the survey. Among the nine game developers specifically, five had been at their position for more than five years; two, for three to five years; and one each for one to three years and under one year.

Almost all participants (fifteen) had been to at least one GDC. Of these, nine had been to more than one GDC. Every respondent had been to multiple events—not only over multiple years but also multiple different games industry conventions. These included (but were not limited to) E3, MIGS, and the Penny Arcade Expo (PAX, which runs annual "PAX East" and "PAX West" events in Boston and Seattle, respectively). Events listed included more specialist games industry conventions, like Games for Change, Indiecade, and Different Games, and fan culture conventions like GenCon, Blizzcon, and Comicon.

With regard to the most recent convention they had attended, the majority of participants answered that costs had been covered by their employer, including six of the nine game developers (of the other three, two had costs covered by a scholarship program and one had paid out of pocket). This reliance on employer funding is significant, as a week at GDC in particular can cost upward of USD 5,000, factoring conference registration (around USD 2,000 for nonpresenters), travel, accommodations, and food. ECGC, by contrast, costs less than half of that, given the cheaper accommodation in Raleigh and the lower cost of tickets (USD 540 in 2023 for a VIP pass purchased the day of the event).[23] This makes GDC, *the* games industry convention, almost prohibitively expensive for average games workers. It is not surprising, then, to see not only that most respondents' costs had been covered by their employer but also that most respondents (twelve) answered "yes" to the question "Do you feel like attending games industry conventions an expected or necessary part of your employment?" Interestingly, less than half of game developers responded yes, but the majority of instructors/educators (five out of six) did, perhaps reflecting their role as representatives of their schools' game design programs and, more importantly, as facilitators and chaperones for their game design students. As one instructor/educator remarked in the open comments section of the survey, he had to attend "basically to 'show the flag' for my program."

The survey asked respondents to rank eight different activities common to GDC and other industry events in order of importance (one being the most important, eight being the least). To help make sense of the responses, we can group activities that showed up most often among respondents' top three choices, activities that most frequently appeared among the bottom three of respondents' rankings, and the activities that showed up in the middle (table 5.1). Based on this clustering, "professional development," "socializing," and "connecting with organizations" ranked as the most popular activities. Among the least popular activities were "looking for employment," "seeking investors," and "hearing from major games industry figures." "Learning more about game development" was ranked highly by

Table 5.1. Grouping convention activities by order of popularity.

	Top three	Middle two	Bottom three
Professional development	15	4	1
Socializing	14	4	2
Connecting with organizations	11	6	3
Learning about game development	7	7	5
Other	5	1	14
Hearing from major industry figures	4	6	10
Seeking investors	4	5	11
Looking for employment	0	7	13

seven participants but was otherwise not very popular. With regard to the "other" category, four participants ranked it highest; write-in answers included "networking more broadly, in face-to-face contexts," "conducting academic research," "meeting developers or press for collaborations, getting industry news," and "presenting game on behalf of employer." It seems that respondents were more interested in using events to connect with colleagues and network and less interested in content-related programming (sessions, keynotes).

From this demographic snapshot, we can tentatively sketch a composite figure: a white woman, relatively young (late twenties to early forties), in the middle of her career in either academia or game development. She has attended GDC multiple times, in addition to one or two other conventions; her attendance is covered by her employer, though she is ambivalent as to whether going to these conventions is an expected part of her job. She is primarily interested in socializing, professional development, and connecting with communities and less in using the event to find funding or employment opportunities or hear from major games industry figures. What is in her starter pack? More accurately, to quote the survey itself, what four items are indispensable to her "successful outing at a games industry convention like GDC or MIGS" (however she may define "successful")?

Digging into Three Starter Packs

Figure 5.2 is the starter pack of a participant who more or less embodies this composite sketch. This participant is a white woman, between thirty-five and forty-four years old; she has worked in her current game development

Figure 5.2. One of the "games industry convention starter packs" for this study. Clockwise from top left: "phone charger," "lozenges," "business cards (~100)," and "written backup meeting schedule for the day."

position for more than five years. She has attended numerous conventions and sees them as necessary for her employment. The most recent one she attended prior to participating in the study was paid for by her employer. Apart from this contextualizing information, it is possible to glean the following from her starter pack: she typically interacts with large numbers of people (hence the need for one hundred business cards). A phone charger ensures that she can stay connected and online throughout the event without having to park herself at a charging station. She maintains a busy schedule of meetings throughout the day—this work is so important that she has a handwritten backup of her meeting schedule for when her phone inevitably runs out of power. Lozenges soothe her throat after or during sustained bouts of talking, presumably with everyone she has met and to whom she has handed out business cards. Certain items are perhaps conspicuous for their absence: articles of clothing, for instance. For this participant, the first two items sustain her ability to circulate through the event, carrying out work that requires a considerable amount of coordination and network

Figure 5.3. Another games industry convention starter pack. Clockwise from top left: "a fully charged portable battery pack to charge various electronics (and charge cables!)," "a multipack of mini Hand Sanitizers," "an emergency pack of individually packaged snacks (so it is safe to share) and water bottle to refill," and "an easily identifiable and memorable hat with lots of personality."

formation—the kind of work expected of managerial or executive positions in the games industry.

The participant whose starter pack is shown below (fig. 5.3) is also a white woman between thirty-five and forty-four who has been in her current position in the games industry for more than five years, has attended numerous conventions, and sees them as necessary for her employment, though she noted in the open comment section on the survey that "I think it SHOULDN'T be but it is because of the way the industry is—it feels like a necessity." Like the participant discussed above, she has included items that allow both her body and her phone to keep going without interruption (snacks and portable battery pack, respectively). Her hat—"easily identifiable"—fulfills a sort of inverse function to that of the business card. Where the stack of business cards allows attendees to distribute their information to new acquaintances and contacts, the hat allows existing acquaintances to pick this participant out from a crowd: a technique oriented more toward reconnection than new connections. Likewise, both the snacks ("safe

Figure 5.4. The starter pack of a games researcher. Clockwise from top left: "good backpack," "comfortable shoes," "smartphone + battery pack," and "notepad with hard cover."

to share") and small bottles of glittery hand sanitizer suggest an emphasis on being with people already known. Whereas the items in figure 5.2 seem intended to allow the participant to *extend* her professional network, the items in figure 5.3 seem intended to allow the participant to *renew* her personal network. These are two fundamentally different orientations to games industry events that a close comparison of starter packs reveals, despite so many shared demographic characteristics.

Figure 5.4 offers yet another orientation. The participant who put this starter pack together is a games researcher who ranks "conducting academic research" as his top priority in attending. He is a white man, between thirty-five and forty-four, who has been to multiple games industry conventions; because they are a key research site for his scholarly research and networking, they have become a necessity. As with the two starter pack

Table 5.2. Starter pack objects, grouped thematically.

Type of objects	Number of instances
Personal effects (clothing, shoes, hair accessories, hat, headphones, backpack/bag)	17
Know-show (business cards, pronoun pins, schedules)	11
Mobile digital media (smartphones, charging cords, laptops)	16
Sustenance (water, other beverages, food)	10
Bodily care (medical products, hygiene products)	13
Recording media (pens, books)	5
Other (abstract concepts or comments about specific events)	8

participants considered above, this participant includes items that sustain his ability to be on his feet and moving around for long periods of time (comfortable shoes and, once again, a battery pack for his phone). He also includes a "good backpack" and a "notepad with hard cover": two items that speak of storing and collecting information (field notes, contact information, and so on) rather than networking or coordinating. Notebooks and notepads were included a small number of times across the other starter packs, but almost always by men, and three out of four male participants included some kind of notebook or notepad. The fact that they are all university instructors and researchers, people whose job involves a great deal of writing, is as salient here as their gender, if not more.

Much to Unpack

A consideration of each starter pack created for this study is beyond the scope of this chapter, however fruitful that might be. But a close reading of individual starter packs only goes so far. To make further sense of them, I aggregated the items listed across all the starter packs, akin to dumping all their contents onto (or into) a table and sorting them. The result is a long and fairly cumbersome list of item categories, how many times categories appear across all starter packs, and specific examples of them. From this list, I further clustered items by purpose, creating a thematic grouping of artifacts (table 5.2). This allowed me to more adequately account for a few of the more surprising insights we gleaned from our interviews with seven participants regarding these mundane and unassuming items—insights that were not attainable through the simple presence of these items in a starter pack.

Personal Effects: Detection and Deflection

"Personal effects" are items that convey identity and belonging at an intensely public and social event like GDC. Through both surveys and interviews, participants articulated a keen sense of the ways in which clothes communicate gender, certainly, but also "insider" status in the games industry. For instance, Interviewee 1, a university researcher who included "black zip-up hoodie" and "black indie game development company logo shirt" in her starter pack, recalled receiving mentorship from her colleague and friend (Interviewee 6) as she was packing for her first GDC, which they attended together: "I started packing my teacher clothes, like my normal conference attire, and I'm not that dressy of a person; I usually wear kind of casual pants with a button-down shirt or something, so nothing fancy. But Interviewee 6 kind of gave me a heads up, like they're very casual; you're going to want hoodies, or you'll want to, you know, bring sneakers." Later she told me, "I like blending in more than standing out, so I'm glad I got that tip from Interviewee 6 to dress more casually." She recalled noticing people at GDC dressed in the more formal clothes she was originally packing, "like a random blazer," and coding them as fellow university professors. For this participant, the advice received from a female friend in how to "blend in" at her first GDC was significant enough to constitute half her starter pack. When I had the chance to chat with Interviewee 6, she elaborated on the volatile gender politics of fitting in at a games industry conference:

> I don't want to wear like cargo shorts and button down. I mean you've seen those starter packs, right? You know, like "dude at a game conference"; this picture of ten guys in blue flannel with big backpacks on, standing around together. But then it's like oh, do you want to be so almost hyperfemme that you stand out and look really distinctive? Which in my everyday life I do sometimes like to dress that way, but you don't always want that kind of attention maybe. So I feel like there's always this interesting line of how you dress for these situations. (Interviewee 6)

Here, Interviewee 6 articulates a line between the meme-ready "blue flannel with big backpacks on" apparel of "dude at a game conference" versus the "hyperfemme" look she sometimes sports in everyday life, which she is cautious about at games industry conventions because of the unwanted attention it might attract. This balance is achieved with what she calls a game design "uniform": "jeans and a T-shirt with some accessories; just like necklaces and stuff and a backpack. And then I usually will have a hoodie or something with me too, and sneakers." Casual and informal clothing thus, perhaps ironically, becomes a uniform—a way of blending in and not attracting attention. There are, of course, powerful gender politics at work here. That women must think carefully about whether and how their clothing choices will warrant unwanted attention at games industry events is no surprise, given what we know about the games industry and its persistent failure to adequately reckon with misogyny and gender-based harassment.[24]

In addition to clothing, some interviewees mentioned techniques for deflecting attention away using headphones. Interviewee 2, who helps direct a nonprofit organization for women in games, stressed the importance of bright, visible headphones at games industry conventions. She stated that of all the items in her starter pack, headphones are the most important, because they "allow me to move through a space when no one's going to talk to me." When I invited her to elaborate on the kinds of spaces in which headphones come in handy—spaces through which she needs to be able to move without interruption—she described a series of interactions she had on the main expo floor of the Moscone Center, the GDC venue.

> There's so much marketing and promo happening. Once you enter the space, you're being photographed . . . Or they're trying to get you to interact with their stuff, whether or not you're going to buy it. I noticed the last time when I was walking around with my friend, and she's East Asian; I was like I feel like I'm getting more approached now because there's two of us. It looks good to have women interacting with their shit. Again, it's the performance. It's not just bros, but it's also kind of like there's women and it's safe. And you kind of end up feeling like you're being used. They don't give a shit I think like whether or not I'm enjoying myself or if I'm going to buy it. I think it's more just like if those two women are there, that might signal to other women to try this or it's worth their time. (Interviewee 2)

The expo floor of GDC, as this interviewee describes it, is a larger, more capital-intensive, more congested version of the bazaar-style concourse Aaron and I encountered at ECGC. For Interviewee 2, such heavily trafficked zones are fraught, as she finds herself constantly solicited to engage with a booth and interact with a product—or more accurately, to be *seen* interacting with a product. We are in a moment when the use of "booth babes" at convention exhibitor booths has been roundly critiqued, and events like GDC and E3 have committed to doing away with it.[25] Interviewee 2's heightened awareness of how her presence at a booth can be "used"—configured as a kind of ad hoc promotional modeling—speaks to the persistence of a masculine logic still at work in the operation of these ostensibly booth-babe-less spaces. If booth babes are hired to cultivate "a managed eroticism on behalf of the companies whose products they exhibit," then the interactions described here position the presence of younger women, however incidental and uneroticized, as an enticement for other potential buyers.[26] This is what headphones allow Interviewee 2 to avoid. To those on the event floor who would attempt to frame her interaction with them or their product, her headphones say, "I can't fucking hear you, so don't even try."

Know-Show: Dis/engagement

The range of items I group together as "know-shows" are technologies that store information for the express purposes of display and exchange: schedules, pronoun pins, business cards. Lisa Gitelman productively theorizes the epistemic and performative function of these media in *Paper Knowledge*. To show the information is to know it; to know it is enter into a social relation where the knowledge must be acted on. Documents hold the recipient to account. As Gitelman notes, "if all documents share a certain 'horizon of expectation,' then, the name of that horizon is accountability."[27] Wearing a pronoun pin signals to those you encounter that you expect them to address you according to your actual gender identity. Handing out a business card produces the expectation that the recipient will add you to their network— maybe reach out to you on LinkedIn or send you a follow-up email. That is the *strategic* expectation of business cards, at any rate, the use of business cards most amenable to accumulating capital.[28] Two of the interviewees I spoke with included business cards in their starter pack for this reason. Interviewee 4, who had spent decades in the games industry before becoming a game design instructor, showed me the two tiers of cards she takes with her to games industry conventions: the "nice one," with her name embossed on one side against a black background and her contact information on the other, and a "lower-grade one" for people she is less eager to impress. She also recounted her system for cards she received:

> Each time I met someone, I would make a note, right. And then I would go back to my room, before I would go back out and get more cards, and I would do my LinkedIn right then and there while it was still fresh in my mind, saying, 'Hey, it was so great to meet you tonight. I know you won't get to this until you get back to work, but you know, I really loved talking to you.' Boom, right. And so I was able to make a connection.

Interviewee 7, the sole man we interviewed, alluded to a similar practice, albeit without Interviewee 4's urgency. He stores business cards he has collected from conventions in a prominent position in his workplace, "then I can go find their LinkedIn or Twitter or whatever." Interviewee 4 put great stock in the relation between business cards, games industry conventions, and networking. She stated that "my whole career has been based on the connections and networks I made at conferences." Business cards are the material conduits of her network-building practices and, subsequently, her livelihood.

This function contrasts with the ways other interviewees described their inclusion (or exclusion) of business cards in their starter packs. Interviewee 2's reasons for deploying business cards are similar to when she dons her bright yellow Beats by Dre headphones: to extract herself. She noted that the business cards she distributes at games industry conventions do not have her own personal or work emails but display the generic email address for the nonprofit organization she represents, shared by multiple people in the organization. Such boundary-making practices are central to her efforts to protect both her time and her safety. While she acknowledged that handing out business cards can be a key step in securing corporate donations, she said that the majority of sponsorship relations are initiated through other means. The act of exchanging business cards, rather than the informational content circulated by the exchange, is most important to her. Exchanging cards effectively concludes an interaction; "it's a way to end things" cordially and without giving offense because, as a woman at the conference, "you can never be rude." Interviewee 5, whose starter pack included the "easily identifiable and memorable hat" (fig. 5.3), took this protective logic with business cards a step further. She told me that she collected business cards at her first few conventions, which she recalled as generally negative experiences—

exhausting both because of the pressure "to keep always on" and the extra emotional, mental, and physical labor required to keep safe. She described this work in the following terms:

> Do people know where I am? Is this invite to the party legitimate? Who's going to be at this party? Okay, if it's a work sponsored party, which not-safe people are going to be there, and do I know any safe people that are going? Are we going as a group or is it going to be individual, like why is this party there? And it's just like—it's exhausting to do all of that 'cause you have to organize all of that.

The business cards she collected from her first couple of GDCs became an archive for her experiences of unease and exhaustion. She described her collection of cards from these events as "the rolodex of sketchy people. It was just like oh, yeah, this dude was really sketchy at GDC, so I would keep his business card because of that." As alluded to in the consideration of her starter pack, Interviewee 5's recent conference experiences were more focused on reconnecting with friends and spending time with those she trusts rather than "the linkup," a shift she said resulted in "the best [experience] I've ever had at any GDC." Crucially, she went not for work but through a scholarship made available by a feminist nonprofit organization. She characterized her earlier emphasis on networking as "making cheap connections," whereas she is now able to "draw that line and have that like nice, safe space where it's just like okay, I don't have to always be on." As part of this shift, Interviewee 5 said she has done away with business cards altogether, having thrown away her "rolodex of sketchy people" during a recent move. This does not mean that she is no longer as concerned with avoiding sketchy people. Rather, as I explain further below, the function of the sketchy people rolodex—as a kind of analog, anti-LinkedIn—has been made redundant by Discord servers devoted to circulating information for women and nonbinary folks on how to stay safe at industry conventions.

Business cards are thus central to much of the tension that participants' stories illuminate regarding the kinds of work they carry out at GDC and other conventions. Here, I use the distinction Michel de Certeau makes between "strategies" and "tactics" to help explain drastically different uses of the same objects. Strategies are techniques exercised by institutions to impel and circumscribe the activities of ordinary people; tactics are the defensive, contingent, and opportunistic means for navigating, circumventing, or simply surviving conditions made inhospitable or unsustainable by institutions and their strategies.[29] For those using business cards strategically, cards form the vital and material first link in an expanding professional network. Take the card, store it, use the information on it to find someone's online presence, send them a message, extend the network. "Mobilize inscriptions" on the card toward further professional growth and capital accumulation; they are catalysts, quite literally, for "net work."[30] Tactical use of business cards, by contrast, follows the logics of deflection and protection. Business cards become a material means for *disconnecting*, either from awkward or pointless interactions (as illustrated by Interviewee 2) or from people considered "sketchy" and unsafe (Interviewee 5). As with the stories around using clothing to deter unwanted attention, insights about these tactical deployments of business cards further reveal the almost ever-present threats that events like GDC present to women and gender minorities and the forms of care they develop to stay safe.

Mobile Digital Media

The ubiquity and inescapability of smartphones makes them difficult to talk about; how ought we grasp the significance of a device that embodies so many histories and forms of communication and fits neatly in one's pocket (at least, if you are wearing men's jeans)? Yet for all their importance, smartphones only showed up in seven respondents' starter packs—fewer instances than pharmaceutical products. Their inconsistent showing might be simply because they are, as Interviewee 2 remarked, as unavoidable as shoes. Everyone's going to bring theirs to a games industry event, though they may not include it as one of their "essential" items for a "successful time," to once again quote the survey itself. The fact that extra phone batteries appeared in starter packs almost as much as smartphones themselves (and often in tandem—see fig. 5.4's "smartphone + battery pack") speaks to this: the smartphone itself is obvious, so best to include a tool for extending its charge. For this reason, my conversations with interviewees about smartphones focused more on specific applications than smartphones themselves. As an example, Twitter provided Interviewee 3 with a way to monitor the buzz generated by the new game they were helping to hype at their studio's E3 booth. For Interviewee 4, whose primary concern at industry conventions is to network as much as possible, the locative affordances of smartphones are key to her efficient navigation; "you actually can GPS your way through a conference, and like 'where the Hell is that room' is no longer an ordeal." In effect, her smartphone facilitates her distribution of business cards. Interviewee 5, conversely, mentioned the smartphone's camera in describing how she has ditched business cards; if she wants to exchange contact information with someone, she takes a photograph of their lanyard.

Perhaps the most prevalent use of smartphones among interviewees, however, was as a means to stay connected with a support network—to stay safe, through a variety of techniques. For Interviewee 2, it is the smartphone's capacity to act, quaintly, as a telephone; at the orientation event her nonprofit organization held for the women it sponsored to attend GDC, she and other facilitators distributed phone numbers to call in an emergency. As she described:

> When you're out and you get into trouble, you call your friends. So you're talking about people who this is sometimes their first visit to the US, and who are they going to call? One of the things that we have at our orientation lunch is 'everyone put my number in your phone right now.' And we have things like inserts into their badges, where it's like if you find this person, here are the emergency numbers to call.

Interviewee 2 further described setting up a buddy system with program participants via text, whereby participants could inform each other of their whereabouts—particularly if going off-site. For her, this was about "encouraging people to always stay connected and know what you need to stay safe." She went on: "We had a participant one time who wanted us to check in with them before, during and after meetings with people because she was going along to spaces off-site. And they were legit business meetings, but she was like because you hear about stuff that happens to other people, and it's just her, we'll do that kind of stuff for you." These kinds of support networks are not specific to this feminist organization, either. Like the program participant Interviewee 2 described, Interviewee 6 said she heard a lot of "really not great stories" about GDC. She described coming across a Discord server specifically for women's safety during her preparation for GDC: "I don't remember what groups specifically I was on where then somebody on that group was like 'hey women, join this.' But I think it's something that could easily bounce off—it's subtle, right? It's like something that would easily bounce off of a non–female identifying person." She said this Discord server, hidden in plain sight, connected users with a safety system. Similar to the in-person buddy system coordinated by Interviewee 2 at her organization's orientation event, this Discord server enabled members to "know where you are" so that other users would "call for assistance" if needed; "if you're feeling unsafe somewhere," Interviewee 6 said, "come get your Discord by you; we'll walk you home." She described this server as "a little whispery networky," referring to the communicative tactic (in de Certeau's sense) that women and gender minorities have deployed to circulate stories of harassment and violence through otherwise undetected channels.[31] These kinds of stories became viral through the #Metoo movement (and earlier, in 2012, the "#1reasonwhy" campaign among games industry workers).[32] In the rush to account for the virality and force of #Metoo, what perhaps got overlooked in subsequent reporting and scholarship around whisper networks is the material practices of care and protection that often accompany them. #Metoo, as our primary example of a whisper network gone public, is seen as empowering women by forcing the public to pay attention, but this emphasis on the communicative and discursive aspects of whisper networks perhaps overshadows the work they have done historically. Whisper networks are not purely informational phenomena. The Discord server Interviewee 6 mentioned, the buddy system Interviewee 2 helped organize, the "rolodex of sketchy people" compiled by Interviewee 5—these communicative tactics are not intended primarily for the circulation of stories. Rather, they are oriented toward the coordination and mobilization of material support. The whisper networks around GDC, at least, are (like battery packs and snacks) part of infrastructures of care.

Sustenance and Substance

Food and beverages did not appear consistently in participants' starter packs, but they did loom significantly in interviewees' stories about the strain industry conferences take on the body and the efforts put into staying alert and (relatively) comfortable. Interviewee 5, for instance, emphasized that she always packs abundant snacks in individual serving sizes for both herself, because she needs to not become "hangry," and her friends and close colleagues. This is part of her convention planning. When she arrives on location, she says, she will go to Target and pick up snacks, as well as tissues and water bottles. She underscored the importance of being able to provide colleagues with sustenance: "If somebody was like oh man, I'm really hungry but I don't have time between my two panels to go get food, I can be like oh, have a CLIFF bar, there you go."[33] Interviewee 6, likewise, connected food and drink with the need to keep her body going during the long hours spent at GDC and ECGC. She articulated the multiple purposes of the "disposable coffee cup" included in her starter pack.

> To me you don't get the best quality sleep at these things, and you also want to stay up and go to stuff. And the result of that is I end up drinking way more coffee than I normally would because I'm usually worn out. And part of that too is if you really want to do the networking and stuff, a lot of that happens after the conference, so it's like you're out really, really late. You're probably getting intoxicated if you're somebody that drinks. So I feel like the coffee is just a counterweight to all of that, and I feel like constantly I just have that in my hand. (Interviewee 6)

Interviewee 6 described herself as having attention deficit hyperactivity disorder (ADHD, which, in her estimation, is remarkably commonplace in the games industry), so coffee becomes a way for her to focus because of the difficulty of sitting through multiple presentations. Aside from the chemical regulation coffee provides, she described it as a "social presentation"—a way of signaling openness to a particular kind of networking. Meeting someone over a meal is a substantial commitment of time, money, and energy, and usually involves going off-site—something other participants described as potentially unsafe. Coffee, on the other hand, is casual, relatively quick, and (with a disposable coffee cup) mobile. It is easier to remove oneself from an interaction over coffee than over a meal.

Food and nutrition loomed largest in my conversation with Interviewee 3, a nonbinary game developer who had been in their position for under five years when we spoke. They described going to E3, paid for by their company (which they had since left), to help operate the company's booth and promote its new game. They claimed that they were vegan when they went to E3 and no longer vegan when they left. They had become vegan for environmental reasons but had decided before going to E3 to "be kind of like pescatarian for this to enjoy the experience." "But then," they went on, describing the group meals and parties they attended, "people were like leaving steak barely eaten and other kinds of land animals. Are they going to waste? It was on the menu and looked amazing and everyone was eating it. So I was like maybe

I'll just let E3 be kind of a cheat; I'm not going to tilt the scales in the climate emergency myself, so I'll just do this. But then I was so negatively impacted psychologically by the whole experience that it was harder for me to go back onto veganism because it takes more planning." For them, the simple fact of needing "a lot of calories" to get through long and stressful days of operating a booth—and crucially, interacting with fans of the studio and game—ruled out the possibility of staying consistent with their normally mindful choices around food and nutrition.[34] This participant spoke to an acute awareness of the importance of protein in sustaining one's energy and staving off frustration (getting "hangry"); faced with looking after themselves while avoiding their colleagues' teasing about veganism or sticking to their dietary choices and feeling fatigued, undernourished, and belittled, their choice was difficult but clear.

Alcohol

While no one put alcoholic beverages in their starter kit, alcohol (and the dangers it presents to women and gender minorities at games industry conventions) was brought up in several interviews. Interviewees described off-site parties, held at night, in which alcohol is consumed in abundance—a culture of late-night partying and heavy drinking portrayed as contiguous with the intensive networking that goes on during the day. Interviewee 3 described "hearing stories of people getting back to their rooms at like three and four a.m., and then having to be on the show floor at like eight thirty. I'm like how in the world?" According to Interviewee 2, whose responsibilities to her nonprofit organization involve setting up women- and nonbinary-focused events at GDC, demarcations between safe and unsafe events sponsored by game publishers, tech companies, and other organizations are "literally night and day." On one hand are luncheons, tea parties, and afternoon socials, for "ultra-safe allies"; "there's booze at those ones," she said, "but there'll also be things like here's our juice bar, and here's our smoothie bar, and our latte bar, and way less emphasis on alcohol." By contrast, she went on, "the ones that happen at night, like Xbox, totally different. Those are like at a club. It's like a bachelor party. They have dancers on cubes, which is fine, but you know what I mean? When you people talk about industry parties that are degrading and whatnot, that's happening at night."[35] She noted that these "club" parties are often the most exclusive and coveted—as if the most desirable places to be are the ones in which women are most objectified and least safe. For Interviewee 2, this reality is entirely consistent with her understanding of the work cultures of many game studios, in which "having a drink and having a good time" on Friday afternoons (often paid for by studios) is seen as vital team building.

Much of the work of care that several participants (including Interviewee 2) carry out involves implementing support systems specifically for colleagues and friends who attend these and other off-site, alcohol-fueled nighttime events. Again, this reason was given by both Interviewee 2 and Interviewee 5 for including smartphone batteries in their starter packs: in case someone needs to call a rideshare after hours. Interviewee 5 said that she often "jokes" at GDC about including in the conference's swag bag "that nail polish that you can use to make sure that there's not drugs in your drink."[36] She went on: "But I was like jokingly serious because I think if GDC had those in the kit it would send a message to say, 'We know this happens, so knock it off,' and it would also say 'we want people to be safe.' But I don't think GDC would ever do that because if they stated that they would have to admit that that kind of stuff does happen at GDC parties." The grounds for this "joke" are neither hyperbolic nor paranoid. According to Interviewee 5, "I have more than one friend who has been drugged at a GDC event." Interviewee 2, for her part, noted how her nonprofit organization (which sponsors women and nonbinary folks to attend GDC) was planning to include date-rape drug–detecting products in kits it made for program participants at the 2020 GDC, before the conference got canceled due to COVID-19; canceled, in other words, to keep *everyone* safe. I say this not to critique the sound public health rationale for canceling this event (and countless others) but to underscore that for many attendees, GDC and other industry events have *never* been safe.

Bodily Care: Service and Repair

Often accompanying food and beverage, both in participants' starter packs and in interviewees' depictions of how they stay healthy and safe during events, is a class of items broadly grouped together as "things you would get at a pharmacy." This is where accounts of the toll games industry conventions take on bodies become most pronounced. As part of the tactical and infrastructural work her organization carries out for the gender minority workers it sponsors to attend GDC, Interviewee 2 says that program participants receive their own starter pack of sorts. It includes painkillers, antacid tablets, cough drops, hand sanitizer, and lip balm and (as indicated above) would have included a date rape drug detection kit for GDC 2020. Every interviewee, as well as a large number of participants who completed a starter pack but declined an interview, referenced how tiring games industry events can be. Long hours of being "always on" (in Interviewee 5's words); constant hand shaking and close talking; not eating well and not drinking enough water; sleeping little or poorly; being hungover; standing or walking longer than one is accustomed to—these and other conditions, in addition to the strain of so many people, interactions, and energies, wears bodies down. No matter how careful people are, many inevitably get sick. Interviewee 2 referred to the "GDC plague," noting that it is a fairly commonplace term, usually striking halfway through the week-long convention.

Interviewee 3, who had not attended GDC but had helped operate the booth at E3 the year their studio released a new game, offered a vivid description of the connection between the kind of affective labor they were required to carry out and an industry culture that routinely denies people's need and ability to care for their bodies. They put both Motrin and Pepto-Bismol in their starter pack; half of its limited inventory went toward bodily care and repair. They remarked that if they had been given room to put more items, they would have included feminine hygiene products because, in their words, "stress can do weird things to your hormones, and your calendar says it's coming one day, and suddenly your friend says oh my God. And you want to be there for your few uterus-having people on the team, because dudes aren't going to have pads in their bags." Throughout our conversation, Interviewee 3 demonstrated an acute awareness of the damage events like E3 can do to bodies. Both the Motrin and Pepto-Bismol were included to fix this damage, allowing them to continue to carry out the work they were flown there to do: interact with fans at their studio's booth for ten to eleven hours a day as a service to the fans who themselves had traveled to attend the event. They remarked that the Motrin in particular helped in this regard:

> Like your whole body is clenched all day, basically, and especially when you're on the floor you can't really show it. Because these people have often traveled a long way and they're excited to meet the devs [developers] and play the game. So that and for my own sake—I don't want to suffer—so the Motrin helps me feel assured that when the almost inevitable physical pain of some degree shows up, I can deal with it and keep going.

Pain and fatigue are as inevitable as GDC plague; given the crucial role that attending these events is (or was) for so many participants, the best one can do is plan for it and bring pharmaceutical products to help their body through it.

Interviewee 3 went on to describe how the intensive travel involved in many facets of the games industry (at least before the pandemic), including to and from industry conventions, led to them being almost constantly sick in their prior job, for which they had traveled to E3. "If they don't get sick at the con," they remarked, "they're sick when they get home. And then they spread it around the whole friggen' floor, because even though we have sick days it's not seen as good to take it if you just have a cough, but then everyone gets it." They described open office plans, routine travel, a cavalier attitude toward public health on the part of the colleagues (mostly men) they worked with, human resources management organized around "crunch," and a desire to be there for your colleagues as all contributing to being almost constantly sick.

> That's the culture, right? You push yourself to show up because otherwise people will be left hanging. And I get it, because I used to be that way. But after a while I realized no, it's not on me. If they've scheduled me so tightly, that's their problem. So I became a bit of a crochety person, I guess, after a while of having to deal with getting sick. I've never been so sick as the few years I worked there, just because of the open office and how many people would bring their illnesses all the time. Oh, it's just a cough, and then it gets to you. You can hear it spreading in the open office; each row started coughing. Next week, my turn. (Interviewee 3)

The emphasis on coming into the office even while sick seems deeply ironic for an industry at the forefront of transformations in casualized, globally distributed, highly mobile labor pools.[37] Yet this "warrior mentality," persistent even under conditions of intense political economic transformation and, more recently, a global pandemic that has made working remotely the default for large swaths of the white-collar workforce, certainly predates the games industry. Under the patriarchal organization of capitalism, the prioritization of capital accumulation over the safety of workers' bodies has become instrumentalized as a distinctly masculine imperative to push through the pain.[38] As Interviewee 3 put it, "make sure you hide your weaknesses; show no vulnerability; if you're hurt like suck it up, keep going." This masculinized value on "sucking it up" is mobilized, in contemporary conditions, through the games industry's reliance on crunch, its soft policies around not taking the time off to which one is entitled, and certainly its arrangement of industry conferences, in which getting the GDC plague and taking it back home to give to all your coworkers is seen as just part of the job.

Cargo Shorts Simulators

In preparing to write the conclusion for this chapter, I went for a walk in the woods. As with many of this book's chapters, I composed this one during a writing retreat at the height of the COVID-19 pandemic, at a secluded cabin in North Carolina halfway between Raleigh and Charlotte. The closest trailhead was a ten-minute drive away through winding back roads. Once I parked at the trailhead, I grabbed my jacket, keys, wallet, mask, and smartphone—my own "pandemic walk in the woods starter kit," perhaps. Trudging along the trail, I thought about the kinds of AAA games that frequently get announced, marketed, and dissected at games industry events— games like those in the *Assassin's Creed*, *FarCry*, and *Witcher* franchises, or *Skyrim* and *Fallout*, open worlds that give players almost unfettered mobility through lush, atmospheric environments populated with colorful, canny (and uncanny) nonplayer characters and massive bestiaries' worth of enemies. Storage systems are fundamental to the design of these experiences. Capacious inventories allow playable characters to cart entire armories around with them, not to mention near endless amounts of potions, traps, raw materials, and so on. In *Diablo 2: Resurrected*, considered by modern genre standards to have a relatively limited inventory, my character can cart around multiple suits of armor, polearms and crossbows, quivers of arrows, and dozens of potions. These games may entice players with characters whose fantastical skills and abilities are always just enough to scrape by in a hostile world, but perhaps the characters' most fantastic superpowers lie in their carrying capacities. That said, these worlds always offer more to collect than a character can possibly store, making gameplay a cyclical routine of adventuring, gathering loot, sorting loot to find space in the inventory, traveling back to a vendor to turn inventory into currency, improving weapons and armor, and heading back out. Small wonder they are called, colloquially, "backpack simulators"—though perhaps a more apt name, given what we know about the gendered politics of both pockets and game studios, might be "cargo short simulators."

Ruminating on these games and what they might mean for the inventory-simulation exercise I had used with study participants to learn about the gendered politics of games industry conventions, I realized at the halfway point in my walk that my smartphone had fallen out of my jacket. I checked and rechecked my pockets, my mind refusing to believe what my senses were telling me. I patted myself down from neck to feet as if my phone could have somehow fallen not *out* of my pocket but *into* me. It was late in the day; I was by myself in the woods one and a half hours from my home in Raleigh without a way to navigate back to my cabin, which did not even have Wi-Fi. For perhaps the first time in my recent memory, I felt acute concern for my own safety *not* related to the pandemic or driving a car—not out of any immediate threat but because of what the loss of my smartphone might mean for my ability to find my way back to my cabin and communicate with my family.[39] I retraced my steps and found the smartphone some ten minutes back along the trail, face down on fallen leaves by a bend in the path. The first thing I did was to text my partner to tell her that everything was okay, even though for a few minutes, I had felt like it was certainly not.

What might cargo short simulators, games industry convention starter packs, and my bumbling misadventure in the woods have in common? Each reveals something about the ways we experience connections between mobility, storage, and safety and how these experiences are *always* conditioned by social location and gender identity (among other markers of difference).[40] My age, race, gender, class, and ability intersect to ensure that the only threats to my safety while I am alone walking in the woods, through campus or city streets at night, or while doing fieldwork arise from my own carelessness. My partner, in contrast, often walks with one or both hands in her pockets, keys jutting out of her clenched fist in case of an attack. When we lived in Raleigh, she would not walk home from work in the winter, because it was dark out by the time she left and Raleigh's city streets are poorly lit. For her, and maybe for women and gender minority folks reading this, none of the stories I have collected in this chapter come as a surprise. Those who may be surprised are people like me, who embody a similar set of privileges and might rarely have to shoulder the burden of protecting themselves. Considering the gender and racial demographics of the games industry, we can safely say that this privileged group also includes the majority of people who *make* and *play* cargo short simulators—those virtual experiences of forceful motion and capacious storage in which the intersections of mobility and danger are not triggering but pleasurable and where every challenge can be met by digging something out of your cartoonishly large inventory.[41] Games in this genre often make a big splash in gaming communities and at industry conventions. They also come out of major studios (Activision Blizzard, CD Projekt Red, Rockstar, Ubisoft) with troubling records of misogyny and sexual harassment in the workplace, exploitative workplace practices, or both.

The quasiplayful study of starter packs around which this chapter is built is, in many ways, the inverse of a cargo short simulator. While the meme format engaged the imagination of the games industry workers, educators, and researchers who participated, it was deliberately and explicitly about their embodied and emplaced experiences, and it enforced a rigidly constrained economy of items. In doing so, it revealed some of the highly inventive forms of work that participants carry out to keep women and nonbinary folk safe at events in which the threats are not fantastical and alien but urgent, utterly predictable, and far too common. I feel fortunate to have talked with them and collected their stories. The interviews unfolded in the wake of a lawsuit by the US Equal Employment Opportunity Commission against Activision Blizzard, alleging multiple employees' claims of sexual harassment and a "frat boy" culture openly hostile to women. None of the interviewees were surprised, of course, just tired. Shortly after I composed the initial draft of this chapter, Activision Blizzard reached a sexual harassment settlement that amounts to pennies for the massive company (USD 18 million) and in which it continues to deny any wrongdoing.[42] This reminder of the games industry's disregard for women's safety and autonomy forms the context for understanding the tiring, tactical work participants carry out, crafting pockets of care, support, and safety out of this misogynistic fabric.

NOTES

1. D'Anastasio, "Inside the Culture of Sexism at Riot Games"; Lorenz and Browning, "Dozens of Women in Gaming Speak Out about Sexism and Harassment"; Egan, "New Suit against Activision Blizzard Alleges 'Rampant Sexism' and Retaliation."
2. Taylor and Dial, "Fuel, Fatigue, Fashion."
3. Fuller, *Media Ecologies*, 16.
4. Cargo shorts are a perennial object of polarizing debate among cultural observers, so much so that *Mel Magazine* ranks the top eleven defenses of cargo shorts (Klee, "11 Defenses of Cargo Shorts, Ranked"; see also Armstrong, "I Am a Pair of

Eddie Bauer Cargo Shorts, and I Have a Tasteful Number of Pockets"; Baer, "Anthropologists Analyze the Cargo-Short Boom"; Hong, "Nice Cargo Shorts! You're Sleeping on the Sofa"). Apparently, while cargo shorts are bad for men's fashion, they are good for platformized news production.

5. Edelman, "It's Time to Bring Back Cargo Pants."

6. Sofia, "Container Technologies," 182. See also Duffy and Packer, "Wifesaver."

7. Unsworth, "Hands Deep in History," 149.

8. Unsworth, "Hands Deep in History," 150.

9. Unsworth, "Hands Deep in History," 158.

10. Schwanz, "Thanks! It Has Pockets!"

11. Yau, "A Visual Analysis of Jean Pockets and Their Lack of Practicality."

12. See, for instance, Bulut, "White Masculinity, Creative Desires, and Production Ideology in Video Game Development"; Kerr and Kelleher, "Recruitment of Passion and Community in the Service of Capital"; Harvey and Fisher, "'Everyone Can Make Games!'"; Johnson, "Technomasculinity and Its Influence in Video Game Production."

13. Butt, "Alcohol and Alienation in Moscone"; Fisher, "Diary of a GDC Party Girl."

14. Eschler and Menking, "'No Prejudice Here,'" 2.

15. Crowe and Bradford, "'Hanging Out in Runescape,'" 331.

16. Milner, *World Made Meme*, 5.

17. Eschler and Menking, "'No Prejudice Here,'" 9.

18. Unsworth, "Hands Deep in History," 163.

19. Eschler and Menking, "'No Prejudice Here,'" 2.

20. I carried out six of the interviews, and Aaron carried out one. Of the interviewees I met with, five identify as women and one as nonbinary. Aaron interviewed the only man involved in this part of the study.

21. A 2021 survey published by the International Game Developers Association (IGDA) reports that 61 percent of respondents identified as men, 30 percent as women, 8 percent as nonbinary, gender fluid, genderqueer, or two spirited, and 7 percent as transgender (Weststar, "Developer Satisfaction Survey 2021," 8).

22. The same IGDA report states that the average age of respondents was thirty-seven years, and most (52 percent) were between twenty-six and thirty-five. With regard to race, two-thirds of the IGDA survey respondents identified solely as white, 9 percent as Hispanic or Latino/Latina/Latinx, and 7 percent as East Asian (Weststar, "Developer Satisfaction Survey 2021," 8).

23. ECGC, "Passes & Prices."

24. Egan, "New Suit against Activision Blizzard Alleges 'Rampant Sexism' and Retaliation"; D'Anastasio, "Inside the Culture of Sexism at Riot Games."

25. Cornfeld, "Babes in Tech Land," 206. At GDC, the same year as the interactions Interviewee 2 describes, Microsoft hired skimpily clad women dancers for its after-party, a move that (once leaked) was described as reversing progress on

the "shameful history of objectifying women in major promotional venues." Sottek, "Microsoft's GDC Party Extends Tradition of Sexism in the Gaming Industry."

26. Cornfeld, "Babes in Tech Land," 209.

27. Gitelman, *Paper Knowledge*, 2.

28. Taiwo, "'Take My Card,'" 45.

29. de Certeau, *Practice of Everyday Life*, 34–39.

30. Gitelman, *Paper Knowledge*, 20.

31. Babel, "Invisible Walls of the Whisper Network," 1.

32. Blodgett and Salter, "#1ReasonWhy."

33. This kind of care might resonate with parents of young children, who understand how a well-timed snack bar or pack of crackers can mean the difference between tantrum and relative peace.

34. They mentioned, as well, that their ongoing choice to consume meat occasionally is accompanied by a realization that while individual choices matter in curbing climate change, "I'm not making a rocket going into space, or all this other stuff that's way more polluting."

35. Here, she is referring to the aforementioned Microsoft after-party in 2016 involving dancers in skimpy schoolgirl outfits. Sottek, "Microsoft's GDC Party Extends Tradition of Sexism in the Gaming Industry."

36. There are now a range of consumer goods designed to detect the presence of date-rape drugs including those based on Xanax (alprazolam) and diazepam, though the initial inventors of the nail polish (students from NCSU) opted instead for a discreet, disposable sample kit (LaVito, "Date Rape Drug Test Allows Women to Discreetly Check for Spiked Drinks with a Few Drops").

37. Bulut, *A Precarious Game*; Kerr, *Global Games*; Dyer-Witheford and Peuter, *Games of Empire*.

38. Vigna and Zancarini-Fournel, "Gender History and Labour History," 191.

39. These concerns were mostly irrational, of course. The trailhead was relatively busy; I could have found my way back to my cabin with some assistance and could easily have driven to a place with Wi-Fi access to contact my partner.

40. Questions of how mobility and privilege intersect are at the core of the "mobility turn" heralded by Mimi Sheller and John Urry (Sheller and Urry, "New Mobilities Paradigm," 208). A powerful critique of this turn comes from Zoe Sofia, however, who insists that foregrounding mobilities in our accounts of networked media hides the importance of *storage* and the ways storage media are themselves frequently feminized (Sofia, "Container Technologies," 182). The tensions between transportation and storage, at both the embodied and metatheoretical levels, are what I am trying to capture in this anecdote about my walk in the woods and this chapter more broadly.

41. Weststar, "Developer Satisfaction Survey 2021"; Brune, "Zooming in on Female Gamers with Consumer Insights Data."

42. Limbong, "Judge Approves Activision Blizzard $18 Million Settlement in Sexual Harassment Suit."

CONCLUSION

Boundaries, (Re)taking the Field

Boundary Work

The motif for this brief concluding chapter is the boundary. Customarily, the conclusion of an academic book is where authors discuss the boundaries of their own work, gesturing to sites and terrains opened up by their analysis and marking lines beyond which their work does not extend. Karen Barad remarks that boundaries are interventions into the world, interventions that both define differences and make them real: boundaries are "material-discursive practices" through which "matter is differentially engaged and articulated."[1] For Barad, boundaries are incredibly productive in the sense of (re)generating relations of difference—as such, they are never innocent. In a sense, this entire book has been about the boundary making carried out by and for digital games; boundaries inhere in any act of enframing (chap. 1) and place making, from the domestic apparatuses of white masculine escape discussed in chapter 2 to the infrastructural gridwork of LANs considered in chapter 3, the decisions around where and how to build collegiate esports in chapter 4, and the boundaries between day and night, on-site and off-site, safe and unsafe, navigated by women and nonbinary games workers at industry conventions, whose experiences I recounted in chapter 5. Each of these essays has considered the production of boundaries between who belongs and who does not in places where games are played, discussed, made, and watched, and each has considered, in turn, how these boundaries work to (re)produce the inequalities that characterize so many gaming cultures. But I have also attempted to show how the boundary-making work of digital play is never limited to the localized sites of gaming, that the boundaries that define contemporary sites of play are productive of a host of interconnected sets of relations, including gender and racial difference; economic privilege and exploitation (including how land and resources are allocated for gaming); and the increasing capture of communicative practices and social belonging by the extracting and sorting apparatuses of platformization. But we can also think of boundaries in academic knowledge production: those used to separate academic disciplines, determine legitimate knowledge claims and ways of knowing from illegitimate ones, and demarcate what lies within and beyond the scope of any given account.

Beyond a Canon

To explore these disciplinary and epistemic senses of boundary making, I offer one last story—one not about endings, which perhaps might be more fitting a conclusion, but about origins. It is about how the academic study of digital games took shape in a particular place and time and became "game studies," the field in which, more than any other, this book might claim to belong. I am piecing this story together from a pair of podcast episodes. The first is an episode of *Designer Notes*, a series about the craft of game design, in which Soren Johnson (a game designer himself) interviews veteran game designer and educator Frank Lantz. The second is an episode of *Game Studies Study Buddies* in which the hosts—Cameron Kunzelman and Michael Lutz, two humanities scholars deeply versed in the study, design, and play of games—critically engage academic books relevant to these pursuits. In the episode I draw from here, Kunzelman and Lutz discuss *Beyond a Boundary*, the autobiography of Marxist historian and Pan-Africanist C. L. R. James, which recounts his experiences as a cricket player in British-colonized Trinidad in the early 1900s. This game studies origin story goes something like this. Back in the late 1990s, Frank Lantz and his colleague Eric Zimmerman (who coined the "magic circle jerk" discussed in chap. 2) approached the head of New York University's interactive telecommunications program about the possibility of offering an elective graduate course on game design. According to Lantz, this course was among the first of its kind in North America, and the two game developer entrepreneurs and would-be university instructors ventured "to the library, and just like started doing research" looking for scholarly accounts of games from "sociology or anthropology or psychology" that could place their game design instruction in "a bigger context."[2] Lantz specifically mentions coming across the works of Johann Huizinga, Roger Caillois, and Brian Sutton-Smith: the first two were armchair ethnologists writing in the early and mid-twentieth century, while the third was a prolific developmental psychologist who wrote about the evolutionary and psychosocial functions of play. All were concerned with developing transhistorical and culturally generalizable theories of games and play and their role in human civilization.

Lantz and Zimmerman's library dive occurred at a time when games were beginning to draw considerable scholarly attention from multiple fields, including education, literature studies, and gender studies. Janet Murray's *Hamlet on the Holodeck*, Espen Aarseth's *Cybertext: Perspectives on Ergodic Literature*, and the edited collection on gender and digital games by Justine Cassell and Henry Jenkins, *From Barbie to Mortal Kombat*, were all published between 1997 and 1999.[3] That said, it is clear from Lantz's account that he and Zimmerman, at least, were looking to anchor their own pioneering work in university-level game design instruction in a longer intellectual tradition—perhaps out of a concern for justifying the study of games and game making as academic pursuits. They were looking for a canon. That these trips to the library proved highly agential to the fledgling amalgamation of scholars interested in games, particularly in the Global North and the humanities, is obvious from the frequency with which Huizinga's *Homo Ludens* and Caillois's *Man, Play and Games* began to land in course syllabi and bibliographies related to games research and university-based game design starting in the early 2000s.[4] According to Cameron Kunzelman, Lantz himself is fairly frank about the "implicit selection bias" at work in his and Zimmerman's trips into the stacks.[5] We might imagine that they saw in Huizinga's and Caillois's texts civilization-spanning accounts that situate games and play as foundational elements of all human culture, an intellectual lineage that could legitimize video games as an object of scholarly pursuit and a way of framing digital games as the inheritors, under novel technological conditions, of humanity's universal drive to play.

I appreciate this story of early game studies canon building for several reasons. First, it is above all a story of place and of how our practices of knowledge building are always situated, mediated, and shaped by the infrastructures (including, centrally, libraries) and locations available to us. This is as true for Lantz and Zimmerman, scouring the library for a longer intellectual history of games and play, as it was for Caillois and Huizinga, armchair ethnologists who scoured texts by colonial anthropologists and comparative sociologists for their transhistorical theorizations of games. And it is certainly true for me, given all the forms of passage I am granted within masculinized gaming cultures (not to mention within academia) on account of my subjectivity, the "assimilative capacity" I borrow from the fields of anticolonial critique and environmental studies in chapter 1. Of course, we cannot treat Lantz's account as *the* origin story for game studies—this would constitute an inaccurate and neocolonialist rendering of what has always been a globalized and intellectually diverse field of academic knowledge production, reestablishing the metropole (in this case, New York) as the rightful center of game studies. There are multiple game studies and multiple origin stories: stories of how games attracted scholars in the Nordic countries, India, Brazil, Latin America, Australia, Canada, Japan, and so on and how these locations, their histories, and their infrastructural conditions have allowed regional games networks with specific concerns, methodologies, and perspectives to take root and grow. Nevertheless, it would be naive to pretend that the dynamics highlighted in *this* origin story are not agential, as Huizinga and Caillois are positioned, frequently and problematically, as game studies canon.

The second reason I appreciate this story, then, is that it is a fable both *of* and *about* contemporary colonialism and the politics of our knowledge-building and citational practices—about who and what gets canonized, why, and by whom. The features that perhaps drew Lantz and Zimmerman to *Homo Ludens* and *Man, Play and Games* are, of course, some of the very characteristics that have led scholars across numerous academic fields to problematize the formation of canons constituted primarily by Western and Eurocentric perspectives, scholars, and knowledge-building practices. In more incisive critiques, existing canons do not simply "reflect bias" toward Western and Eurocentric scholarship; the work of canon building has been one of privileging objectivism, entrenching a liberal humanism that presumes an unmarked and universalized subject (who is thereby assumed to be white, settler, cis, and male) and reifying hierarchies produced through and for colonial rule.[6] In other words, canon building in the humanities has been carried out as an extension of colonialist modes of boundary making, an insight that returns to themes developed in chapter 1 and chapter 4.

A similar critique has been leveled specifically against the game studies canon that was (perhaps inadvertently) summoned into being through the earnest and well-intentioned work of Lantz and Zimmerman, among other scholars and practitioners casting about in the late 1990s and early 2000s for serious theorizations of games and play. Tara Fickle's chapter in her book *The Race Card* on "the Orientalist origins of game studies" offers a trenchant discussion of the colonialist worldview underpinning Huizinga's and Caillois's canonical works. Both Huizinga and Caillois used "the Orientalist imaginary"—the Eurocentric reliance on and continual reproduction of the Orient as an inverse mirror of European civilization—"as the formal logic guiding their theories."[7] In the case of Huizinga, who "trained as an Orientalist" and whose examples in *Homo Ludens* draw from a wide range of knowledge about Asian and South American histories and practices (produced by Europeans, of course), Fickle notes a "striking formal parallelism" between the "absolute divide between East and West" in Huizinga's work and his conviction in an "absolute, zero-sum divide" between play and real life. The result is an account of play as a universal impulse in which the magic circle and the strict division between Occident and Orient are both used as "boundary-drawing" exercises—one institutional, the other cartographic— that intertwine to assert the supremacy of European civilization.[8] As for Caillois, Fickle demonstrates how his categorization of play is built on the taxonomic preoccupations of the Enlightenment and specifically Carl Linneas's hierarchical organization of humanity into "four racial 'subspecies.'"[9] Animating *Man, Play and Games* is a concern with grafting the four types of play (competition, chance, simulation, and vertigo) to an evolutionary teleology of race in which competition, as the most virtuous form of play, is the hallmark of the most advanced societies. Extending Fickle's critique of this oft-used taxonomy, Aaron Trammell points out how "competition and chance," which for Caillois "yield the meritocratic structures that underlie much of white European society," are seen as more sophisticated forms of play. These are nonetheless corruptible by "mimicry and vertigo," which are in turn associated with "primitive" societies encountered through (and often devastated by) European imperialism.[10] To Fickle and Trammell's critical interrogations of the Orientalism undergirding the game studies canon, we might also point out that the boundaries and taxonomies Huizinga and Caillois construct not only *reflect* Orientalist renderings of the Other. They were produced through Huizinga and Caillois's reliance on the works of

early anthropology and sociology: knowledge-building practices that relied on and helped extend colonizers' extractive relations to Indigenous
land and peoples and that, in turn, produced comparative (which is to say,
hierarchical) accounts of the differences between European and Indigenous
cultures.[11] In the glib terms offered by Kunzelman and Saltsman on their
podcast, "Caillois is racist"—not just because he and Huizinga parrot racial
stereotypes rooted in colonial relations of dispossession and genocide but
also because the accounts they draw on both legitimize and were made
possible by the manifold boundaries that colonialism produced, separating
European and white from Other.[12]

A further reason why I appreciate this story is because it leads Kunzelman to a speculative prompt, which he poses briefly in the same podcast
episode: "What if we read James instead of Caillois?" In this, he is referring to *Beyond a Boundary*, the largely autobiographical account of cricket
in the West Indies under British colonial rule written by C. L. R. James.
While Kunzelman has not yet explored this question himself (as of the
time of this writing in late 2022), I am very grateful that he put it to his and
Lutz's podcast audience. It is a question about operating from different
grounds—epistemically and methodologically—in constructing understandings of digital games. *Beyond a Boundary* is held up by sport scholars
and journalists as one of the most important books on sports and culture
ever produced. It is at once an exhaustive description of the key players,
clubs, leagues, and social and political conditions that characterized cricket
play in the West Indies in the early twentieth century; a reflection on the
aesthetics and politics of the sport; and an exploration of the ways in which
cricket, as a cultural institution, instrument of colonial rule, and place-
making practice, engaged and transformed the fabric of James's world. This
is a subtle but absolutely vital insight into how we make sense of games.
The theorizations of Caillois and Huizinga were generated through textual
engagement with accounts of other/Other cultures, accounts furnished by
the colonial and colonizing encounters of comparative anthropology and
sociology. According to their armchair epistemology, games themselves
are texts from which we can read off inherent characteristics of the societies that play them. For James, on the other hand, cricket is a powerful
mechanism of becoming: both a cultural institution and a set of abstract
ideals and embodied practices that do not simply express ideologies about
race, and class, and nation but transform them. Cricket provided means for

darker-skinned Trinidadians and those from lower socioeconomic rungs to ascend to positions of wealth and status beyond their otherwise racially or economically designated stations, a way for racial or class solidarities to form and dissolve, and so on. For James, cricket refracted and reproduced logics of class, colonialism, and race, reworking them in ways that were perhaps not revolutionary but were certainly transformative beyond the space and time of the cricket pitch.

James regards the idea that cricket could function as if set apart from the political and cultural fabric of everyday life as an imperial (im)position, one impossible for those racially Othered through colonial relationality. He writes that "the British tradition soaked deep into me was that when you entered the sporting arena you left behind you the sordid compromises of everyday existence. Yet for us to do that we would have had to divest ourselves of our skins."[13] Only those privileged by colonial rule could believe that play can ever be separated from politics. As Kunzelman and Lutz discuss, this is a far cry from the notion of play existing within a magic circle in Huizinga's *Homo Ludens*, which I reimagined as a practice of white masculine domestic boundary making in chapter 2.[14] But if this imperialist and imperializing notion continues to manifest in subtle ways in games scholarship, such as in the representationalist notion that games merely reflect or express social and political orders rather than transform and reproduce them, it shows up much more explicitly in conventional (and frequently reactionary) discourses about video games and sports alike. It is why the many exhortations to keep politics out (of "our" games, sports, discussion forums, and so on) only ever serve as rhetorical boundary-making mechanisms that allow for the linked operations of settler capitalism, racism, and patriarchy to continue unchallenged.[15] This is precisely the material-discursive boundary beyond which James encourages us to cross as we make sense of the cultural and political significance of play—at once referring to the physical line in cricket marking the perimeter of the pitch and, simultaneously, the ideological line produced by and for colonial rule, separating what is inside and of the game and what is outside. And while James is passionate about the rules of cricket and the game's integrity, he is also clear in his rebuke of the boundary between play and the political: "The reader is here invited to make up his mind. If for him all this is 'not cricket,' then he should take friendly warning and go in peace (or in wrath). These are no random reminiscences. This is the game as I have known it and this is the game I am going to write about. How could it be otherwise?"[16] Kunzelman and Lutz's podcast episode on *Beyond a Boundary* proceeds by highlighting sections of the book and, frequently, specific passages that they consider of interest to an audience of game studies scholars. This is a productive and thoughtful exercise, but it is Kunzelman's initial prompt that I regard as more generative in the long term: how would we approach the study of digital play if we took *Beyond a Boundary* as our foundation rather than *Man, Play and Games*? Learning from James's book as a whole, this might mean, among other things, privileging narrative as a generous wellspring of theoretical knowledge and with it, modes of knowing that value partiality, situatedness, relationality, and embodiment over objectivism, taxonomization, and generalizability.[17] And certainly, James's work invites a reflexive and rich understanding of boundaries—not as static demarcations but as active, dynamic, material-discursive interventions into the world that ought to be problematized rather than accepted as fact. This goes as much for disciplinary boundaries (such as those that tell us our stories are "just anecdotes" and our firsthand experiences are mere "bias") as those spatial, technical, and temporal ones that separate the inside of a game from the outside.

These are the lessons from *Beyond a Boundary* I have in mind in thinking through what my own book might offer as a collection of attempts at coming to terms with the ways whiteness, masculinity, and gaming are bound together in place-making projects. A reflexive and deliberate playing with boundaries guides my consideration of boutique hotels and server farms (chap. 1), wires and wall hangings (chap. 2), pubs and railroads (chap. 3), student centers and land scrips (chap. 4), and cargo shorts and tea socials (chap. 5) while barely considering games or, for that matter, players themselves. This approach also explains my citational and knowledge-making practices, in which I have drawn extensively from scholarly traditions outside the usual boundaries of game studies scholarship (and media studies more broadly), traditions that nonetheless enable me to connect questions of interactive media and its cultural politics to considerations about infrastructure and land: hence this book's indebtedness to anticolonial critique, cultural geography, critical infrastructure studies, and feminist new materialism. This scholarship has allowed me to locate the conditions of gaming's manifold inequalities beyond the boundaries of representationalist analysis. In doing so, I have sought to problematize the ways games scholars often define the proper objects of study solely in terms of the figures in the frame.

I have drawn critical attention to how gaming's cultural and ideological boundaries are always also spatial, formed *in* place and *as* place making.

Reconstituting the Grounds of Gaming

The connective fabric running through this entire book is the notion that certain toxic formations of masculinity are *infrastructural* to contemporary gaming cultures. These formations are both made possible by and engaged in the reproduction of the conjoined projects of patriarchy, racism, colonialism, and capitalism and expressed acutely through the cultivation and demonstration of mastery with apparatuses of digital play. They circulate through the various contexts I have explored in this book (and many more that I have not—I would have loved to consider esports team houses, game development studios, and other important sites) as readily as data, internet connectivity, and electricity. As infrastructure, these formations support the communicative practices and processes of becoming and belonging of players, developers, researchers, and so on who enjoy the most unfettered access to physical contexts of gaming.

Holding this theoretical position means casting a skeptical eye toward solutions for gaming's inequalities and exclusions that begin and end with games themselves—for instance, by tweaking the ways games portray race and gender, a solution frequently invoked by games researchers and development studios alike. But contaminated water crises are not fixed by replacing individual faucets. Likewise, I am grateful to Aaron Trammell for his argument that "a postcolonial approach to play must begin by centering people, not games"; I understand this claim as urging game scholars to specifically consider the play practices of BIPOC individuals and communities.[18] At the same time, we ought to acknowledge the ways in which much player-centered research on games—and there is a considerable amount—is engaged explicitly in settler capitalist logics of capture, categorization, and commodification. As I argue in chapter 1, a focus on the figures in the frame does not itself constitute the kinds of good relations to which an anticolonial and antiracist approach to gaming and social justice might aspire. Rather, in the theoretical position I hold here, attempts to make gaming cultures more hospitable and sustainable *must* address the politics of place. This runs contrary to games industries' long-standing efforts to sell us on notions of transportation and immersion, as documented in chapter 2, and in certain prevalent threads of theory building in game studies that enclose digital play in epistemic boundaries only slightly more expansive, if at all, than those peddled by the games industry. Contrary to these visions, gaming is resolutely space-taking and place-making: we make space for gaming in our homes, our places of work and learning, our lives, our neighborhoods, our environment, and as we do, gaming takes place. If we accept that—and if we acknowledge that in our given social, political, and technological milieu, white masculinity is infrastructural to gaming's space-taking and place-making ways—then we would do well to pursue projects that reconstitute the relations between space, place, and play in whichever localized and temporary ways are available to us. These projects are already underway and take myriad forms: daytime tea socials for women and gender minorities at games industry conventions (as discussed in chap. 5); collegiate esports programs that make space and time for casual players and invite multiple forms of participation in the production and play of competitive gaming, as discussed in chapter 4 (and that post clear and consequential codes of conduct!); game playing and crafting circles in feminist bookstores, Indigenous community centers, and similar sites of community gathering and solidarity.[19] These place-making practices disrupt the infrastructural flow of white masculinity by quite literally *reconstructing* the spaces in which we play, from the ground up.

NOTES

1. Barad, "Posthumanist Performativity," 822.

2. Johnson and Saltsman, "Designer Notes: Frank Lantz."

3. Aarseth, *Cybertext*; Cassell and Jenkins, *From Barbie to Mortal Kombat*; Murray, *Hamlet on the Holodeck*.

4. This is an evocative and gestural claim rather than a strictly objective one. That said, a quick Google Scholar search for "video games" within the over seven thousand works that cite *Man, Play and Games* yields over four thousand articles since the year 2000. The same exercise for *Homo Ludens* yields almost nine thousand as of the time of this writing (late 2022).

5. Kunzelman, Personal communication.

6. Braidotti, *Posthuman*; Chakravartty et al., "#CommunicationSoWhite"; Trammell, "Decolonizing Play."

7. Fickle, *Race Card*, 118.

8. Fickle, *Race Card*, 123.

9. Fickle, *Race Card*, 132.

10. Trammell, "Decolonizing Play," 241.

11. Beresin, "A More Serious Introduction," 136.

12. Kunzelman and Lutz, "James—Beyond A Boundary."

13. James, *Beyond a Boundary*, 66.

14. Kunzelman and Lutz, "James—Beyond A Boundary."

15. Trammell, *Repairing Play*.

16. James, *Beyond a Boundary*, 51. As the language in this passage indicates, gender relations are not at the fore of James's concerns. The masculinity of cricket players, and of his readership, is not problematized in the same ways as class, race, and nationality.

17. This same lesson has been offered up repeatedly by generations of feminist and Indigenous ethnographers, Black feminist writers, and autoethnographers, among others.

18. Trammell, "Decolonizing Play," 241.

19. See, for instance, QGCon, "What Is QGCon?"; LaPensée and Lewis, "Skins"; Schoemann, "Power of Community Organizing."

BIBLIOGRAPHY

Aarseth, Espen. "Allegories of Space: The Question of Spatiality in Computer Games." In *Cybertext Yearbook 2000*, edited by Markku Eskelinen and Raine Koskimaa, 152–71. Jyväskylä: University of Jyväskylä, 2001. https://jyx.jyu.fi /handle/123456789/77567.

———. *Cybertext: Perspectives on Ergodic Literature*. Baltimore: JHU Press, 1997.

Alexander, Michelle. *The New Jim Crow: Mass Incarceration in the Age of Color-blindness*. New York: New Press, 2020.

Allen, Louisa, John Fenaughty, and Lucy Cowie. "Thinking with New Materialism about 'Safe-Un-Safe' Campus Space for LGBTTIQA+ Students." *Social & Cultural Geography* 23, no. 5 (August 18, 2020): 1–17. https://doi.org/10.1080 /14649365.2020.1809012.

Amenabar, Teddy. "Teachers Say PlayVS Wields Partnerships to Monopolize Scholastic Esports." *Washington Post*, April 11, 2022. https://www.washingtonpost .com/video-games/esports/2022/04/11/playvs-high-school-esports/.

Anable, Aubrey. *Playing with Feelings: Video Games and Affect*. St. Paul: University of Minnesota Press, 2018.

Andrejevic, Mark. "Ubiquitous Computing and the Digital Enclosure Movement." *Media International Australia* 125, no. 1 (2007): 106–17.

———. "Ubiquitous Surveillance." In *Routledge Handbook of Surveillance Studies*, edited by Kirstie Ball, Kevin Haggerty, and David Lyon, 91–98. New York: Taylor & Francis, 2012.

AnyKey. "Diversity & Inclusion in Collegiate Esports: Challenges, Opportunities, and Interventions." October 2019. https://www.anykey.org/resources.

Aouragh, Miriyam, and Paula Chakravartty. "Infrastructures of Empire: Towards a Critical Geopolitics of Media and Information Studies." *Media,*

Culture & Society 38, no. 4 (May 1, 2016): 559–75. https://doi.org/10.1177
/0163443716643007.

Apperley, Thomas. "Digital Gaming, Social Inclusion, and the Right to Play: A
Case Study of a Venezuelan Cybercafe." In *The Routledge Companion to Digital
Ethnography*, edited by Larissa Hjorth, Heather Horst, and Genevieve Bell,
235–43. New York: Routledge, 2017.

Armstrong, Bobbie. "I Am a Pair of Eddie Bauer Cargo Shorts, and I Have a
Tasteful Number of Pockets." *McSweeney's Internet Tendency*, July 17, 2020.
https://www.mcsweeneys.net/articles/i-am-a-pair-of-eddie-bauer-cargo
-shorts-and-i-have-a-tasteful-number-of-pockets.

Ash, James. "Technologies of Captivation: Videogames and the Attunement
of Affect." *Body & Society* 19, no. 1 (March 1, 2013): 27–51. https://doi.org
/10.1177/1357034X11411737.

Ask, Kristine, and Stine H. Bang Svendsen. "Sexual Harassment in Online
Games: Bug or Feature?" *AoIR Selected Papers of Internet Research*, October 31,
2014. https://journals.uic.edu/ojs/index.php/spir/article/view/8847.

Augé, Marc. *Non-places: Introduction to an Anthropology of Supermodernity*. New
York: Verso, 1995.

Avancini, Danielly B., Joel J. P. C. Rodrigues, Simion G. B. Martins, Ricardo
A. L. Rabêlo, Jalal Al-Muhtadi, and Petar Solic. "Energy Meters Evolution in
Smart Grids: A Review." *Journal of Cleaner Production* 217 (April 20, 2019):
702–15. https://doi.org/10.1016/j.jclepro.2019.01.229.

Babel, Anna. "The Invisible Walls of the Whisper Network." *Anthropology News*
59, no. 3 (May 2018): e67–e72. https://doi.org/10.1111/AN.859.

Baer, Drake. "Anthropologists Analyze the Cargo-Short Boom." *The Cut*, September 26, 2016. https://www.thecut.com/2016/09/anthropologists-analyze
-the-cargo-short-boom.html.

Bakke, Gretchen. "Chapter 2. Electricity Is Not a Noun." In *Electrifying Anthropology: Exploring Electrical Practices and Infrastructures*, edited by Simone
Abram, Brit Ross Winthereik, and Thomas Yarrow, 25–42. London: Bloomsbury Academic, 2019. https://doi.org/10.5040/9781350102675.

Barad, Karen. "Posthumanist Performativity: Toward an Understanding of
How Matter Comes to Matter." *Signs* 28, no. 3 (2003): 801–31. https://doi
.org/10.1086/345321.

Baym, Nancy K. *Personal Connections in the Digital Age*. New York: John Wiley &
Sons, 2015.

BBC News. "Amazon, Facebook and Apple Thriving in Lockdown." July 30, 2020,
sec. Business. https://www.bbc.com/news/business-53602596.

Benjamin, Ruha. *Race after Technology: Abolitionist Tools for the New Jim Code*.
Hoboken, NJ: John Wiley & Sons, 2019.

Bennett, Jane. *Vibrant Matter: A Political Ecology of Things*. Durham, NC: Duke University Press, 2010.

Beresin, Anna. "A More Serious Introduction: A Critique of the Inherent Racism in Early Comparative Play Theory." *International Journal of Play* 10, no. 2 (April 3, 2021): 133–38. https://doi.org/10.1080/21594937.2021.1934945.

Bergstrom, Kelly, Stephanie Fisher, and Jennifer Jenson. "Disavowing 'That Guy': Identity Construction and Massively Multiplayer Online Game Players." *Convergence* 22, no. 3 (June 1, 2016): 233–49. https://doi.org/10.1177/1354856514560314.

Berlant, Lauren. "The Commons: Infrastructures for Troubling Times*." *Environment and Planning D: Society and Space* 34, no. 3 (June 1, 2016): 393–419. https://doi.org/10.1177/0263775816645989.

Bhatia, Shekhar. "Daryush 'Roosh' Valizadeh at Center of International 'Pro-rape' Storm Pictured." *Daily Mail*, February 4, 2016. https://www.dailymail.co.uk/news/article-3432531/Pictured-pick-artist-center-international-pro-rape-storm-t-shirt-shorts-door-mother-s-home-lives-basement.html.

Biswas, Asit K., and Cecilia Tortajada. "COVID-19 Heightens Water Problems around the World." *The Conversation*, June 8, 2020. http://theconversation.com/covid-19-heightens-water-problems-around-the-world-140167.

Bjarnason, Nökkvi Jarl. "Playing as Travelling: At the Border of Leisure and Learning." In *Proceedings of the 2020 DiGRA International Conference: Play Everywhere*, 1–15. Tampere: Digital Games Research Association. http://www.digra.org/digital-library/publications/playing-as-travelling-at-the-border-of-leisure-and-learning/.

Blaisdell, Benjamin, and Ronda Taylor Bullock. "White Imagination, Black Reality: Recentering Critical Race Theory in Critical Whiteness Studies." *International Journal of Qualitative Studies in Education* 36, no. 8 (2023): 1450–58. https://doi.org/10.1080/09518398.2022.2025484.

Blodgett, Bridget, and Anastasia Salter. "#1ReasonWhy: Game Communities and the Invisible Woman." Foundations of Digital Games. Association for Computing Machinery, New York, 2014. http://www.fdg2014.org/papers/fdg2014_paper_02.pdf.

Blomley, Nicholas. "Law, Property, and the Geography of Violence: The Frontier, the Survey, and the Grid." *Annals of the Association of American Geographers* 93, no. 1 (2003): 121–41.

Bollmer, Grant. *Inhuman Networks: Social Media and the Archaeology of Connection*. New York: Bloomsbury, 2016.

Boluk, Stefanie, and Patrick LeMieux. *Metagaming: Playing, Competing, Spectating, Cheating, Trading, Making, and Breaking Videogames*. St. Paul: University of Minnesota Press, 2017.

Borowy, Michael, and Dal Yong Jin. "Pioneering E-sport: The Experience Economy and the Marketing of Early 1980s Arcade Gaming Contests." *International Journal of Communication* 7 (October 15, 2013): 21.

Bowker, Geoffrey. "How to Be Universal: Some Cybernetic Strategies, 1943–70." *Social Studies of Science* 23 (June 29, 2016): 107–27. https://doi.org /10.1177/030631293023001004.

Braidotti, Rosi. *The Posthuman*. New York: John Wiley & Sons, 2013.

Bratich, Jack Z. "Amassing the Multitude: Revisiting Early Audience Studies." *Communication Theory* 15, no. 3 (2005): 242–65. https://doi.org/10.1111/j.1468 -2885.2005.tb00335.x.

Bratton, Benjamin H. *The Stack: On Software and Sovereignty*. Cambridge, MA: MIT Press, 2015.

Brock, André. *Distributed Blackness: African American Cybercultures*. New York: NYU Press, 2020.

Browne, Simone. *Dark Matters: On the Surveillance of Blackness*. Durham, NC: Duke University Press, 2015.

Brune, Mary. "Zooming in on Female Gamers with Consumer Insights Data." *Newzoo* (blog), March 8, 2022. https://newzoo.com/insights/articles /zooming-in-on-female-gamers-with-consumer-insights-data.

Bryce, Jo, and Jason Rutter. "The Gendering of Computer Gaming: Experience and Space." In *Leisure Cultures: Investigations in Sport, Media and Technology*, edited by Scott Fleming and Ian Jones, 3–22. Essex, UK: Leisure Studies Association, 2003.

Bulut, Ergin. *A Precarious Game: The Illusion of Dream Jobs in the Video Game Industry*. Ithaca, NY: Cornell University Press, 2020.

———. "White Masculinity, Creative Desires, and Production Ideology in Video Game Development." *Games and Culture* 16, no. 3 (May 1, 2021): 329–41. https://doi.org/10.1177/1555412020939873.

Butt, Mahli-Ann. "Alcohol and Alienation in Moscone." *Unwinnable*, April 18, 2018. https://unwinnable.com/2018/04/18/alcohol-and-alienation-in -moscone/.

Cacciatore, Michael A., Dietram A. Scheufele, and Shanto Iyengar. "The End of Framing as We Know It . . . and the Future of Media Effects." *Mass Communication and Society* 19, no. 1 (January 2, 2016): 7–23. https://doi.org/10.1080 /15205436.2015.1068811.

Calleja, Gordon. *In-Game: From Immersion to Incorporation*. Cambridge, MA: MIT Press, 2011.

Campbell, Hugh. "The Glass Phallus: Pub (Lic) Masculinity and Drinking in Rural New Zealand." *Rural Sociology* 65, no. 4 (2000): 562–81.

Can, Önder, and Maxwell Foxman. "Out of the Café and into the Arena: Esports Spaces and Neoliberalization in Turkey." *ROMchip* 3, no. 1 (August 19, 2021). https://romchip.org/index.php/romchip-journal/article/view/144.

Candy, Graham. "In Video Games We Trust." *Fast Capitalism* 9, no. 1 (2012): 133–41.

Cassell, Justine, and Henry Jenkins. *From Barbie to Mortal Kombat: Gender and Computer Games*. Cambridge, MA: MIT Press, 1998.

Castronova, Edward. *Synthetic Worlds: The Business and Culture of Online Games*. Chicago: University of Chicago Press, 2008.

Chakravartty, Paula, Rachel Kuo, Victoria Grubbs, and Charlton McIlwain. "#CommunicationSoWhite." *Journal of Communication* 68, no. 2 (April 1, 2018): 254–66. https://doi.org/10.1093/joc/jqy003.

Chambers, Deborah. "'Wii Play as a Family': The Rise in Family-Centred Video Gaming." *Leisure Studies* 31, no. 1 (2012): 69–82. https://doi.org/10.1080/02614367.2011.568065.

Chee, Florence M. *Digital Game Culture in Korea: The Social at Play*. Lanham, MD: Lexington Books, 2023.

Chee, Florence, and Veli-Matti Karhulahti. "The Ethical and Political Contours of Institutional Promotion in Esports: From Precariat Models to Sustainable Practices." *Human Technology* 16, no. 2 (August 19, 2020): 200–26.

Chee, Florence M., Nicholas T. Taylor, and Suzanne de Castell. "Re-mediating Research Ethics: End-User License Agreements in Online Games." *Bulletin of Science, Technology & Society* 32, no. 6 (December 1, 2012): 497–506. https://doi.org/10.1177/0270467612469074.

Chess, Shira. *Ready Player Two: Women Gamers and Designed Identity*. St. Paul: University of Minnesota Press, 2017.

Chess, Shira, and Adrienne Shaw. "A Conspiracy of Fishes, or, How We Learned to Stop Worrying about #GamerGate and Embrace Hegemonic Masculinity." *Journal of Broadcasting & Electronic Media* 59, no. 1 (January 2, 2015): 208–20. https://doi.org/10.1080/08838151.2014.999917.

Condis, Megan. *Gaming Masculinity: Trolls, Fake Geeks, and the Gendered Battle for Online Culture*. Iowa City: University of Iowa Press, 2018.

Connell, R. W. "Periphery and Metropole in the History of Sociology." *Sociologisk Forskning* 47, no. 1 (2010): 72–86.

Connell, R. W., and James W. Messerschmidt. "Hegemonic Masculinity: Rethinking the Concept." *Gender & Society* 19, no. 6 (2005): 829–59. https://doi.org/10.1177/0891243205278639.

Consalvo, Mia. "There Is No Magic Circle." *Games and Culture* 4, no. 4 (October 1, 2009): 408–17. https://doi.org/10.1177/1555412009343575.

Cornfeld, Li. "Babes in Tech Land: Expo Labor as Capitalist Technology's Erotic Body." *Feminist Media Studies* 18, no. 2 (March 4, 2018): 205–20. https://doi.org/10.1080/14680777.2017.1298146.

Cote, Amanda C. *Gaming Sexism: Gender and Identity in the Era of Casual Video Games*. New York: NYU Press, 2020.

Cote, Amanda C., Önder Can, Maxwell Foxman, Brandon C. Harris, Jared Hansen, Md Waseq Ur Rahman, and Tara Fickle. "The COVID Season: U.S.

Collegiate Esports Programs' Material Challenges and Opportunities During the 2020–21 Pandemic." *Games and Culture* 18, no. 2 (March 1, 2023): 229–50. https://doi.org/10.1177/15554120221088116.

Cote, Amanda C., and Brandon C. Harris. "'Weekends Became Something Other People Did': Understanding and Intervening in the Habitus of Video Game Crunch." *Convergence* 27, no. 1 (2021): 161–176. https://doi.org/10.1177/1354856520913865.

Couldry, Nick, and Ulises A. Mejias. *The Costs of Connection: How Data Is Colonizing Human Life and Appropriating It for Capitalism.* Stanford, CA: Stanford University Press, 2019.

Crogan, Patrick. *Gameplay Mode: War, Simulation, and Technoculture.* St. Paul: University of Minnesota Press, 2011. https://www.upress.umn.edu/book-division/books/gameplay-mode.

Cross, Katherine. "'We Will Force Gaming to Be Free.'" *First Person Scholar,* October 8, 2014. http://www.firstpersonscholar.com/we-will-force-gaming-to-be-free/.

Crowe, Nic, and Simon Bradford. "'Hanging out in Runescape': Identity, Work and Leisure in the Virtual Playground." *Children's Geographies* 4, no. 3 (December 1, 2006): 331–46. https://doi.org/10.1080/14733280601005740.

Csikszentmihalyi, Mihaly. *Flow: The Psychology of Optimal Experience.* New York: Harper Collins, 2009.

Dahdouh-Guebas, Farid, J. Ahimbisibwe, Rita Van Moll, and Nico Koedam. "Neo-colonial Science by the Most Industrialised upon the Least Developed Countries in Peer-Reviewed Publishing." *Scientometrics* 56, no. 3 (March 1, 2003): 329–43. https://doi.org/10.1023/A:1022374703178.

D'Anastasio, Cecilia. "Inside the Culture of Sexism at Riot Games." Kotaku, August 7, 2018. https://kotaku.com/inside-the-culture-of-sexism-at-riot-games-1828165483.

Data USA. "Communication and Media Studies." Accessed June 8, 2021. https://datausa.io/profile/cip/communication-and-media-studies#demographics.

de Certeau, Michel. *The Practice of Everyday Life.* Berkeley: University of California Press, 1988.

Denoon, Donald. *Settler Capitalism: The Dynamics of Dependent Development in the Southern Hemisphere.* Oxford: Clarendon Press, 1983.

Deterding, Sebastian. "Modes of Play: A Frame Analytic Account of Video Game Play." Doctoral thesis, Staats-und Universitätsbibliothek Hamburg Carl von Ossietzky, 2013. https://ediss.sub.uni-hamburg.de/handle/ediss/5508.

de Wildt, Lars, Thomas H. Apperley, Justin Clemens, Robbie Fordyce, and Souvik Mukherjee. "(Re-)Orienting the Video Game Avatar." *Games and Culture* 15, no. 8 (December 1, 2020): 962–81. https://doi.org/10.1177/1555412019858890.

Disalvo, Betsy, and Amy Bruckman. "Race and Gender in Play Practices: Young African American Males." *FDG 2010—Proceedings of the 5th International Conference on the Foundations of Digital Games*, January 1, 2010. https://doi .org/10.1145/1822348.1822356.

Donaldson, Scott. "Mechanics and Metagame: Exploring Binary Expertise in League of Legends." *Games and Culture* 12, no. 5 (July 1, 2017): 426–44. https://doi.org/10.1177/1555412015590063.

Doughty, Richard. "The Future of Online Learning: The Long-Term Trends Accelerated by Covid-19." *The Guardian*, February 16, 2021. http:// www.theguardian.com/education/2021/feb/16/the-future-of-online -learning-the-long-term-trends-accelerated-by-covid-19.

Dourish, Paul. "Protocols, Packets, and Proximity: The Materiality of Internet Routing." In *Signal Traffic: Critical Studies of Media Infrastructures*, edited by Lisa Parks and Nicole Starosielski, 183–204. Champaign: University of Illinois Press, 2015.

Dovey, Jon, and Helen W. Kennedy. *Game Cultures: Computer Games as New Media*. London: Open University Press, 2006.

Duffy, Brooke Erin, and Jeremy Packer. "Wifesaver: Tupperware and the Unfortunate Spoils of Containment." In *Re-understanding Media: Feminist Extensions of Marshall McLuhan*, edited by Sarah Sharma and Rianka Singh, 98–118. Durham, NC: Duke University Press, 2022. https://doi.org/10.1515/9781478022497-009.

Dyer-Witheford, Nick, and Greig De Peuter. *Games of Empire: Global Capitalism and Video Games*. St. Paul: University of Minnesota Press, 2009.

ECGC. "Passes & Prices." April 8, 2020. https://ecgconf.com/.

Edelman, Gilad. "It's Time to Bring Back Cargo Pants." *Wired*, August 18, 2021. https://www.wired.com/story/bring-back-cargo-pants/.

Editor. "From Plantation to Prison: How Oppression Led to High Rates of Disease, Death for Black North Carolinians." *North Carolina Health News*, February 23, 2021. http://www.northcarolinahealthnews.org/2021/02/23/from -plantation-to-prison-how-oppression-led-to-high-rates-of-disease-death -for-black-north-carolinians/.

Edwards, Paul N. "Infrastructure and Modernity: Force, Time, and Social Organization in the History of Sociotechnical Systems." In *Modernity and Technology*, edited by Thomas J. Misa, Philip Brey, and Andrew Feenberg, 185–226. Cambridge, MA: MIT Press, 2003.

Egan, Toussaint. "New Suit against Activision Blizzard Alleges 'Rampant Sexism' and Retaliation." *Polygon* (blog), March 24, 2022. https://www.polygon .com/22994994/activision-blizzard-lawsuit-sexism.

Elam, Jessica. "Automated: The Life and Death of the Human Subject." Doctoral diss., North Carolina State University, 2018. https://repository.lib.ncsu.edu /bitstream/handle/1840.20/35334/etd.pdf?sequence=1&isAllowed=y.

El-Nasr, Magy Seif, Anders Drachen, and Alessandro Canossa. *Game Analytics: Maximizing the Value of Player Data*. New York: Springer Science & Business Media, 2013.

Ensmenger, Nathan L. *The Computer Boys Take Over: Computers, Programmers, and the Politics of Technical Expertise*. Cambridge, MA: MIT Press, 2012.

Ermi, Laura, and Frans Mäyrä. "Fundamental Components of the Gameplay Experience: Analysing Immersion." In *DiGRA '05—Proceedings of the 2005 DiGRA International Conference: Changing Views: Worlds in Play*, vol. 3. Vancouver: Digital Games Research Association, 2005. http://www.digra.org/wp-content/uploads/digital-library/06276.41516.pdf.

Eschler, Jordan, and Amanda Menking. "'No Prejudice Here': Examining Social Identity Work in Starter Pack Memes." *Social Media + Society* 4, no. 2 (April 1, 2018): 2056305118768811. https://doi.org/10.1177/2056305118768811.

Esports Connect International. "Play Esports in College." ECInternational. Accessed July 10, 2023. https://www.esportsconnectinternational.com.

Feste, Karen A. "Frame Theory." In *America Responds to Terrorism: Conflict Resolution Strategies of Clinton, Bush, and Obama*, edited by Karen A. Feste, 15–32. The Evolving American Presidency Series. New York: Palgrave Macmillan US, 2011. https://doi.org/10.1057/9780230118867_2.

Fickle, Tara. *The Race Card: From Gaming Technologies to Model Minorities*. New York: NYU Press, 2019.

Fine, Gary Alan. *Shared Fantasy: Role Playing Games as Social Worlds*. Chicago: University of Chicago Press, 1983.

Fisher, Stephanie. "Diary of a GDC Party Girl: Inequity and Inclusion in Games Industry Events." Presented at Party! The Nineteenth Annual Tampere University Game Research Lab, Tampere, May 5, 2023.

Fisher, Stephanie, and Alison Harvey. "Intervention for Inclusivity: Gender Politics and Indie Game Development." *Loading* 7, no. 11 (2012): 25–40. http://journals.sfu.ca/loading/index.php/loading/article/view/118.

Fletcher, Akil. "Esports and the Color Line: Labor, Skill and the Exclusion of Black Players." In *Proceedings of the 53rd Hawaii International Conference on System Sciences*. Hawaii: Association for Information Systems, 2020. http://hdl.handle.net/10125/64067.

Flynn, Bernadette. "Geography of the Digital Hearth." *Information, Communication & Society* 6, no. 4 (December 1, 2003): 551–76. https://doi.org/10.1080/1369118032000163259.

Foucault, Michel. *Discipline and Punish: The Birth of the Prison*. Translated by Alan Sheridan. 2nd ed. New York: Vintage Books, 1995.

———. *Power/Knowledge: Selected Interviews and Other Writings, 1972–1977*. New York: Pantheon Books, 1980.

Frank, Allegra. "Ninja Explains His Choice Not to Stream with Female Gamers." *Polygon* (blog), August 11, 2018. https://www.polygon.com/2018/8 /11/17675738/ninja-twitch-female-gamers.

Frederici, Silvia. *Wages against Housework*. Bristol: Falling Wall Press, 1975.

Friends of Telford Town Park. "Heritage." *Friends of Telford Town Park* (blog), July 23, 2012. https://friendsoftelfordtownpark.org/heritage/.

Fullagar, Simone, Wendy O'Brien, and Kathy Lloyd. "Feminist Perspectives on Third Places." In *Rethinking Third Places: Informal Public Spaces and Community Building*, edited by Joanne Dolley and Caryl Bosman, 20–37. Cheltenham: Edward Elgar, 2019.

Fuller, Matthew. *Media Ecologies: Materialist Energies in Art and Technoculture*. Cambridge, MA: MIT Press, 2005.

Funk, Daniel C., Anthony D. Pizzo, and Bradley J. Baker. "Esport Management: Embracing Esport Education and Research Opportunities." *Sport Management Review* 21, no. 1 (January 1, 2018): 7–13. https://doi.org/10.1016/j .smr.2017.07.008.

Garrett, Bradley. *Bunker: What It Takes to Survive the Apocalypse*. New York: Simon and Schuster, 2021.

Geoghegan, Bernard Dionysius. "After Kittler: On the Cultural Techniques of Recent German Media Theory." *Theory, Culture & Society* 30, no. 6 (November 2013): 66–82. https://doi.org/10.1177/0263276413488962.

Gillespie, Tarleton. "The Politics of 'Platforms.'" *New Media & Society* 12, no. 3 (May 1, 2010): 347–64. https://doi.org/10.1177/1461444809342738.

Ging, Debbie. "Alphas, Betas, and Incels: Theorizing the Masculinities of the Manosphere." *Men and Masculinities* 22, no. 4 (October 1, 2019): 638–57. https://doi.org/10.1177/1097184X17706401.

Giroux, Henry A. "Public Intellectuals against the Neoliberal University." In *Qualitative Inquiry Outside the Academy*, edited by Norman K. Denzin and Michael D. Giardina, 35–60. New York: Routledge, 2014.

Gitelman, Lisa. *Paper Knowledge: Toward a Media History of Documents*. Durham, NC: Duke University Press, 2014.

Glaser, Barney G., and Anselm L. Strauss. *The Discovery of Grounded Theory: Strategies for Qualitative Theory*. New Brunswick, NJ: Aldine Transaction, 1967.

Goffman, Erving. *Frame Analysis: An Essay on the Organization of Experience*. New York: Harper & Row, 1974.

———. *The Presentation of Self in Everyday Life*. New York: Knopf Doubleday, 2021.

Grant, Jill. "The Dark Side of the Grid: Power and Urban Design." *Planning Perspectives* 16, no. 3 (January 1, 2001): 219–41. https://doi.org/10.1080 /02665430152469575.

Gray, Kishonna L. "Intersecting Oppressions and Online Communities." *Information, Communication & Society* 15, no. 3 (April 1, 2012): 411–28. https://doi.org/10.1080/1369118X.2011.642401.

Guins, Raiford. *Atari Design: Impressions on Coin-Operated Video Game Machines.* New York: Bloomsbury, 2020.

Hall, Gary. *The Uberfication of the University.* St. Paul: University of Minnesota Press, 2016.

Hamer, Jennifer F., and Clarence Lang. "Race, Structural Violence, and the Neoliberal University: The Challenges of Inhabitation." *Critical Sociology* 41, no. 6 (September 1, 2015): 897–912. https://doi.org/10.1177/0896920515594765.

Hanson, Christopher. *Game Time: Understanding Temporality in Video Games.* Bloomington: Indiana University Press, 2018.

Haraway, Donna. "Situated Knowledges: The Science Question in Feminism and the Privilege of Partial Perspective." *Feminist Studies* 14, no. 3 (1988): 575–99.

Hart, Gillian. "Becoming a Geographer: Massey Moments in a Spatial Education." In *Doreen Massey Critical Dialogues,* edited by Marion Werner, Jamie Peck, Rebecca Lave, and Brett Christophers, 75–88. Newcastle upon Tyne: Agenda, 2018. https://doi.org/10.2307/j.ctv5cg810.9.

Harvey, Alison. *Gender, Age, and Digital Games in the Domestic Context.* New York: Routledge, 2015.

Harvey, Alison, and Stephanie Fisher. "'Everyone Can Make Games!': The Postfeminist Context of Women in Digital Game Production." *Feminist Media Studies* 15, no. 4 (July 4, 2015): 576–92. https://doi.org/10.1080/14680777.2014.958867.

Harvey, Alison, and Tamara Shepherd. "When Passion Isn't Enough: Gender, Affect and Credibility in Digital Games Design." *International Journal of Cultural Studies* 20, no. 5 (September 1, 2017): 492–508. https://doi.org/10.1177/1367877916636140.

Harvey, David. "Flexible Accumulation through Urbanization Reflections on 'Post-modernism' in the American City." *Perspecta* 26 (1990): 251–72. https://doi.org/10.2307/1567167.

Heljakka, Katriina, and J. Tuomas Harviainen. "From Displays and Dioramas to Doll Dramas: Adult World Building and World Playing with Toys." *American Journal of Play* 11, no. 3 (2019): 351–78.

Hill, Jasmine Diana. "The Hustle Ethic and the Spirit of Platform Capitalism." PhD diss., Stanford University, 2020. https://www.proquest.com/docview/2603931767/abstract/CD2795CBB7D74FABPQ/1.

Hogan, Mél. "Big Data Ecologies." *Ephemera* 18, no. 3 (2018): 631–57.

Hong, Nicole. "Nice Cargo Shorts! You're Sleeping on the Sofa." *Wall Street Journal,* August 1, 2016. https://www.wsj.com/articles/nice-cargo-shorts-youre-sleeping-on-the-sofa-1470082856.

Howard, Matthew Jungsuk. "Rendering Hallyu: Gyopo Media Histories of the Korean Wave." PhD diss., North Carolina State University, 2023.

Hsu, J. "Inside the Largest Virtual Psychology Lab in the World." *Medium* (blog), January 27, 2015. https://medium.com/backchannel/inside-the-largest-virtual-psychology-lab-in-the-world-7c0d2c43cda5.

Huh, Searle, and Dmitri Williams. "Dude Looks Like a Lady: Gender Swapping in an Online Game." In *Online Worlds: Convergence of the Real and the Virtual*, edited by William Sims Bainbridge, 161–74. Human-Computer Interaction Series. London: Springer, 2010. https://doi.org/10.1007/978-1-84882-825-4_13.

Huizinga, Johan. *Homo Ludens*. London: Taylor & Francis, 1949.

Ingle, Sean. "Money Talks: How Saudi Arabia's Soft Power Project Is Shaking up Sport." *The Guardian*, June 7, 2023, sec. Sport. https://www.theguardian.com/sport/blog/2023/jun/07/saudi-arabia-deal-pga-major-step-sportswashing-golf.

Ingraham, Chris. "Fake Plastic Trees." In *LEGOfied: Building Blocks as Media*, edited by Nicholas T. Taylor and Chris Ingraham, 109–36. New York: Bloomsbury Academic, 2021.

James, C. L. R. *Beyond a Boundary: 50th Anniversary Edition*. Durham, NC: Duke University Press, 2013.

Jane, Emma A. "'Dude . . . Stop the Spread': Antagonism, Agonism, and #Manspreading on Social Media." *International Journal of Cultural Studies* 20, no. 5 (September 1, 2017): 459–75. https://doi.org/10.1177/1367877916637151.

Jansz, Jeroen, and Lonneke Martens. "Gaming at a LAN Event: The Social Context of Playing Video Games." *New Media & Society* 7, no. 3 (June 30, 2016): 333–55. https://doi.org/10.1177/1461444805052280.

Jayemanne, Darshana. "Game Studies' Material Turn." *Westminster Papers in Communication and Culture* 9, no. 1 (June 13, 2017): 5–25. https://doi.org/10.16997/wpcc.145.

Jayne, Mark, Gill Valentine, and Sarah L. Holloway. "The Place of Drink: Geographical Contributions to Alcohol Studies." *Drugs: Education, Prevention & Policy* 15, no. 3 (June 2008): 219–32.

Johnson, Robin. "Technomasculinity and Its Influence in Video Game Production." In *Masculinities in Play*, edited by Nicholas T. Taylor and Gerald Voorhees, 249–62. Palgrave Games in Context. New York: Palgrave Macmillan, 2018. https://doi.org/10.1007/978-3-319-90581-5_14.

Johnson, Soren, and Adam Saltsman. "Designer Notes: Frank Lantz." *Designer Notes* (podcast). Accessed November 15, 2022. https://www.idlethumbs.net/designernotes/episodes/frank-lantz.

Johnston, Andrew R. *Pulses of Abstraction: Episodes from a History of Animation*. St. Paul: University of Minnesota Press, 2021.

Jones, Stephen G. "Labour, Society and the Drink Question in Britain, 1918–1939." *The Historical Journal* 30, no. 1 (1987): 105–22.

Jonsson, Fatima, and Harko Verhagen. 2011. "Senses Working Overtime: On
   Sensuous Experiences and Public Computer Game Play." In *ACE'11: Proceed-
   ings of the 8th International Conference on Advances in Computer Entertainment
   Technology*, 1–8. New York: Association for Computing Machinery. https://doi
   .org/10.1145/2071423.2071493.
Joseph, Daniel James. "The Discourse of Digital Dispossession: Paid Modifica-
   tions and Community Crisis on Steam." *Games and Culture* 13, no. 7 (Novem-
   ber 1, 2018): 690–707. https://doi.org/10.1177/1555412018756488.
Kakkar, Ankur. "'Education, Empire and the Heterogeneity of Investigative
   Modalities': A Reassessment of Colonial Surveys on Indigenous Indian Edu-
   cation." *Paedagogica Historica* 53, no. 4 (July 4, 2017): 381–93. https://doi.org
   /10.1080/00309230.2016.1270338.
Kalpagam, U. *Rule by Numbers: Governmentality in Colonial India.* Lanham, MD:
   Lexington Books, 2014.
Kauweloa, Nyle Sky, and Jenifer Sunrise Winter. "Taking College Esports
   Seriously." *Loading . . .* 12, no. 20 (October 15, 2019): 35–50.
Keightley, Keir. "'Turn It Down!' She Shrieked: Gender, Domestic Space, and
   High Fidelity, 1948–59." *Popular Music* 15, no. 2 (1996): 149–77.
Kelly, Casey Ryan. *Apocalypse Man: The Death Drive and the Rhetoric of White
   Masculine Victimhood.* Columbus: Ohio State University Press, 2020.
Kendall, Lori. "'White and Nerdy': Computers, Race, and the Nerd Stereo-
   type." *Journal of Popular Culture* 44, no. 3 (2011): 505–24. https://doi.org
   /10.1111/j.1540-5931.2011.00846.x.
Kerr, Aphra. *Global Games: Production, Circulation and Policy in the Networked
   Era.* New York: Routledge, 2017.
Kerr, A., S. De Paoli, and M. Keatinge. "Surveillant Assemblages of Governance
   in Massively Multiplayer Online Games: A Comparative Analysis." *Surveil-
   lance and Society* 12, no. 3 (2014): 330–36.
Kerr, Aphra, and John D. Kelleher. "The Recruitment of Passion and Community
   in the Service of Capital: Community Managers in the Digital Games Indus-
   try." *Critical Studies in Media Communication* 32, no. 3 (May 27, 2015): 177–92.
   https://doi.org/10.1080/15295036.2015.1045005.
Kinsella, William J. "Heidegger and Being at the Hanford Reservation:
   Standing Reserve, Enframing, and Environmental Communication Theory."
   Environmental Communication 1, no. 2 (November 1, 2007): 194–217.
   https://doi.org/10.1080/17524030701642728.
Kittler, Friedrich. *Optical Media: Berlin Lectures 1999.* Translated by Anthony
   Enns. Cambridge: Polity, 2010.
Klee, Miles. "11 Defenses of Cargo Shorts, Ranked." *MEL Magazine* (blog),
   July 27, 2017. https://melmagazine.com/en-us/story/11-defenses-of-cargo
   -shorts-ranked-2.

Kocurek, Carly A. *Coin-Operated Americans: Rebooting Boyhood at the Video Game Arcade*. St. Paul: University of Minnesota Press, 2015.

Kunzelman, Cameron. "Story about Early Game Studies." November 14, 2022.

Kunzelman, Cameron, and Michael Lutz. "James—Beyond A Boundary." *Game Studies Study Buddies* (podcast). Accessed November 15, 2022. https://rangedtouch.com/2019/07/30/14-james-beyond-a-boundary/.

LaPensée, Elizabeth, and Jason Edward Lewis. "Skins: Designing Games with First Nations Youth." *Journal of Game Design and Development Education* 1, no. 1 (2011). https://www.obxlabs.net/obx_docs/Journal-of-Game-Design-and-Development-Education-Skins-abstract.pdf.

Larkin, Brian. "The Politics and Poetics of Infrastructure." *Annual Review of Anthropology* 42 (2013): 327–43.

Latour, Bruno. "Why Has Critique Run out of Steam? From Matters of Fact to Matters of Concern." *Critical Inquiry* 30, no. 2 (January 2004): 225–48. https://doi.org/10.1086/421123.

LaVito, Angelica. "Date Rape Drug Test Allows Women to Discreetly Check for Spiked Drinks with a Few Drops." *CNBC*, September 6, 2018. https://www.cnbc.com/2018/09/05/date-rape-drug-test-allows-women-to-discreetly-check-for-spiked-drinks.html.

LeCavalier, Jesse. *The Rule of Logistics: Walmart and the Architecture of Fulfillment*. St. Paul: University of Minnesota Press, 2016.

Lee, Robert, and Tristan Ahtone. "Land-Grab Universities." *High Country News*, March 30, 2020. https://www.hcn.org/issues/52.4/indigenous-affairs-education-land-grab-universities.

Lefebvre, Henri. "Notes on the New Town." In *Introduction to Modernity: Twelve Preludes, September 1959–May 1961*, Translated by John Moore, 116–27. New York: Verso, 1995.

Liboiron, Max. *Pollution Is Colonialism*. Durham, NC: Duke University Press, 2021.

Limbong, Andrew. "Judge Approves Activision Blizzard $18 Million Settlement in Sexual Harassment Suit." *NPR*, March 29, 2022. https://www.npr.org/2022/s03/29/1089577389/judge-activision-blizzard-settlement-sexual-harassment.

Lin, Holin, and Chuen-Tsai Sun. "The Role of Onlookers in Arcade Gaming: Frame Analysis of Public Behaviours." *Convergence* 17, no. 2 (May 1, 2011): 125–37. https://doi.org/10.1177/1354856510397111.

Linderoth, Jonas. "The Effort of Being in a Fictional World: Upkeyings and Laminated Frames in MMORPGs." *Symbolic Interaction* 35, no. 4 (2012): 474–92. https://doi.org/10.1002/symb.39.

Lombard, Matthew, and Theresa Ditton. "At the Heart of It All: The Concept of Presence." *Journal of Computer-Mediated Communication* 3, no. 2 (September 1, 1997): JCMC321. https://doi.org/10.1111/j.1083-6101.1997.tb00072.x.

Lorenz, Taylor, and Kellen Browning. "Dozens of Women in Gaming Speak
   Out about Sexism and Harassment." *New York Times*, June 23, 2020, sec. Style.
   https://www.nytimes.com/2020/06/23/style/women-gaming-streaming
   -harassment-sexism-twitch.html.
Luongo, Cody. "NC State Receives $16M to Build Esports Facilities on Campus."
   Esports Insider (blog), February 21, 2022. https://esportsinsider.com/2022/02
   /nc-state-university-esports-facility-grant.
Lyotard, Jean-François. *The Postmodern Condition: A Report on Knowledge.*
   Translated by Geoff Bennington and Brian Massumi. St. Paul: University of
   Minnesota Press, 1984.
MACE Archive. "From Dawley to Telford: Building a Community." Video. 2013.
   https://vimeo.com/81006283.
Mackenzie, Adrian. *Wirelessness: Radical Empiricism in Network Cultures.*
   Cambridge, MA: MIT Press, 2010.
Marwick, Alice E., and Robyn Caplan. "Drinking Male Tears: Language, the
   Manosphere, and Networked Harassment." *Feminist Media Studies* 18, no. 4
   (July 4, 2018): 543–59. https://doi.org/10.1080/14680777.2018.1450568.
Maryville Strategic Plan. "Vision & Mission." Accessed June 7, 2021.
   https://www.maryville.edu/strategicplan/vision-and-mission/.
Massanari, Adrienne L. "#Gamergate and the Fappening: How Reddit's
   Algorithm, Governance, and Culture Support Toxic Technocultures."
   New Media & Society 19, no. 3 (March 1, 2017): 329–46. https://doi.org
   /10.1177/1461444815608807.
Massey, Doreen. *For Space.* London: SAGE, 2005.
———. "Masculinity, Dualisms and High Technology." *Transactions of the
   Institute of British Geographers* 20, no. 4 (1995): 487–99. https://doi.org
   /10.2307/622978.
———. *Space, Place and Gender.* New York: John Wiley & Sons, 2013.
Massumi, Brian. *Parables for the Virtual: Movement, Affect, Sensation.* Durham,
   NC: Duke University Press, 2002.
Mattson, Richard Leonard. *The Evolution of Raleigh's African-American Neighbor-
   hoods in the 19th and 20th Centuries.* Charlotte, NC: Mattson, Alexander, 1988.
McLuhan, Marshall. *Understanding Media: The Extensions of Man.* Cambridge,
   MA: MIT Press, 1964.
Mills, Evan, Norman Bourassa, Leo Rainer, Jimmy Mai, Arman Shehabi, and
   Nathaniel Mills. "Toward Greener Gaming: Estimating National Energy Use
   and Energy Efficiency Potential." *Computer Games Journal* 8, no. 3 (December
   1, 2019): 157–78. https://doi.org/10.1007/s40869-019-00084-2.
Milner, Ryan M. *The World Made Meme: Public Conversations and Participatory
   Media.* Cambridge, MA: MIT Press, 2016.

Minh-ha, Trinh T. *Framer Framed: Film Scripts and Interviews*. New York: Routledge, 2012.

Molinaro, Matie, Corinne McLuhan, and William Toye, eds. *Letters of Marshall McLuhan*. Oxford: Oxford University Press, 1987.

Monserrate, Steven Gonzalez. "The Cloud Is Material: On the Environmental Impacts of Computation and Data Storage." *MIT Case Studies in Social and Ethical Responsibilities of Computing*, Winter (January 27, 2022). https://doi .org/10.21428/2c646de5.031d4553.

Morales, Christina, and Allyson Waller. "A Gender-Reveal Celebration Is Blamed for a Wildfire. It Isn't the First Time." *New York Times*, September 7, 2020, sec. U.S. https://www.nytimes.com/2020/09/07/us/gender-reveal -party-wildfire.html.

Mortensen, Torill Elvira. "Anger, Fear, and Games: The Long Event of #Gamer-Gate." *Games and Culture* 13, no. 8 (December 1, 2018): 787–806. https://doi .org/10.1177/1555412016640408.

Mukherjee, Souvik. *Videogames and Postcolonialism: Empire Plays Back*. New York: Palgrave Macmillan, 2017.

Murray, Janet Horowitz. *Hamlet on the Holodeck: The Future of Narrative in Cyberspace*. New York: Simon and Schuster, 1997.

Murray, Soraya. *On Video Games: The Visual Politics of Race, Gender and Space*. New York: IB Tauris, 2017.

———. "The Work of Postcolonial Game Studies in the Play of Culture." *Open Library of Humanities* 4, no. 1 (March 1, 2018): 1–25. https://doi.org/10.16995 /olh.285.

Muse, Eben. "The Event of Space: Defining Place in a Virtual Landscape." In *Creating Second Lives: Community: Identity and Spatiality as Constructions of the Virtual*, edited by Astrid Ensslin and Eben Muse, 190–211. New York: Routledge, 2011.

NC State University. "Pathway to the Future." Strategic Planning. Accessed June 8, 2021. https://strategicplan.ncsu.edu/archive/pathway-to-the-future/index .html.

Nieborg, David B., and Thomas Poell. "The Platformization of Cultural Production: Theorizing the Contingent Cultural Commodity." *New Media & Society* 20, no. 11 (November 1, 2018): 4275–92. https://doi.org /10.1177/1461444818769694.

Nitsche, Michael. *Video Game Spaces: Image, Play, and Structure in 3D Worlds*. Cambridge, MA: MIT Press, 2008.

Nooney, Laine. "A Pedestal, a Table, a Love Letter: Archaeologies of Gender in Videogame History." *Game Studies* 13, no. 2 (December 2013). http://gamestudies .org/1302/articles/nooney.

Oldenburg, Ray. *The Great Good Place: Cafés, Coffee Shops, Community Centers, Beauty Parlors, General Stores, Bars, Hangouts, and How They Get You through the Day.* St. Paul: Paragon House, 1989.

Olssen, Mark, and Michael A. Peters. "Neoliberalism, Higher Education and the Knowledge Economy: From the Free Market to Knowledge Capitalism." *Journal of Education Policy* 20, no. 3 (January 1, 2005): 313–45. https://doi.org/10.1080/02680930500108718.

Özden-Schilling, Canay. "Chapter 9. Big Grid: The Computing Beast That Preceded Big Data." In *Electrifying Anthropology: Exploring Electrical Practices and Infrastructures,* edited by Simone Abram, Brit Ross Winthereik, and Thomas Yarrow, 161–80. London: Bloomsbury Academic, 2019.

Packer, Jeremy. "The Conditions of Media's Possibility." In *The International Encyclopedia of Media Studies,* edited by John Nerone, 1–34. New York: John Wiley & Sons, 2012. https://doi.org/10.1002/9781444361506.wbiems005.

Packer, Jeremy, and Stephen B. Crofts Wiley. *Communication Matters: Materialist Approaches to Media, Mobility and Networks.* New York: Routledge, 2013.

paperson, la. *A Third University Is Possible.* St. Paul: University of Minnesota Press, 2017.

Parisi, David. "A Counterrevolution in the Hands: The Console Controller as an Ergonomic Branding Mechanism." *Journal of Games Criticism* 2, no. 1 (January 22, 2015): 1–23.

Parker, Kim, and Wendy Wang. "Modern Parenthood." *Pew Research Center,* March 14, 2013. https://www.pewsocialtrends.org/2013/03/14/modern-parenthood-roles-of-moms-and-dads-converge-as-they-balance-work-and-family/.

Parks, Lisa, and Nicole Starosielski. "Introduction." In *Signal Traffic: Critical Studies of Media Infrastructures,* edited by Lisa Parks and Nicole Starosielski, 1–30. Chicago: University of Illinois Press, 2015.

Partin, William Clyde. "Bit by (Twitch) Bit: 'Platform Capture' and the Evolution of Digital Platforms." *Social Media + Society* 6, no. 3 (July 1, 2020): 2056305120933981. https://doi.org/10.1177/2056305120933981.

———. "The 'E' in Sports: The Platformization of Professional Gaming," PhD diss., University of North Carolina, 2024.

———. "The Esports Pipeline Problem." *Polygon* (blog), July 11, 2019. https://www.polygon.com/features/2019/7/11/18632716/esports-amateur-pro-players-teams-talent-process.

Pasquale, Frank. "Two Narratives of Platform Capitalism." *Yale Law & Policy Review* 35, no. 1 (2016): 309–19.

Patterson, Christopher B. *Open World Empire: Race, Erotics, and the Global Rise of Video Games.* New York: NYU Press, 2020.

Paul, Christopher A. *The Toxic Meritocracy of Video Games: Why Gaming Culture Is the Worst.* St. Paul: University of Minnesota Press, 2018.

Pawlicka-Deger, Urszula. "Place Matters: Thinking about Spaces for Humanities Practices." *Arts and Humanities in Higher Education* 20, no. 3 (2021): 320–38. https://doi.org/10.1177/1474022220961750.

Phillips, Amanda. *Gamer Trouble: Feminist Confrontations in Digital Culture.* New York: NYU Press, 2020.

Preciado, Paul B. *Pornotopia: An Essay on Playboy's Architecture and Biopolitics.* New York: Zone Books, 2014.

———. *Testo Junkie: Sex, Drugs, and Biopolitics in the Pharmacopornographic Era.* New York: Feminist Press at CUNY, 2013.

Puar, Jasbir K. "'I Would Rather Be a Cyborg Than a Goddess': Becoming-Intersectional in Assemblage Theory." *PhiloSOPHIA* 2, no. 1 (October 2, 2012): 49–66.

QGCon. "What Is QGCon?" Accessed November 30, 2022. https://qgcon.com /what-is-qgcon/.

Ratan, Rabindra A., Nicholas T. Taylor, Jameson Hogan, Tracey Kennedy, and Dmitri Williams. "Stand by Your Man: An Examination of Gender Disparity in League of Legends." *Games and Culture* 10, no. 5 (September 1, 2015): 438–62. https://doi.org/10.1177/1555412014567228.

Read, Sarah, and Jason Swarts. "Visualizing and Tracing: Research Methodologies for the Study of Networked, Sociotechnical Activity, Otherwise Known as Knowledge Work." *Technical Communication Quarterly* 24, no. 1 (January 2, 2015): 14–44. https://doi.org/10.1080/10572252.2015.975961.

Red Bull Gaming. *Step into Ninja's Ultimate Stream Room!* YouTube video. 2018. https://www.youtube.com/watch?v=QgRVDRpLbbc.

Richard, Gabriela T., and Kishonna L. Gray. "Gendered Play, Racialized Reality: Black Cyberfeminism, Inclusive Communities of Practice, and the Intersections of Learning, Socialization, and Resilience in Online Gaming." *Frontiers: A Journal of Women Studies* 39, no. 1 (2018): 112–48.

Rivera, Isaac. "Digital Enclosure and the Elimination of the Oceti Sakowin: The Case of the Dakota Access Pipeline." *Society + Space.* Accessed October 28, 2022. https://www.societyandspace.org/articles/digital-encosure-and-the -elimination-of-the-oceti-sakowin-the-case-of-dapl.

Rodgers, Thomas Arthur. "Into the Social Factory: An Investigation into Labour & Value in the Video-Games Industry." PhD diss., University of York, 2016. https://etheses.whiterose.ac.uk/17634/.

Rodino-Colocino, Michelle, Lauren J. DeCarvalho, and Aaron Heresco. "Neo-orthodox Masculinities on Man Caves." *Television & New Media* 19, no. 7 (November 1, 2018): 626–45. https://doi.org/10.1177/1527476417709341.

Rolt, L. T. C. *Thomas Telford*. London: Longman, Greens, 1969.

Rosario, Isabella. "When the 'Hustle' Isn't Enough." *NPR*, April 3, 2020, sec. Word Watch. https://www.npr.org/sections/codeswitch/2020/04/03/826015780/when-the-hustle-isnt-enough.

Rosenberg, Adam. "NeoGAF Is Back Online, but It's Turned into an Undead Nazi Version of Its Former Self." *Mashable*, October 24, 2017. https://mashable.com/2017/10/24/neogaf-tyler-malka-statement/.

Rosenblat, Alex. *Uberland: How Algorithms Are Rewriting the Rules of Work*. Oakland: University of California Press, 2018.

Rose-Redwood, Reuben. "With Numbers in Place: Security, Territory, and the Production of Calculable Space." *Annals of the Association of American Geographers* 102, no. 2 (2012): 295–319.

Ruberg, Bonnie "Bo," and Amanda L. L. Cullen. "Feeling for an Audience: The Gendered Emotional Labor of Video Game Live Streaming." *Digital Culture & Society* 5, no. 2 (December 1, 2019): 85–102. https://doi.org/10.14361/dcs-2019-0206.

Ruberg, Bonnie "Bo," and Daniel Lark. "Livestreaming from the Bedroom: Performing Intimacy through Domestic Space on Twitch." *Convergence* 27, no. 3 (June 1, 2021): 679–95. https://doi.org/10.1177/1354856520978324.

Rusk, Fredrik, and Matilda Ståhl. "Coordinating Teamplay Using Named Locations in a Multilingual Game Environment—Playing Esports in an Educational Context." *Classroom Discourse* 13, no. 2 (April 3, 2022): 164–87. https://doi.org/10.1080/19463014.2021.2024444.

———. "Esports—the New White Boys' Club? Problematizing Structures Limiting Diversity and Inclusion in an Educational Gaming Context." In *Challenges and Opportunities Facing Diversity in Nordic Education*, edited by Vander Tavares and Thor-André Skefsrud, 213–30. Lanham, MD: Lexington Books.

Salter, Anastasia, and Bridget Blodgett. "Hypermasculinity & Dickwolves: The Contentious Role of Women in the New Gaming Public." *Journal of Broadcasting & Electronic Media* 56, no. 3 (July 1, 2012): 401–16. https://doi.org/10.1080/08838151.2012.705199.

———. *Toxic Geek Masculinity in Media: Sexism, Trolling, and Identity Policing*. New York: Springer, 2017.

Sarkar, Samit. "Valve Hires Economist to Assist with Linking Its Virtual Economies." *Polygon* (blog), June 15, 2012. https://www.polygon.com/gaming/2012/6/15/3089588/valve-hires-economist-varoufakis-linking-virtual-economies.

Saval, Nikil. *Cubed: A Secret History of the Workplace*. New York: Doubleday, 2014.

Scheufele, Dietram A., and David Tewksbury. "Framing, Agenda Setting, and Priming: The Evolution of Three Media Effects Models: Models of Media

Effects." *Journal of Communication* 57, no. 1 (March 2007): 9–20. https://doi
.org/10.1111/j.0021-9916.2007.00326.x.

Schippers, Mimi. "Recovering the Feminine Other: Masculinity, Femininity,
and Gender Hegemony." *Theory and Society* 36, no. 1 (2007): 85–102.

Schmalzer, Madison. "Janky Controls and Embodied Play: Disrupting the
Cybernetic Gameplay Circuit." *Game Studies* 20, no. 3 (September 2020).
https://gamestudies.org/2003/articles/schmalzer.

———. "Transition Games: Speedrunning Gender." PhD diss., North Carolina
State University, 2022. https://repository.lib.ncsu.edu/handle/1840.20/39869
?show=full.

Schoemann, Sarah. "The Power of Community Organizing." In *The Queer Games
Avant-Garde: How LGBTQ Game Makers Are Reimagining the Medium of Video
Games*, edited by Bonnie "Bo" Ruberg, 223–32. Durham, NC: Duke University
Press, 2020. https://doi.org/10.1515/9781478007302-029.

Schoemann, Sarah, and Mariam Asad. "Design for the Margins: Creating an
Inclusive Space at the Different Games Conference." In *Diversifying Barbie and
Mortal Kombat: Intersectional Perspectives and Inclusive Designs in Gaming*, ed-
ited by Yasmin B. Kafai, Gabriela T. Richard, and Brendesha M. Tynes, 173–85.
Pittsburgh: ETC Press, 2017.

Schwanz, Charlie. "Thanks! It Has Pockets!" *Medium* (blog), March 11, 2023.
https://medium.com/@clozigs/thanks-it-has-pockets-331d0b5f57eb.

Sharma, Ajay. "STEM-Ification of Education: The Zombie Reform Strikes
Again." *Journal for Activist Science and Technology Education* 7, no. 1 (June
29, 2016): 42–51. https://jps.library.utoronto.ca/index.php/jaste/article
/view/26826.

Sharma, Sarah. "Going to Work in Mommy's Basement." *Boston Review*, June
19, 2018. https://www.bostonreview.net/articles/sarah-sharma-programmers
-mommys-basement/.

———. *In the Meantime: Temporality and Cultural Politics*. Durham, NC: Duke
University Press, 2014.

———. "Introduction." In *Re-understanding Media: Feminist Extensions of
Marshall McLuhan*, edited by Sarah Sharma and Rianka Singh, 1–20. Durham,
NC: Duke University Press, 2022.

Sharma, Sarah, and Rianka Singh. *Re-understanding Media: Feminist Extensions
of Marshall McLuhan*. Durham, NC: Duke University Press, 2022.

Shaw, Adrienne. "Do You Identify as a Gamer? Gender, Race, Sexuality, and
Gamer Identity." *New Media & Society* 14, no. 1 (February 1, 2012): 28–44.
https://doi.org/10.1177/1461444811410394.

Shaw, Susan M. "Family Leisure and Changing Ideologies of Parenthood."
Sociology Compass 2, no. 2 (2008): 688–703. https://doi.org/10.1111/j.1751-9020
.2007.00076.x.

Sheller, Mimi, and John Urry. "The New Mobilities Paradigm." *Environment and Planning A: Economy and Space* 38, no. 2 (February 1, 2006): 207–26. https://doi.org/10.1068/a37268.

Sherry, John L. "Flow and Media Enjoyment." *Communication Theory* 14, no. 4 (November 1, 2004): 328–47. https://doi.org/10.1111/j.1468–2885.2004.tb00318.x.

Shropshire Star. "Watch: The Birth of Telford . . . New Town, Old Worries." February 7, 2015. https://www.shropshirestar.com/news/2015/02/07/watch-the-birth-of-telford-new-town-old-worries/.

Siegert, Bernhard. *Cultural Techniques: Grids, Filters, Doors, and Other Articulations of the Real.* New York: Fordham University Press, 2015.

Simon, Bart. "Beyond Cyberspatial Flaneurie: On the Analytic Potential of Living with Digital Games." *Games and Culture* 1, no. 1 (January 1, 2006): 62–67. https://doi.org/10.1177/1555412005281789.

———. "Geek Chic: Machine Aesthetics, Digital Gaming, and the Cultural Politics of the Case Mod." *Games and Culture* 2, no. 3 (July 1, 2007): 175–93. https://doi.org/10.1177/1555412007304423.

Simson, Alan James. "The Post-Romantic Landscape of Telford New Town." *Landscape and Urban Planning* 52, no. 2 (December 25, 2000): 189–97. https://doi.org/10.1016/S0169-2046(00)00133-X.

Singh, Rianka. "Platform Feminism: Feminist Protest Space and the Politics of Spatial Organization." PhD diss., University of Toronto, 2020. https://tspace.library.utoronto.ca/handle/1807/103313.

Skardzius, Karen. "I Stream, You Stream, We All Stream: Gender, Labour, and the Politics of Online Streaming." PhD diss., York University, 2020. https://yorkspace.library.yorku.ca/xmlui/handle/10315/37971.

Smith, Brian C. "This Guy Studies Man Caves for a Living; Here's What He's Learned." *MEL Magazine*, August 29, 2016. https://melmagazine.com/en-us/story/this-guy-studies-man-caves-for-a-living-heres-what-hes-learned-2.

Smith, Dave. "Meet Jessica Blevins, the 26-Year-Old Wife and Manager of the Most Popular Video-Game Player in the World Right Now." *Business Insider*, August 16, 2018. https://www.businessinsider.com/jessica-blevins-tyler-ninja-interview-2018-8.

Smith, Lisa D., and Jo White Linn. "Central Prison." In *Encyclopedia of North Carolina*, edited by William S. Powell, 513–14. Chapel Hill: University of North Carolina Press, 2006. https://www.ncpedia.org/central-prison.

Smith-Biwer, Kelli. "The Hi-Fi Man: Masculinity, Modularity, and Home Audio Technology in the U.S. Midcentury." PhD diss., University of North Carolina at Chapel Hill, 2023. https://doi.org/10.17615/6jcq-fa15.

Sofia, Zoë. "Container Technologies." *Hypatia* 15, no. 2 (2000): 181–201. https://doi.org/10.1353/hyp.2000.0029.

Sontag, Susan. *On Photography.* London: Picador, 2001.

Sottek, T. C. "Microsoft's GDC Party Extends Tradition of Sexism in the Gaming Industry." The Verge, March 18, 2016. https://www.theverge.com/2016/3/18 /11262888/microsoft-gdc-2016-party.

Spigel, Lynn. *Make Room for TV: Television and the Family Ideal in Postwar America*. Chicago: University of Chicago Press, 1992.

Srauy, Sam, and Valerie Palmer-Mehta. "Tools of the Game: The Gendered Discourses of Peripheral Advertising." In *Masculinities in Play*, edited by Nicholas Taylor and Gerald Voorhees, 185–207. Palgrave Games in Context. New York: Palgrave Macmillan, 2018. https://doi.org/10.1007/978-3-319-90581-5_11.

Srnicek, Nick. *Platform Capitalism*. New York: John Wiley & Sons, 2017.

Stafford, Barbara. M., and Frances Trepak. *Devices of Wonder: From the World in a Box to Images on a Screen*. Los Angeles: Getty Publications, 2001.

Star, Susan Leigh, and Karen Ruhleder. "Steps toward an Ecology of Infrastructure: Design and Access for Large Information Spaces." *Information Systems Research* 7, no. 1 (March 1, 1996): 111–34. https://doi.org/10.1287/isre.7.1.111.

Starosielski, Nicole. "Fixed Flow: Undersea Cables as Media Infrastructure." In *Signal Traffic: Critical Studies of Media Infrastructures*, edited by Lisa Parks and Nicole Starosielski, 53–70. Urbana: University of Illinois Press, 2015.

Steinkuehler, Constance A., and Dmitri Williams. "Where Everybody Knows Your (Screen) Name: Online Games as 'Third Places.'" *Journal of Computer-Mediated Communication* 11, no. 4 (2006): 885–909. https://doi .org/10.1111/j.1083-6101.2006.00300.x.

Stenros, Jaakko. "In Defence of a Magic Circle: The Social and Mental Boundaries of Play." In *DiGRA Nordic '12: Proceedings of 2012 International DiGRA Nordic Conference*, vol. 10. Tampere: DiGRA, 2012. http://www.digra.org/wp -content/uploads/digital-library/12168.43543.pdf.

Stone, Allucquère Rosanne. *The War of Desire and Technology at the Close of the Mechanical Age*. Cambridge, MA: MIT Press, 1996.

Stout, Bryce. "Smashing Some Bros: A Feminist Analysis of Governance in Super Smash Bros." Master's thesis, North Carolina State University, 2020. https://search.proquest.com/openview/5f518a3205ec26e1e6e793994ffad3c0 /1?pq-origsite=gscholar&cbl=18750&diss=y.

Strom, David. "For Riot Games, Big Data Is Serious Business." Dice Insights, December 7, 2012. https://insights.dice.com/2012/12/07/for-riot-games-big-data -is-serious-business/.

Student Life. "Esports Clubs at Maryville University." Accessed June 7, 2021. https://www.maryville.edu/studentlife/esports-clubs/.

Suits, Bernard. *The Grasshopper: Games, Life and Utopia*. Peterborough: Broadview Press, 2005.

Swalwell, Melanie. "LAN Gaming Groups: Snapshots from an Australasian Case Study, 1999–2008." In *Gaming Cultures and Place in Asia-Pacific*, edited by Larissa Hjorth and Dean Chan, 117–36. Oxon: Routledge, 2009. https://researchnow.flinders.edu.au/en/publications/lan-gaming-groups -snapshots-from-an-australasian-case-study-1999-.

Szablewicz, Marcella. *Mapping Digital Game Culture in China: From Internet Addicts to Esports Athletes.* New York: Palgrave Macmillan, 2020.

Taiwo, Wendy Thompson. "'Take My Card': Analyzing the Business Cards of Nigerian Entrepreneurs in Guangzhou." *Material Culture* 53, no. 1 (Spring 2021): 27–60.

TallBear, Kim. "Standing with and Speaking as Faith: A Feminist-Indigenous Approach to Inquiry." *Journal of Research Practice* 10, no. 2 (July 1, 2014): 1–8.

Taylor, Laurie. "Toward a Spatial Practice in Video Games." *Gameology*, March 30, 2008. https://web.archive.org/web/20080330042537/http://www.game ology.org/node/809.

Taylor, Nicholas T. "Hardwired." In *MsUnderstanding Media*, edited by Sarah Sharma and Rianka Singh, 51–67. Durham, NC: Duke University Press, 2022.

———. "I'd Rather Be a Cyborg Than a Gamerbro: How Masculinity Mediates Research on Digital Play." *MedieKultur: Journal of Media and Communication Research* 34, no. 64 (June 14, 2018): 21. https://doi.org/10.7146/mediekultur .v34i64.96990.

———. "Kinaesthetic Masculinity and the Prehistory of Esports." *ROMchip* 3, no. 1 (August 19, 2021). https://romchip.org/index.php/romchip-journal /article/view/131.

———. "Now You're Playing with Audience Power: The Work of Watching Games." *Critical Studies in Media Communication* 33, no. 4 (2016): 293–307. https://doi.org/10.1080/15295036.2016.1215481.

———. "The Numbers Game: Collegiate Esports and the Instrumentation of Movement Performance." In *Sports, Society, and Technology: Bodies, Practices, and Knowledge Production*, edited by Jennifer J. Sterling and Mary G. McDonald, 121–44. New York: Palgrave Macmillan, 2020. https://doi .org/10.1007/978-981-32-9127-0_6.

———. "Postscript on Postdisciplinarity." *ToDiGRA* 7, no. 1 (2024).

———. "Reimagining a Future for Game Studies, from the Ground Up." *Eludamos: Journal for Computer Game Culture* 14, no. 1 (2023): 9–29.

Taylor, Nicholas T., and A. Joseph Dial. "Fuel, Fatigue, Fashion: Towards a Media Ecology of Game Industry Conventions." In *Proceedings of the 2020 DiGRA International Conference: Play Everywhere*, 1–3. Tampere: Digital Games Research Association,. http://www.digra.org/digital-library/publications /fuel-fatigue-fashion-towards-a-media-ecology-of-game-industry-conventions/.

Taylor, Nicholas T., and Jessica Elam. "'People Are Robots, Too': Expert Gaming as Autoplay." *Journal of Gaming & Virtual Worlds* 10, no. 3 (October 1, 2018): 243–60. https://doi.org/10.1386/jgvw.10.3.243_1.

Taylor, Nicholas T., Jennifer Jenson, and Suzanne de Castell. "Cheerleaders/
    Booth Babes/*Halo* Hoes: Pro-gaming, Gender and Jobs for the Boys." *Digi-*
    tal Creativity 20, no. 4 (December 2009): 239–52. https://doi.org/10.1080
    /14626260903290323.
Taylor, Nicholas T., Jennifer Jenson, Suzanne de Castell, and Barry Dilouya.
    "Public Displays of Play: Studying Online Games in Physical Settings." *Jour-*
    nal of Computer-Mediated Communication 19, no. 4 (2014): 763–79. https://doi
    .org/10.1111/jcc4.12054.
Taylor, Nicholas T., and Bryce Stout. "Gender and the Two-Tiered System of
    Collegiate Esports." *Critical Studies in Media Communication* 37, no. 5 (2020):
    451–65. https://doi.org/10.1080/15295036.2020.1813901.
Taylor, Nicholas T., and Gerald A. Voorhees, eds. "Introduction: Masculinity
    and Gaming: Mediated Masculinities in Play." In *Masculinities in Play*, 1–18.
    Palgrave Games in Context. New York: Palgrave Macmillan, 2018. https://doi
    .org/10.1007/978-3-319-90581-5.
Taylor, T. L. *Play between Worlds: Exploring Online Game Culture.* Cambridge,
    MA: MIT Press, 2009.
———. *Raising the Stakes: E-sports and the Professionalization of Computer*
    Gaming. Cambridge, MA: MIT Press, 2015.
———. *Watch Me Play: Twitch and the Rise of Game Live Streaming.* Princeton,
    NJ: Princeton University Press, 2018.
Taylor, T. L., and Emma Witkowski. 2010. "This Is How We Play It: What a Mega-
    LAN Can Teach Us about Games." In *FDG '10: Proceedings of the Fifth Interna-*
    tional Conference on the Foundations of Digital Games, 195–202. New York:
    Association for Computing Machinery. https://doi.org/10.1145/1822348
    .1822374.
Tekinbas, Katie Salen, and Eric Zimmerman. *Rules of Play: Game Design Funda-*
    mentals. Cambridge, MA: MIT Press, 2003.
Telford International Centre. "About—TIC." Accessed August 1, 2020.
    https://www.theinternationalcentretelford.com/about/.
———. "Hall 1 Specifications." 2019. https://www.theinternationalcentretelford
    .com/wp-content/uploads/2019/05/1.-The-International-Centre-A4-Suites
    -Floor-Plan-Leaflets-2019-Hall-1.pdf.
Temple, Paul. "From Space to Place: University Performance and Its Built
    Environment." *Higher Education Policy* 22, no. 2 (June 1, 2009): 209–23.
    https://doi.org/10.1057/hep.2008.30.
Tesseract, Lethalo1, MasterCornholio, Wings 嫩翼翻せ, and xyrho_44. "Terms
    of Service." *NeoGAF* (blog), March 20, 2010. https://www.neogaf.com/threads
    /terms-of-service.390708/.
The Roestone Collective. "Safe Space: Towards a Reconceptualization." *Antipode*
    46, no. 5 (2014): 1346–65. https://doi.org/10.1111/anti.12089.

The White House. "Biden-Harris Administration Actions to Attract STEM Talent and Strengthen Our Economy and Competitiveness." January 21, 2022. https://www.whitehouse.gov/briefing-room/statements-releases/2022/01/21/fact-sheet-biden-harris-administration-actions-to-attract-stem-talent-and-strengthen-our-economy-and-competitiveness/.

Thompson, Tiffy. "The Weird Things You Learn as a 'Booth Babe.'" *Vice*, September 5, 2017. https://www.vice.com/en/article/599vwa/the-weird-things-you-learn-as-a-booth-babe.

Tobin, Samuel. "Cocktail Cabinets: A Critique of Digital and Ludic Essentialism." *Analog Game Studies*, January 1, 2015. https://analoggamestudies.org/2015/01/cocktail-cabinets/.

———. *Portable Play in Everyday Life: The Nintendo DS*. New York: Palgrave Macmillan, 2013.

———. "Time and Space in Play: Saving and Pausing with the Nintendo DS." *Games and Culture* 7, no. 2 (July 13, 2012): 127–41. https://doi.org/10.1177/1555412012440313.

Tolley, Rodney S. "Telford New Town: Conception and Reality in West Midlands Industrial Overspill." *Town Planning Review* 43, no. 4 (1972): 343–60.

Towns, Armond R. *On Black Media Philosophy*. Oakland: University of California Press, 2022.

Trammell, Aaron. "Decolonizing Play." *Critical Studies in Media Communication* 39, no. 3 (May 27, 2022): 239–46. https://doi.org/10.1080/15295036.2022.2080844.

———. "Deodorizing the Geek Gamer." *First Person Scholar*, June 20, 2018. http://www.firstpersonscholar.com/deodorizing-the-geek-gamer/.

———. *The Privilege of Play: A History of Hobby Games, Race, and Geek Culture*. New York: NYU Press, 2023.

———. *Repairing Play: A Black Phenomenology*. Cambridge, MA: MIT Press, 2023.

Tran, Christine H. "Twitch Spouse: Livestreaming and the Legacy of Spousal Labour in the Video Game Industry." *Global Media and China* 9, no. 2 (2024): 173–87. https://doi.org/10.1177/20594364241247675.

Traub, Matt. "Maryville University to Redevelop Center for Esports Space." *SportsTravel* (blog), April 4, 2022. https://www.sportstravelmagazine.com/maryville-university-to-redevelop-center-for-esports-space/.

Tuck, Eve. "Suspending Damage: A Letter to Communities." *Harvard Educational Review* 79, no. 3 (September 1, 2009): 409–28. https://doi.org/10.17763/haer.79.3.n0016675661t3n15.

Tuck, Eve, and K. Wayne Yang. "Decolonization Is Not a Metaphor." *Decolonization: Indigeneity, Education & Society* 1, no. 1 (2012): 1–40.

UCI Esports. "2017–2018 Inclusivity Plan." UC Irvine, 2017. https://esports.uci.edu/wp-content/uploads/sites/3/2017/09/Inclusivity-Plan.pdf.

"UCI Esports Conference 2018 Schedule." Accessed July 10, 2023. https://uciesports conference2018.sched.com/.

Unsworth, Rebecca. "Hands Deep in History: Pockets in Men and Women's Dress in Western Europe, c. 1480–1630." *Costume* 51, no. 2 (September 1, 2017): 148–70. https://doi.org/10.3366/cost.2017.0022.

Uszkoreit, Lena. "With Great Power Comes Great Responsibility: Video Game Live Streaming and Its Potential Risks and Benefits for Female Gamers." In *Feminism in Play*, edited by Kishonna L. Gray, Gerald Voorhees, and Emma Vossen, 163–81. Palgrave Games in Context. New York: Palgrave Macmillan, 2018. https://doi.org/10.1007/978-3-319-90539-6_10.

Viana, Bhernardo. "How Much Money Has Mixer Paid Ninja to Stream on Its Platform?" *Dot Esports*, August 2, 2019. https://dotesports.com /streaming/news/how-much-money-has-mixer-paid-ninja-to-stream-on -its-platform.

Vigna, Xavier, and Michelle Zancarini-Fournel. "Gender History and Labour History: Intersections." Translated by Siân Reynolds. *Clio: Women, Gender, History*, no. 38 (September 15, 2014): 176–203. https://doi.org/10.4000 /cliowgh.306.

Virilio, Paul. *Bunker Archaeology.* Translated by George Collins. Princeton, NJ: Princeton Architectural Press, 1994.

———. *War and Cinema: The Logistics of Perception.* New York: Verso, 1989.

visitRaleigh. "Raleigh's Heights House Hotel Named among World's Best New Hotels." April 20, 2022. https://www.visitraleigh.com/plan-a-trip/visitraleigh -insider-blog/post/raleighs-heights-house-hotel-named-among-worlds-best -new-hotels/.

Voorhees, Gerald A., Joshua Call, and Katie Whitlock, eds. *Guns, Grenades, and Grunts: First-Person Shooter Games.* London: Continuum, 2012.

Voorhees, Gerald A., and Alexandra Orlando. "Performing Neoliberal Masculin- ity: Reconfiguring Hegemonic Masculinity in Professional Gaming." In *Masculinities in Play*, edited by Nicholas T. Taylor and Gerald A. Voorhees, 211–27. Palgrave Games in Context. New York: Palgrave Macmillan, 2018. https://doi.org/10.1007/978-3-319-90581-5_12.

Wakeman, Rosemary. *Practicing Utopia: An Intellectual History of the New Town Movement.* Chicago: University of Chicago Press, 2016.

Ward, Jane. *Not Gay: Sex between Straight White Men.* New York: NYU Press, 2015.

Welter, Barbara. "The Cult of True Womanhood: 1820–1860." *American Quarterly* 18, no. 2 (1966): 151–74. https://doi.org/10.2307/2711179.

Weststar, Johanna. "Developer Satisfaction Survey 2021: Report on the Impact of COVID-19." International Game Developers Association, July 18, 2021. https://igda-website.s3.us-east-2.amazonaws.com/wp-content/uploads /2021/07/31184838/IGDA-DSS-2021-COVID-Report_July-18-2021-1.pdf.

Whitson, Jennifer R. "The New Spirit of Capitalism in the Game Industry." *Television & New Media* 20, no. 8 (December 1, 2019): 789–801. https://doi .org/10.1177/1527476419851086.

Whitton, Peter David. "The New University: Space, Place and Identity." Doctoral diss., Manchester Metropolitan University, 2018. https://e-space.mmu.ac .uk/620806/.

Wilde, Tyler. "Major Esports Host ESL Gaming Is Now Owned by Saudi Arabia." *PC Gamer*, January 25, 2022. https://www.pcgamer.com/esl -and-dreamhack-are-now-owned-by-saudi-arabia/.

Williams, Chris. "About Multiplay." Multiplay. Accessed August 1, 2020. https://multiplay.com/about/.

Williams, Ian. "Death to the Gamer." *Jacobin*, September 2014. https://jacobin .com/2014/09/death-to-the-gamer/.

Williams, Ian, and Samuel Tobin. "The Practice of Oldhammer: Re-membering a Past Through Craft and Play." *Games and Culture* 17, no. 4 (June 1, 2022): 576–92. https://doi.org/10.1177/15554120211049577.

Williamson, Sarah. "Exploration: Cabinets of Curiosities—Playing with Artefacts in Professional Teacher Education." In *The Power of Play in Higher Education*, edited by Alison James and Chrissi Nerantzi, 103–11. New York: Palgrave Macmillan, 2019. https://doi.org/10.1007/978-3-319-95780-7.

Willis, Susan. *A Primer for Daily Life*. Studies in Culture and Communication. New York: Routledge, 1991.

Winthrop-Young, Geoffrey. "Material World: An Interview with Bernhard Siegert." *Artforum*, Summer 2015. https://www.artforum.com/print/201506 /material-world-an-interview-with-bernhard-siegert-52281.

Witkowski, Emma. "Doing/Undoing Gender with the Girl Gamer in High-Performance Play." In *Feminism in Play*, edited by Kishonna Gray, Emma Vossen, and Gerald Voorhees, 185–203. Palgrave Games in Context. New York: Palgrave Macmillan, 2018.

———. "Eventful Masculinities: Negotiations of Hegemonic Sporting Masculinities at LANs." In *Sports Videogames*, edited by Mia Consalvo, Konstantin Mitgutsch, and Abe Stein, 217–35. New York: Routledge, 2013. https://doi .org/10.4324/9780203084496-20.

———. "Growing Pains in Esports Associationalism: Four Modes of National Esports Associational Development." *Games and Culture* 18, no. 2 (March 1, 2023): 147–69. https://doi.org/10.1177/15554120221084449.

Woodcock, Jamie. *Marx at the Arcade: Consoles, Controllers, and Class Struggle*. Chicago: Haymarket Books, 2019.

Woodcock, Jamie, and Mark R. Johnson. "The Affective Labor and Performance of Live Streaming on Twitch.Tv." *Television & New Media* 20, no. 8 (December 1, 2019): 813–23. https://doi.org/10.1177/1527476419851077.

Yau, Nathan. "A Visual Analysis of Jean Pockets and Their Lack of Practicality." *FlowingData* (blog), August 16, 2018. https://flowingdata.com/2018/08/16/a-visual-analysis-of-jean-pockets/.

Zhu, Lily. "Masculinity's New Battle Arena in International E-sports: The Games Begin." In *Masculinities in Play*, edited by Nicholas Taylor and Gerald Voorhees, 229–47. Palgrave Games in Context. New York: Palgrave Macmillan, 2018. https://doi.org/10.1007/978-3-319-90581-5_13.

Zylinska, Joanna. "The Vanishing Object of Technology." *Catalyst: Feminism, Theory, Technoscience* 1, no. 1 (May 26, 2015): 1–4. https://doi.org/10.28968/cftt.v1i1.28814.

INDEX

Page numbers in *italics* refer to figures and illustrations.

Aarseth, Espen, 20, 204
academia. *See* universities and
    colleges
Activision Blizzard, 199
Alder, Katreena, 66, 73
Andrejevic, Marc, 48
animated media, 42
anticolonial critique, 38–39. *See also*
    colonialism; settler capitalism
AnyKey, 161
apparatus, 11–12, 69, 118. *See also*
    frames; gaming setups; immersion
    and escapism; photograph at
    Insomnia 42
Arora, Sahil "Universe," 158

Bakke, Gretchen, 130
Barad, Karen, 41, 202
Bateson, Gregory, 43
Berlant, Jody, 105
Bjarnason, Nökkvi, 20
Blevins, Jessica, 92
Blevins, Tyler "Ninja," 89–94,
    90, 91

Boluk, Stephanie, 65, 97, 99
boundaries, 17, 28–29, 202–3, 298–10
Bridges, Tristan, 66–67
Bryce, Jo, 70
Bulut, Ergin, 6, 8–9, 18, 22, 92
Bush, Vannevar, 130–31
Butt, Mahli-Ann, 173

cabinets of curiosity, 83–84, *84*, 91–92.
    See also gaming setups
Caillois, Roger, 28, 98, 204–5, 206–7
Candy, Graham, 108
capitalism, 8–9, 44–45. *See also*
    colonialism; labor; settler
    capitalism
cargo shorts, 170–71, 184. *See also*
    mobility; pockets
cargo shorts simulators, 197, 198–99
Cassell, Justine, 204
Castronova, Edward, 97
Chambers, Deborah, 68, 86
chronopolitics, 109–10
circles (magic circles), 24–25, 64–65,
    97–99. *See also* gaming setups

colonialism: assimilative capacity, 56; colonial technoscience, 45–53; game studies and, 38–39, 46–51, 205, 206–7; hegemonic masculinity, whiteness, and, 8; historicity of, 48–51; land, digital play, and, 51–55; land exploitation and enframing, 44–46, 51–52, 54–55; land-grant/ land-grab university system, 27, 149–51; ludopolitics of games industry, 8–9; postcolonial approach to play, 210–11; settler capitalism and, 40, 53–55. *See also* capitalism; Insomnia LAN parties; Orientalism; race; whiteness

Connell, Raewyn, 7

Consalvo, Mia, 64

conventions: activities ranked by popularity, 178–79, *179*; alcohol at, 193–94; "booth babes" and models, 186, 200n25; clothing and blending in, 170–71, 184–85; overview, 27–28; tea socials, 193; as temporary platforms, 173. *See also* East Coast Games Conference (ECGC); Games Developer Conference (GDC); LAN (local area network) parties; safety; starter pack meme study

Couldry, Nick, 48–50

cultural techniques, 10, 12, 23, 56. *See also* frames; grids; platforms; pockets

cybernetics theory, 131

data capture, 47–53

de Certeau, Michel, 188

Dial, Aaron, 169–71, 174, 177

domestic space: domestic labor, 87, 92–93; immersion and escapism, 65, 88; man caves, 2–3, 66–67, 88; mancounters, 1–4, 13; media domestication, 67–70, 73, 74–75, 78, 86–87; networks of privilege and, 69–70; white masculinity and, 65–66, 86; wire management techniques, 75–77, 79, 81–82, 87. *See also* feminization and feminism, escape from; gaming setups; labor

Dourish, Paul, 26

DreamHack LAN party, 120, 123–24, 128

Dyer-Witheford, Nicholas, 18, 52

East Coast Games Conference (ECGC), 169–71, 178

energy resources. *See* grids; infrastructures

environmental degradation, 52–53, 56

escapism. *See* immersion and escapism

ESL, 128, 157–58

esports: AnyKey, 161; charter or manifesto for collegiate programs, 159–64; COVID-19 pandemic, 157–58; cultural and economic imperialism, 154; exclusionary patterns and solutions, 140, 154–55, 159, 160–61, 162, 163–64; financial viability, 128; games' meta, 144; gaming setups, 146; Golden Guardians, 145; infrastructure and, 142, 146, 149, 161–62; at LAN parties, 125–27, 128; as media productions, 161–62; overview, 26–27; place making on university campuses, 138; platform contingent, 146–47; player demographics, 146, 147, 155, 160; players as athletes, 141, 146, 147, 155, 159; racial imaginary of, 154–55; sportswashing, 128; STEM and, 138, 140, 145, 147, 154–55, 167n50; technomasculinity, 160; tiers of collegiate esports, 141, 142, 145–47; UCI esports conference, 140; university partnerships, 135–37, 147–49, 155–56; university programs, 140, 145–47, 158–61; university space for, 138, 142–43, 146–47, 162–63, 164, 166n26; women's marginal and hidden presence, 92. *See also League of Legends* (LoL) NCSU team

Esports Connect International, 155

Esports Denmark, 165

ethnographic research: assimilative capacity of researcher agency and positionality, 56–58; at LAN events, 33–37, 46–51; overview, 19–22. *See also* gaming setups; starter pack meme study

exclusion: data capture and, 47; esports, 140, 154–55, 159, 160–61, 162, 163–64; gaming setups, 124; of women and gender minorities, 88, 92, 93–94. *See also* gender; immersion and escapism; safety; women

feminization and feminism, escape from, 88–89, 92–97, 123, 124, 171. *See also* exclusion; immersion and escapism; women

Fickle, Tara, 206

figure motif, defined, 14, 129

Fine, Gary, 43

Fisher, Stephanie, 173

Flynn, Bernadette, 69, 73, 77, 86

Foucault, Michel, 11

frame rates, 42

frames: as apparatus, 43; assimilative capacity, 56; boundaries and, 202–3, 209–10; capitalism and

colonialism, 40, 53–55; capture and, 45–46; as cultural technique, 23, 40, 41–44, 45–46; enframing, 44–45; in game studies, 43–44; mediating function, 42, 45; overview, 23–24, 40–41. *See also* LAN (local area network) parties; photograph at Insomnia 42

GAME, 127

Games Developer Conference (GDC): cost, 178; safety for women and gender minorities, 173, 185–86, 187–89, 190–91, 193–94

game studies, as field, 28–29, 43–44, 203–10

gaming setups: author's own, 74–75; bunker setup, 79–82, *80, 81,* 85, 86, 87, 87–90, 94–97, 122–25, 146; cabinet setup, 82–85, *83, 85,* 86, 87, 87–89, 91–92, 93–94, 123–24; as diagrams of power, 86; escape from domestic life and feminization, 88–89, 92–97, 123, 124; esports, 146; "geek chic," 82; "ghetto geek," 81, 82; hearth setup, 77–78, *78,* 79, 85, 86–87, *87,* 123–24; at LAN parties, 122–25; man caves vs, 66–67; media domestication and, 67–70, 73, 74–75, 78, 86–87; methodology, 73–75; NeoGAF, 66, 77–85, *78,* 96; "Ninja" Blevins's setup, 89–92, *90, 91,* 93–94; Orientalism, 84, 91–92; overview, 24–25; professionalization of home, 93; white masculinity and, 86; wire management techniques, 75–77, 79, 81–82, 87, 122–23; women and, 102n59, 124

GDC. *See* Games Developer Conference (GDC)

gender: chrono- and ludopolitics of
    gaming, 109–10; clothing, 170–72,
    184–85; games for men vs for
    women, 109–10; gender privilege,
    71; sketch of figure at center of
    gaming, 5–6; technogender, 10–11.
    See also conventions; domestic
    space; exclusion; feminization and
    feminism, escape from; gaming
    setups; labor; LAN (local area
    network) parties; man caves;
    mancounters; masculinities;
    mobility; photograph at Insomnia
    42; pockets; race; safety; starter
    pack meme study; women
gentrification, 54
Giroux, Henry A., 152
Gitelman, Lisa, 186
Goffman, Erving, 43, 44
Golden Guardians, 145
grids: as cultural technique, 25, 103–4,
    105, 121, 130; effects on LAN parties,
    121–28, 130; electricity contained
    and used, 130–31; overview, 25–26.
    See also infrastructures; LAN (local
    area network) parties
grounds, 14, 129, 131. *See also* LAN
    (local area network) parties

Hall, Gary, 152
Hamer, Jennifer, 151
Hammar, Emil, 53
Haraway, Donna, 33
Harrisburg University, 162, 164–65
Hart, Gillian, 15
Harvey, Alison, 70
Harvey, David, 15
Hefner, Hugh, 17, 86, 93
Heidegger, Martin, 45, 60n34
higher education. *See* universities and
    colleges

Hogan, Mél, 52–53
Howard, Matthew Jungsuk, 155
Huizinga, Johann, 24, 28, 97, 204–5,
    206–7

Imangi, 53–54
immersion and escapism: domestic
    space's role in, 65, 88; effect of
    privileged arrangements, 66, 99;
    magic circle, 64–65, 97–99; material
    media apparatus, product of, 69, 88,
    97, 99, 104; silencing and excluding
    women, 88, 92, 93. *See also*
    feminization and feminism, escape
    from; gaming setups; manosphere
infrastructures: of care, 191; convention
    centers, 116–17, 173; dependency on
    and invisibility of, 104–5; esports
    and, 142, 146, 149, 157–58, 161–62;
    grids controlling, 105; infrastructural
    understanding of gaming,
    overview, 18, 21; logistification,
    117–18; mancounters, 16; masculinity
    infrastructural to gaming cultures,
    22, 210, 211; safety and, 173; speed in
    gaming, 108–9, 157–58; Telford, UK,
    111–13; temporalities of, 108–9. *See
    also* grids; LAN (local area network)
    parties
Insomnia LAN parties: colonial
    program of field research, 46–51;
    esports tournaments, 125–27; events
    overview, 120–21; fieldwork study,
    overview, 33–37; gaming setups,
    122–25; infrastructure central to,
    111, 116, 122, 129–30; management
    of, 127–28; unsafe for women,
    124–25; wire management etiquette,
    122–23; women's labor, 124. *See
    also* photograph at Insomnia 42;
    Telford, UK

James, C. L. R., 28, 203, 207–9
Jenkins, Henry, 204
Johnson, Soren, 203
Johnston, Andrew, 42

Keightley, Keir, 69, 76, 88
Kerr, Aphra, 18, 48
Keyboard Toss, 106
Kinsella, William, 45
Kittler, Friedrich, 41–42
Kunzelman, Cameron, 203, 204, 207, 208, 209

labor: Asian labor exploitation, 155, 156; "booth babes" and models, 36–37, 39–40, 55–58, 186, 200n25; of care, 28, 174, 190–91, 194; domestic labor, 87, 92–93; gendered divisions in gaming, 87, 92–93, 124; ludopolitics of games industry, 8–9, 22; mancounters, 13
land: assimilative capacity, 56; colonialism in- and out-of-game, 53–55; exploitation and enframing, 44–46, 51–52, 54–55; gentrification, 54; land-grant/land-grab university system, 27, 149–51; zoning regulations, 54. See also colonialism
Lang, Clarence, 151
LAN (local area network) parties: corporatization and financialization, 128; cultures of, 121, 128–29; esports tournaments, 125–27, 128; framing of, 110, 113; gaming setups, 122–25; grids' effects on, 121–28, 130; infrastructure needs, 26, 106–7; multilayered communicative media practices, 36; overview, 25–26, 120–21; white masculinity and

grounds of, 129; wire management etiquette, 122–23. See also conventions; Insomnia LAN parties
Lantz, Frank, 203–4
Lask, Daniel, 102n59
League of Legends (LoL) NCSU team: Circuit Studio, 142–45, 157; COVID-19 pandemic, 157; demographics, 135; place-making activities, 143–44; platform contingent, 145, 146; players as athletes, 141–42, 143–44; space and identity coconstituted, 144–45; team organization and competition overview, 141–42; VR lab, 135–37, 142
LeCavalier, Jesse, 117–18
Lefebvre, Henri, 15
LeMieux, Patrick, 65, 97, 99
Liboiron, Max, 44–45, 51–52, 56, 60n34
Lin, Holin, 44
Linderoth, Jonas, 43–44
Linneas, Carl, 206
local area network (LAN) parties. See LAN (local area network) parties
ludopolitics, 8–9, 22, 109–10
Lutz, Michael, 203, 208, 209
Lyotard, Jean-Francois, 151

Mackenzie, Adrian, 76
magic circles, 24–25, 64–65, 97–99. See also gaming setups
Major League Gaming (MLG), 126
man caves, 2–3, 66–67, 88
mancounters, 1–4, 13–14, 16, 19
manosphere, 6, 89, 94, 97
Maryville University, 145–47, 162, 164–65, 166n26

masculinities: apparatus of, 11–12;
    chrono- and ludopolitics of gaming,
    22, 109–10; defined, 7; domestic
    space constructing, 65–66, 86,
    88, 93; hegemonic masculinity
    and whiteness, 7–9, 22, 86, 92,
    154; hustle and grind, 7–8, 151;
    infrastructural to gaming cultures,
    210, 211; kinaesthetic masculinity,
    12; Mommy's basement, 96–97, 125;
    neoliberalism and, 151; nondiscursive
    practices constituting, 9–10;
    Playboy magazine, 17, 86, 93;
    pushing through pain, 196–97;
    sketch of figure at center
    of gaming, 5–6; suburban
    patriarch, 86; technogender and
    technomasculinity, 11, 96, 130,
    131, 160; white masculinity and
    grounds of LANs, 129. *See also*
    gaming setups; gender; man caves;
    mancounters; manosphere; race
Massey, Doreen, 14–15, 16–17, 98, 117
massively multiplayer online games
    (MMOGs). *See* MMOGs
Massumi, Brian, 131n3
McLuhan, Marshall, 14, 129
Mejias, Ulises, 48–50
Messerschmidt, James, 7
militarization of gaming, 69, 82
Milner, Ryan, 175
MMOGs (massively multiplayer
    online games), 35, 47, 65, 115. *See also*
    Insomnia LAN parties
mobility: cargo shorts simulators, 197,
    198–99; mancounters, 13; pockets,
    171–72; safety and, 173–74, 185–56,
    198–99. *See also* conventions; LAN
    (local area network) parties;
    pockets; starter pack meme study
Mommy's basement, 96–97, 125

Monseratte, Steven, 52
Mortensen, Torill, 37
Mukherjee, Souvik, 53
Multiplay, 116, 126, 127, 128. *See also*
    Insomnia LAN parties
Murray, Janet, 204
Murray, Soraya, 53

Negroponte, Nicholas, 76
NeoGAF, 66, 71–73, 77–85, 78, 96
neoliberalism, 27, 151–52, 153
networked media, 75–77, 79, 81–82, 87,
    122–23. *See also* infrastructures
networks of privilege, 8, 21–22, 66,
    69–70, 71, 99. *See also* LAN (local
    area network) parties; race
Newbury, UK, horse racing track as
    gaming space, 34–35, 116, 118, 121, 125
Ninjas in Pyjamas (NIP), 158
Nintendo DS, 70
Nintendo Wii, 68–69
Nitsche, Michael, 20
nonbinary individuals. *See* gender;
    safety; starter pack meme study
North Carolina State University:
    esports partnerships, 147–50, 155–56;
    esports workgroup and program,
    158–59; space for esports, 142–45,
    164; VR lab, 135–37. *See also* League of
    Legends (LoL) NCSU team

Ohio State University, 161, 162
Oldenburg, Ray, 114
online gaming forums, 70, 71. *See also*
    NeoGAF
Orientalism, 84, 91–92, 206–7. *See also*
    race
Özden-Schilling, Canay, 130–31

Packer, Jeremy, 11
Parks, Lisa, 16

Partin, Will, 157–58, 159, 160
Pawlicka-Deger, Urszula, 143
Penny Arcade online gaming
   community, 70
Peuter, Greg de, 18, 52
photograph at Insomnia 42:
   arrangement of, 36–37; framing
   interaction, 40, 55; objectification
   of women in gaming cultures,
   39–40; toxicity in gaming cultures,
   55–58
place, conceptual overview, 14–22. *See
   also* conventions; land; LAN (local
   area network) parties; *League of
   Legends* (LoL) NCSU team
place-making practices: boundaries
   and, 17, 18; esports, 138, 143–44;
   magic circles, 98; mancounters,
   19; *Playboy* magazine, 17. *See also*
   apparatus; cultural techniques;
   gender; grounds; infrastructures;
   labor; masculinities; networks of
   privilege; space; whiteness
platforms: conventions as temporary
   platforms, 173; COVID-19 pandemic
   and, 156; as cultural technique, 139;
   data capture, 47–48; dislocation
   and disruption, 156–58; overview,
   26–27, 139; platform capitalism, 8;
   platformization, 27, 139–40, 143, 147,
   152. *See also* esports; universities and
   colleges
Playboy, 17, 86, 93
Player1 Events, 127
PlayStation consoles, 64–65, 69, 70
PlayVS, 139, 165n6
pockets, 27–28, 171–72, 174. *See also*
   starter pack meme study
postsecondary institutions. *See*
   universities and colleges
Preciado, Paul B., 10–11, 17, 86, 93

Puar, Jasbir, 131n3
pubs, 113–14

race, 7, 9, 62n78, 154–55, 167n46,
   206–8. *See also* colonialism; gender;
   masculinities; networks of privilege;
   Orientalism; whiteness
Read, Sarah, 142
Reddit, 72
Riot Games, 47, 141, 157
Rosenberg, Adam, 72
Ruberg, Bo, 102n59
Ruhleder, Karen, 108
Rutter, Jason, 70

safety: gaming contexts and, 124–25,
   173, 185–86; infrastructural
   conditions, 173; at LAN parties,
   124–25; mobility and, 173–74,
   185–56, 198–99; pockets, 174; safe
   spaces, 137; for women and gender
   minorities at conventions, 173, 185–
   86, 187–89, 190–91, 193–94. *See also*
   conventions; pockets; women
Saltsman, Adam, 207
Schmalzer, Madison, 29n1
settler capitalism, 38, 40, 48–50, 53–55,
   208, 210–11. *See also* anticolonial
   critique
settler capitalist technoscience, 40
Shannon, Claude, 131
Sharma, Ajay, 153–54
Sharma, Sarah, 96, 97, 109,
   125, 129
Sheller, Mimi, 201n40
Siegert, Bernhard, 10, 23, 103, 130
Simon, Bart, 65, 76, 82
Singh, Rianka, 165
sociality, 70, 85, 87–88, 97, 107
Sofia, Zoe, 171, 201n40
Sontag, Susan, 41

space, overview, 14–22. *See also* colonialism; domestic space; esports; gaming setups; grounds; infrastructures; land; LAN (local area network) parties; third spaces; universities and colleges

Spigel, Lynn, 18, 68, 77, 78, 86

Star, Susan Leigh, 108

Starosielski, Nicole, 16, 108

starter pack meme study: about the meme, 174–76, *175*; alcohol at conventions, 193–94; convention activities by popularity, 178–79, *179*; demographics and backgrounds of participants, 177–79; examples of participant packs, 179–83, *180*, *181*, *182*; methodology, 176–77; objects by theme, 183–84, *183*; objects by theme: bodily care, 195–97; objects by theme: know-shows, 186–89; objects by theme: mobile digital media, 189–91; objects by theme: personal effects, 184–86; objects by theme: sustenance and substance, 191–93; as orientations to games industry events, 181–82; overview, 27–28. *See also* conventions

Stenros, Jaakko, 98

storage. *See* cargo shorts; pockets; starter pack meme study

Stout, Bryce, 141, 142, 154, 160, 163

streaming, 53

Sun, Chuen-tsai, 44

Sutton-Smith, Brian, 204

Swarts, Jason, 142

tabletop gaming, 8, 69–70

Taylor, T. L., 65, 93

Tebinkas, Katie, 97

Telford, Thomas, 111

Telford, UK: city infrastructure, 111–13; cybernetics theory and, 131; as LAN party location, 112–14, 115, 119–20; pubs lacking, 113–14; Telford International Centre (TIC), 115–19, *119*, 130

Temple Run (Imangi), 53–54

third spaces, 114, 115

time, 108–10, 157–58. *See also* infrastructures

Tobin, Sam, 70, 110

toxicity of gaming cultures, 55–58, 72. *See also* exclusion; safety

Trammell, Aaron, 8, 9, 22, 69, 206, 210

Tsuji, Shigeru, 41

Tuck, Eve, 57–58

Unity Technologies, 127

universities and colleges: campus space, 135–38; COVID-19 pandemic, 149, 156; digital humanities, 142, 143; external partnerships, 47–48, 147–49, 152, 155–56; land-grant/ land-grab system, 27, 149–51; as metaplatforms, 152–53; Morrill Act, 149–50, 153; neoliberalism, 27, 153; overview, 26–27; platformization, 27, 139–40, 143, 147, 152; safe spaces, 137; STEM and, 138, 153–55. *See also* esports; North Carolina State University

University of California Irvine (UCI), 140, 161, 162–63

University of Utah, 162

Unsworth, Rebecca, 171–72, 176

Urry, John, 201n40

Valizadeh, Roosh "Roosh V," 95–96

Valve, 47

Varoufakis, Yanis, 47

Virilio, Paul, 109
visual media, 41–42

Wake Technical Community
  College, 169
Weiner, Norbert, 131
whiteness: computation and, 154;
  domestic space and, 65–66, 86,
  93; grounds of LANs and, 129;
  hegemonic masculinity and,
  7–9, 22, 86, 92, 154; networks of
  privilege in tabletop hobbyism,
  8; Orientalism, 84, 91–92, 206–7;
  sketch of figure at center of gaming,
  5–6. *See also* esports; gaming setups;
  masculinities; race
Whitson, Jen, 47
Williams, Dmitri, 47
wire management techniques. *See*
  gaming setups; networked media

Witkowski, Emma, 37, 165, 166n12
women: "booth babes" and models,
  36–37, 39–40, 55–58; care work,
  190–91, 194; clothing choices,
  184–85; convention booths trying
  to attract, 185–86; in esports, 92;
  gaming contexts unsafe for,
  124–25, 173, 185–86; gaming
  setups and, 102n59, 124. *See
  also* conventions; exclusion;
  feminization and feminism, escape
  from; gender; labor; photograph at
  Insomnia 42; safety; starter pack
  meme study

Yee, Nick, 47

Zimmerman, Eric, 65, 97, 99,
  203–4
Zylinska, Joanna, 76

NICHOLAS (NICK) TAYLOR is Associate Professor in the Department of Communication and Media Studies at York University in Toronto, Canada. He is editor with Gerald Voorhees of *Masculinities in Play* and with Chris Ingraham of *LEGOfied: Building Blocks as Media*.

For Indiana University Press

Allison Chaplin, Acquisitions Editor

Anna Garnai, Editorial Assistant

Sophia Hebert, Assistant Acquisitions Editor

Samantha Heffner, Marketing and Publicity Manager

Brenna Hosman, Production Coordinator

Katie Huggins, Production Manager

Darja Malcolm-Clarke, Project Manager/Editor

Dan Pyle, Online Publishing Manager

Michael Regoli, Director of Publishing Operations

Pamela Rude, Senior Artist and Book Designer

www.ingramcontent.com/pod-product-compliance
Lightning Source LLC
Chambersburg PA
CBHW020343270326
41926CB00007B/294